Control and Security of Computer Information Systems

Control and Security of Computer Information Systems

Philip E. Fites, CSP, CDP
Fites and Associates Management Consultants, Ltd.

Martin P. J. Kratz, LLB
Cruickshank Phillips

Alan F. Brebner, CA
Institute of Chartered Accounts of Alberta, Inc.

COMPUTER SCIENCE PRESS

Library of Congress Cataloging-in-Publication Data

Fites, Philip E.
    Control and security of computer information systems/Philip E.
    Fites, Martin P. J. Kratz, Alan F. Brebner.
        p.—cm.
    Bibliography: p.
    Includes index.
    ISBN 0-7167-8191-3
    1. Computers—Access control.   I. Kratz, Martin P. J.
II. Brebner, Alan F.   III. Title.
QA76.9.A25F535 1989   68172   88-19748
005.8—dc19   CIP

Printed in the United States of America

Computer Science Press, Inc.
1803 Research Boulevard
Rockville, MD 20850
An imprint of W. H. Freeman and Company
41 Madison Avenue, New York, NY 10010
20 Beaumont Street, Oxford OX1 2NQ, England

1 2 3 4 5 6 7 8 9 0 RRD 7 6 5 4 3 2 1 0 8 9

CONTENTS

PREFACE

The creation of this textbook was almost an accident. The initial effort was started as part of the work involved in developing a course in computer security for a two-year technical training program in "Computer Programming and Systems Analysis (CPA)" at the Computer Career Institute in Edmonton, Alberta, Canada. We reviewed all the textbooks we could locate; none was really appropriate for an introductory course. Some were IBM- or Honeywell-oriented, and we did not want to limit the course to one manufacturer. Some turned out to be too general, or too "sensational," or outdated. There are many excellent books with very detailed treatments of specific parts of the topic area, but we found none that gave the sort of overview we wanted, without too much vendor-specific material or detailed mathematical treatments. We developed a number of "handouts," often to supplement classroom presentations. When I noticed that the handouts totalled something like 180 pages, I decided to invest another 15 to 20 percent to the work we had to do anyway and make a textbook from the material.

This probably was an error. For anyone who may face a similar situation, let me note that the extra effort has been more like 2015 percent!

As you will note from the title page, I also enlisted the help of two coauthors, specialists in accounting and in computer law, so we could create something which would be useful for instructors in several disciplines who need to help students learn about information systems security.

I think the effort has been worth it. Our original situation was much like that of a tourist trying to get a feel for what a province or state is like, using maps that range from very undetailed maps in an encyclopedia, to maps of individual cities, to topographical maps of tiny areas. Trying to understand what a state or province is like, using only such special purpose maps would be a frustrating exercise. A reasonably good road map would be much more helpful.

There are several general books addressing information systems security -- the encyclopedia map. There are several books going into specific vendors' approaches -- the city maps. Books on such topics as encryption and secure operating systems are available -- the topographical map (or perhaps, a map of a city's utility corridors). We've tried to make this textbook a fairly good road map, with enough detail to give a feel for what the field is like: with enough detail to show the differences between, say, a city of 10,000 such as Edson and a major center of 700,000 such as Edmonton or Calgary. The text should serve as a jumping off place for more detailed study of topics in information systems security, or of a vendor's products.

This book is intended specifically as a *textbook* for an introductory course in information systems security. There is an associated *Instructor's Guide*, with supplemental material, transparency masters, case studies, answers to questions in the text, and other material based on that used by instructors in actual classroom situations.

The text has served well for courses in a programming-oriented stream and an accounting-oriented stream, both offered late in two-year technical college programs. We believe it would serve well as an introduction at the third or fourth-year university level. It is not intended to be a reference manual, nor is there a lot of detail in it, compared to what *could* have been included; however, many references and a bibliography help increase the value of this text as a reference.

Students need a number of prerequisites to take a course using this text: some programming, some accounting, some exposure to organizational analysis, basic business mathematics, and several courses in areas such as "Management Information Systems" and "Database Management," operating systems, and data communications. It is a text not for a first year course but for a course introducing a complex topic area which integrates many previous courses' material. Depending on the instructor's emphasis, different chapters may be omitted; after the first few chapters, most are reasonably self-contained and can be dropped without harming following chapters.

As an example, the chapter on law is somewhat different in format from others and may not be of great interest to computing science students; accounting program students probably should study this chapter, however, and students of law and technology might concentrate on this chapter. For another example, accounting students probably do not need to concern themselves with the chapter on encryption but certainly would spend time on Chapter 15 and the associated accounting profession's guidelines. See the *Instructor's Guide* for more material on use of the book in courses.

No work such as this can be the result of a single person's efforts. My coauthor, Martin P. J. Kratz, has provided most of the law-related material; my other coauthor, Alan F. Brebner, is a Chartered Accountant who has used drafts of the text in teaching courses and whose insight has been invaluable in revising early drafts. Many suffering students have contributed comments, some printable; parts of this book represent considerable reworking from earlier drafts, and suggestions from students were an important aid. The first edition of this text was written and in use before the Canadian Institute of Chartered Accountants (CICA) *Computer Control Guidelines,* Second Edition was available; my studies in preparing for the Certified Information Systems Auditor examination, the CICA book, and feedback from Mr. Brebner, led to restructuring several parts of the book dealing with accounting material.

We express special gratitude to others who contributed: Brenda Dixon; Peter Johnston, P.Eng.; Margaret Nickel; and formal reviewers Prof. Fleming Woo of Kwantlen College in Vancouver and Prof. John J. Rooney of American University in Washington, D. C.

The CICA has given permission to reproduce portions of *Computer Control Guidelines*. The Royal Canadian Mounted Police (RCMP) "T" Directorate (the EDP security group) likewise have allowed use of material from their *Security Information Publications* series and from the *EDP Security Bulletin*. The Institute of Chartered Accountants of Alberta allowed us to adapt a case study which appears in three chapters. Some of the material in Chapter 14 is adapted from uncopyrighted publications of the Institute for Certification of Computer Professionals (ICCP) and of DPMA Canada/ACFOR. Supplementary material in the *Instructors' Guide* is used with permission of the Data Processing Management Association, Wang Canada Limited, and the Organization for Economic Cooperation and Development (OECD). We thank these organizations for helping us to create the best possible textbook.

Except for some diagrams drawn by an artist, this text was created entirely using Microsoft WORD 4.0 on a microcomputer with 640K and a fixed disk. Drafts were printed on various laser printers which could handle PostScript, particularly a system owned by Laserimage Text and Graphics. The final high-resolution typesetting was done from the same PostScript files, using a Linotron 300 at the University of Alberta.

I have done my best to incorporate material from these and other sources accurately. The responsibility for any errors that may have been introduced into others' submissions is mine. If users of this text will let me know about errors they find or areas less than clear, the next edition will be better yet.

Philip E. Fites, CSP, CDP
April, 1988

INTRODUCTION

In December 1987, newspapers reported that a graphics-image Christmas card had proved so popular that enough copies were made and transmitted to fill up IBM's world wide electronic mail communication system. Graphics images take a lot of space, and the space available in any electronic mail system is limited. According to the reports, IBM lost the use of most of its communication system for nearly two days because of this.

In January 1988, newspapers reported that a "virus" was discovered in the computer system at Hebrew University in Jerusalem. The virus had been set to delete all files on Friday, May 13th, 1988.

In January 1988, a program containing a virus was left on a computer in a store for two days. It has been estimated that 350,000 people in countries all over the world saw the "peace message" produced by the virus on March 2nd 1988.

Credit reporting companies maintain millions of files on individuals. The information included may be damaging if released, and is in any case very private. Usually, there is no check on the accuracy of the information; reports from retailers simply are filed. How can privacy be maintained, and how can accuracy be assured?

In California during 1987, a bank switched over from manual methods to an electronic teller system. Due to inadequate testing, very serious problems were reported. Estimates of the loss exceed $23 million. No one knows how many customers were lost.

Some years ago in Australia, a police officer used the computer terminal available to him to locate, from the welfare department's computer system, where his estranged wife was staying. He went to her home and murdered her.

In 1987, the Auditor General of the Canadian Federal Government reported that the several million dollar computerized budgeting system for the Canadian Broadcasting Corporation was not functioning properly, to the extent that CBC could not account for something like $50 million (Canadian).

During the Falklands War, the British destroyer Sheffield was severely damaged by a French-made Exocet missile. Published reports indicate that the defense system detected the incoming missile, but since it was French, the fire control computers considered it "friendly" and ignored it.

All of these examples involve computer systems. Computers have grown over the past few years to become one of the main things which affect our lives. As their impact and importance have increased, so has the need to protect computer systems.

These examples illustrate several kinds of problems which have occurred. The problems illustrate *security*: the virus and the Christmas card; *accuracy*: credit files and the Sheffield incident; *privacy*: credit files and the Australian incident; and *control*: the budget and bank problems. These are the topics of this textbook.

Consider one other example, more detailed this time.

One of the many checklists regarding information systems security is reproduced below. Scan through it: how many of the questions can you answer for your organization? For the "no" answers, do you know what to do about a possible problem? The purpose of this book is to provide the background needed to understand these and similar questions, to know why the questions are included, to know how to get answers for them, and to have at least a hint of what to do about revealed exposures.

(This questionnaire was chosen for the example because the police organization which created it has given explicit permission to reproduce it for use in your own organization.)

SECURITY CHECKLIST

Small Systems -- Questionnaire

1.   Is a definite person or area responsible for small systems security?

2.   Is this assigned responsibility documented so the individual/area knows the extent of the expected task?

3.   Has this assignment been distributed to all employees?

4.   Is there a security incident reporting system to notify designated personnel of problems?

5.   Have definite policies and procedures for use of the systems, e. g. copyright laws, been set?

6.   Have rules and regulations for the systems been set?

7.   Is physical access to the systems appropriately controlled?

8.   Is logical access (passwords) to the systems and data necessary and appropriately controlled?

9. Does an up-to-date inventory, including software packages, exist for all systems?

10. Are activities on the systems audited?

11. Are contingency plans for all systems in existence and are they appropriate?

12. Has a complete backup of software and data been taken and, if so, how often?

13. Is the backup kept in a separate, safe place?

14. Are users mutually acceptable, i. e. are all users allowed to access all data on a hard disk system?

15. Do appropriate termination of employment procedures exist, e. g. retrieval of keys and passwords, and are they followed?

16. Have users received proper training?

17. Has smoking, eating and drinking been banned near the systems?

18. Are diskettes locked in appropriate secure containers?

19. Are hard disks locked in an appropriate manner?

20. Is the power to these machines regulated to remove spikes that can cause damage?

21. Are dedicated circuits used for these machines?

22. Is air conditioning necessary and, if so, supplied?

23. Are the machines and their environments cleaned and maintained regularly?

24. Is sufficient fire protection provided?

25. Are defective disks (diskettes), tapes and ribbons destroyed properly?

26. Are the machines, internals, and peripherals secured to prevent theft?

27. Do procedures exist for sharing the systems among several users?

28. Is encryption needed for communications?

29. Is encryption needed for storage?

30. Are systems located to minimize others reading the screen?

31. Is sensitive information removed before maintenance is done?

32. Are disks returned for "over-the-counter" replacements? If so, how is data confidentiality retained?

33. Are communication links disabled when not required?

34. Does internally-generated software conform to pre-defined standards and conventions?

35. Are sufficient recovery routines built into the software?

36. Is there sufficient software piracy protection?

37.   Is there an up-to-date list of users for the systems?

38.   Are appropriate procedures in place for issuing and transmitting passwords?

39.   Are appropriate procedures in place to assist operators in using the systems?

40   Are there appropriate input and output control processes to ensure information is not lost?

41.   Do diskettes contain sufficient markings to identify ownership and contents?

42.   If machines may be used at home, is there a signout procedure?

43.   Are the types of security problems that users should be watching for documented and distributed?

44.   Are communications line errors logged and retained?

45.   Is traffic routed to the proper destination?

46.   Are acknowledgements required?

47.   Is TEMPEST equipment used where necessary?

48.   Are sensitive machines locked when not used?

RCMP EDP Security Bulletin, July 1987, pp. 5-7

System *security* relates to a number of things. Access to computer resources should be denied to some people, while others should be allowed partial access, and some few need complete access. For example, perhaps the policeman in Australia should not have been able to get at the social services department's computer from the terminal in his cruiser. Certainly, the information system manager at Hebrew University would have preferred that whoever entered the virus had not had that sort of access.

System *control* is an issue which affects many people. The examples above of the CBC and the bank in California are illustrations of breakdowns in several places in the computer system development process. The consequences of lapses in control can be, as in these examples, rather extreme.

Control, in this text, refers both to the kind of things which keep the system running properly, and to the accounting idea of control. The accountant's use of "control" is closer to what is usually meant by "safeguards" in this text. (In Chapter 15, "control" is used purely in the accounting sense.)

Accuracy in computer information systems is another problem. Very careful checking is needed to ensure that information entered into a system is correct, and controls in the system should ensure that the information *stays* correct. Most people would not like to think that, for instance, the balance of their bank accounts was likely to be incorrect due to the bank's lack of controls over accuracy, or due to an entry error. Someone's error in not telling a computer that

Argentines were using French missiles contributed to the sinking of a British warship.

Computer information systems maintain all kinds of files on all kinds of people (there are estimates that governments in the United States keep as many as 14 files for every American citizen). The issue of *privacy* is one which affects essentially everyone. Most people probably would prefer that people in general should not be able to access those credit bureau files to look at their financial picture. Medical records are confidential -- but are the computerized files secure?

If you are the manager of an information system, developments in laws may put you in a position of personal risk, especially in the area of privacy. Chapter 13 in this text addresses legal topics so that a basic background will be available.

Security and controls in information systems can be improved. Many things help, and some of these things are quite simple. This book discusses a number of such topics.

While it often may be simple to improve system security and controls, a very broad background is needed to attack the problem area. Some of the things which help are technical in nature, and computer training is needed with these. Many things which help are not technical at all but relate to how the organization is run and how employees are treated; a background in things like organization theory is helpful here. In some cases, the controls or security relate to financial matters, and accounting comes into play. The material following covers many of these areas, with emphasis on items from the various disciplines which are related to information system security and controls.

Before a complex analysis of many parts of an organization should be attempted, a "road map," or plan of action, needs to be in place. The road map -- or methodology -- of this text is simple in concept:

Look at what you are trying to protect.

Look at what you need to protect it from.

Determine how likely threats are.

Implement measures which will protect your assets in a cost-effective manner.

Review the process continuously, and improve things every time a weakness is found.

Technical fixes may be advisable, but they are not the whole answer. It is necessary to look carefully at the overall picture.

The overall system security picture includes:

1. Asset identification;
2. Exposure analysis;

3.   Risk quantification;
4.   Security and control measures based on the qualitative and quantitative
       data developed in the first stages;
5.   Testing measures;
6.   Review of results of testing and actual experience.

The most important elements in any good system control and security picture are administrative and organizational control measures.

Effective security and control is not a one-time event. The overall picture needs to be reviewed periodically as much as the budgeting process does. Conditions change; plans need updating. The critical element of any good management strategy is continued commitment by the organization, and periodic review and upgrading of system security and control plans is one way to maintain organizational awareness and commitment.

SECTION I: RISK MANAGEMENT

"Risk Management," according to the Royal Canadian Mounted Police (RCMP), is:

A scientific, systematic approach to the quantitative analysis of security risks and the introduction of cost effective safeguards to reduce these risks.

In the next two chapters, we examine some of the factors involved in identifying "assets" -- what we want to protect; "threats" -- what we want to protect them from; and what will be called "risk analysis," which will be seen to include figuring out how much effort to expend where in trying to manage the risk. These cover the first five of the elements of risk management listed below. The last two points (and some others as well) are covered later in this material.

The *elements* of risk management, again according to the RCMP, include:

1. A team of people to do the job
2. Identification of assets
3. Identification of threats
4. Determining likelihood of occurrence
5. Calculating the exposure
6. Introducing safeguards
* Reviewing, revising, and refining these processes based on observed results.

(The last item is added to the RCMP's list to emphasize the necessity of periodic review and revision of plans.)

In Section I, Chapter 1 deals with identifying assets and presents some of the simpler methods often used to assign values to assets in risk analysis. Chapter 2 deals with identification of threats and probabilities, and how to combine threats and assets to achieve a realistic assessment of where, and how much, to invest. Sections II and III look at specific control measures (the "safeguards" in item 6 above); Section IV goes into the developing legal and professional areas of control; and Section V is a brief summary of some of the rules and tools the accounting profession recommends.

Chapter 1

ASSET IDENTIFICATION AND VALUATION

INTRODUCTION

Security measures can be very costly and can present a very considerable nuisance and hindrance to "comfortable" working practices. In order to minimize the cost, and to be sure that the most important measures are implemented first, the first step in risk management is to identify the *assets* which are to be protected. Failure to do so leads to a "fortress mentality," where everything is protected to the utmost whether it's valuable or not; or to its opposite, a near complete lack of any security. Only when the assets and their values are clear can an intelligent security system design be created.

What, then, is an "asset?" An accountant would say that an asset is "something of value to the business." Certainly, this is one aspect of what we mean when we use the word "asset" in security and control. The accountant, however, is concerned with measuring precisely and accurately the dollar value of assets. In risk management, we often must work with much less precise values. It is difficult to define the exact value of the "asset" which a trained instructor represents to the educational institution paying this person. Yet, protection of this asset is certainly part of an intelligent security program. Let us accept the definition of asset as "something of value to the business," but with the clear understanding that it is not just dollars and cents we are dealing with.

1.1 PROCESSING VALUATION

Since an asset is something of value, let us consider value analysis next. A computer system, or any other system, presumably has value to a business. If not, it should be scrapped, or never created in the first place. The "processing value" analysis considers what it is worth to the business to have this thing done: from the viewpoint of the user, *and without regard to how the activity is to be performed*, what is the value of the activity. Preferably, this value should be expressed in dollars and cents. The instructor presumably teaches students, who pay the institution for the service. What is this value to the institution? Notice that here, the instruction perhaps could have been delivered by video tape, or laserdisc, or by satellite hookup from another city. We are asking at the moment only about the value of the service. Having established a value, we can then say that this service is an asset, and the value of having it performed is whatever we determined it to be in the analysis. Only the user of the service has the background to assign a value; for security purposes, the more senior the user, the more useful the value assigned is likely to be.

In data processing systems, the value analysis should be restricted to sorting out three properties:

1.   Availability
2.   Confidentiality
3.   Integrity.

In the first instance, what is the value of continued **availability** of the service? Or, turned around, what would happen if the service disappeared entirely? (The computer center burned down, for example.) If the payroll run takes five hours, is normally started at 11:00 AM on payday, and checks must be delivered by 5:00 PM the same day, then the maximum acceptable downtime is probably less than one hour. The value of this service could well be the continued existence of the business, or large legal fees due to violation of a union contract and resulting strike, or similar high figures.

Confidentiality refers to the need to keep data or information from being public. If all the organization's data and information could be published without problems, then there might be no need of confidentiality. In practice, this is rarely, if ever, true. In Canada and the United States, privacy laws require employers to be reticent about personal information of employees. Most financial figures for a company are at least sensitive. For example, a competitor might pay well indeed to know the exact budget allocated to advertising a specific product. Medical records are highly protected in most jurisdictions. One way to get an idea how much the confidentiality attribute of an asset is worth is to imagine how much money a person or group would pay to have the information, or the cost of the loss of the business, if there is a legal requirement to observe privacy.

The third property of the assets in an information system under consideration is **integrity**. Integrity of data or processes is the property which relates to their authenticity, accurateness, and completeness. Has there been an unannounced change in a credit limit? Has all information been reported to the credit granter? Is the information which was reported accurate as well as authentic and complete? It is perhaps easiest to comprehend the value of integrity when a tangible asset is under discussion. For example, if a bank cannot depend on account balances, it could sustain a very large loss through paying checks which are not covered. In an inventory, the potential loss is the amount of material which could be diverted between physical inventory counts. In a more general information system, the loss of goodwill of clients could be a cost. For a newspaper, unreliable data used as backing for a damaging story could incur very great costs.

Through looking at value analysis we have examined the three characteristics of an asset in an information system and we have discussed some examples of how one would set a value on an asset. The three characteristics are **availability**, **confidentiality**, and **integrity**. The general rule for setting a value on an asset is that the user or owner of the asset must be the one to do it (with the help of professionals to be sure). Let us look first at considerations in selecting a risk management team, and then at two classifications of assets, and at some representative assets in each of the classifications.

While "asset" has not been defined other than as "something of value to the business," we have identified a starting point for identification of assets and properties to be examined:

Start by determining the processing value of the service in question.

Examine the properties of
1.   availability
2.   confidentiality
3.   integrity.

This gives a sufficient picture of "asset" to begin the valuation process. Examination of the valuation process has resulted in identifying some of the people who need to be involved; next, we expand upon this to look at the risk management team.

1.2 THE RISK MANAGEMENT TEAM

Value analysis is not a particularly difficult activity, but it does require that fundamental questions be answered carefully by people who have the appropriate background to know the answers. On the data processing group's side, the key team member clearly is that person who has final responsibility for securing the system. The situation from the users' side is more complex.

Every piece of data or information passing through an information system has an *owner* and someone who is *responsible* for the data or information. The **owner** may delegate responsibility; delegation of ownership of course means that the previous owner is no longer involved. For example, the Vice President of Finance probably would be the **owner** of all accounting data; the Accounts Receivable Manager might be **responsible** for the data in the accounts receivable system. At another level, the A/R manager might be the **owner** of the accounts receivable data, and the supervisor of data entry responsible for getting data correctly entered into a computer. In the final analysis, the **owner** must be involved in the value attribution. Since data and information may be changed as they pass through the information system, the persons who hold the ownership and responsibility positions may also change; thus several people may need to be involved on the users' side where only the person with final responsibility is necessary from the data processing department. As stated previously, the more senior the people involved, the better the results are likely to be as answers to fundamental questions about the value of a particular asset to the ongoing organization.

In summary then, the following people must be members of the risk analysis team:

1.   Data Processing: Person with final responsibility for securing the system
2.   Users: Owner(s) of data and information [or their delegates]

Many other team members may be desirable for technical expertise or other reasons, but these two groups *must* be involved or the security effort is doomed to irrelevance.

1.3 CLASSIFICATION OF ASSETS

There are many ways to classify assets. Perhaps the most common is the accounting distinction between "tangible" and "intangible" assets. In essence:

tangible assets are measurable in dollars and cents.
intangible assets are not easily measured in dollars and cents.

This distinction is somewhat arbitrary; greater effort at measurement, or more data to work with, often will allow a measurement in dollars. For example, Johnson & Johnson probably considers the brand name Tylenol to be an intangible asset because its value was very difficult to measure. Since the discovery of packages with broken seals and poisoned capsules added in 1982 and 1986, and the resulting product redesign, the asset is easier to measure, as it has at least the value of the money spent on advertising and management time in allaying public fears and redesigning the product to be more tamper resistant. Of course, much effort was spent; it seems likely that Johnson & Johnson would prefer to have had the value remain intangible rather than spend the money which was invested. The point here is that even "intangible" assets often can have dollar values applied, if enough effort is invested. The risk management team and senior management must trade off measurement effort against value achieved; in asset valuation for security purposes, being out by a factor of two normally is not a problem so long as relative sizes are maintained.

A second, related classification is **physical** versus **logical** assets. A physical asset is also a tangible asset. Many logical assets are intangible. An example could be a computer program stored on a "floppy disk." The physical value of the storage medium is likely about $2. The logical value of the arrangement of data (the "program") may be hundreds of thousands of dollars. It would be difficult to measure this value precisely; the usual way is to estimate how long it would take to recreate the program, or how long it took to create it in the first place. In this case, the *intrinsic* value of the medium has an *acquired* value added to it.

Much, or most, of the value of assets in an information system very well may be represented by intangible logical assets. The value of a document in computer readable format, such as this one, is at least the cost of having it re-entered from a paper backup, assuming all computer readable forms are lost. If the paper backup were lost as well, it would have to be created again, likely from memory, by a senior person who did the original creation. The value of data in an Accounts Receivable subsystem could be as high as the total of all bad accounts, or of all purchases not yet billed. More about actual asset values is discussed below.

There are two main ways to classify assets which are of interest in security work: tangible/intangible, and physical/logical. **Tangible** assets have easily measured dollar values. **Intangible** assets are not easily measured in dollars. **Physical** assets are those you can "feel;" **logical** assets are such things as data and the arrangement of things. Most physical assets are tangible as well. To some extent, the amount of effort expended can change an asset from intangible to tangible; if you spend enough, most intangible assets can be given dollar values with high confidence.

1.4 SUBCLASSIFICATIONS OF ASSETS

The next several subsections show, for several types of assets, physical and logical subclassifications. These lists are not exhaustive; each installation will have at least slight differences. The general types considered in this text are those used by the RCMP [RCMP 1981], but are not unique:

1.   Essential Services
2.   Support Items
3.   Physical EDP Assets
4.   Logical EDP Assets

Another breakdown could be:

1.   People
2.   Physical and Environmental
3.   Communications
4.   Hardware
5.   Software
6.   Data and Information

Yet another breakdown, useful for some purposes, is:

1.   Hardware
2.   Software
3.   Data and Information
4.   People and Procedures

The point of these breakdowns is not to generate lists but to illustrate that each risk analysis will have different needs and perspective and each risk management team will analyze its assets differently. The key is to list assets in such a way as to have a list which is

1.   complete (or as complete as is needed)
2.   not too long
3.   has no duplication

For purposes of this text, these subclasses will be used:

1.   People and Procedures
2.   Physical and Environmental
3.   Communications
4.   Hardware

5.   Software

6.   Data and Information

1.4.1 People and Procedures

In discussions and seminars on computer security, participants often are asked to identify the single most important asset requiring protection. Is it the mainframe computer hardware? The program library? Or whatever? Surprisingly, many make several guesses before they reach the correct answer: "people." (It is worth noting that more senior staff generally get the right answer the first time.) An organization can be defined as a group of **people** gathered to accomplish a **purpose** which they cannot accomplish individually. Machines do not have purposes; people do. Without the people, all other assets are irrelevant. In security, people may have reasons to penetrate, and they nearly always deal with people in a penetration attempt.

Both philosophically and practically, then, the protection of human life is the one overriding concern in any intelligent security plan. The fire extinguisher exists, not to put out the fire, but to ensure a clear path to safety for people in the computer room. Industrial safety is a field with an extensive literature; computer operations are not so different as to require much special treatment in a work of this type. Section II does consider several administrative aspects of security systems. From time to time throughout this treatment, it is noted that selection and proper use of people is a paramount concern (so far, we have touched on this mainly in the example of the instructor and in selection of the risk management team.)

The skills, training, and experience of people are assets. It costs money to find new people and to train them. Examples of people in the information security arena include:

1.   Operators

2.   Programmers

3.   Analysts

4.   Managers

5.   Secretarial staff

6.   Security staff

7.   Custodial staff

8.   Vendors

9.   Customers

All of these and others, depending on the installation, must be considered both as assets and, as discussed in Chapter 2, as threats or exposures.

In the summary for this chapter on identifying and valuing assets, there is a diagram (Figure 1.2). It is one of the familiar "pyramid" representations showing the approximate relationship of four major types of asset and their cost. The cost or value of the people in the organization, their training and experience, and their familiarity with procedures is by far the most significant (and also the most often ignored in evaluating a change to a new system). This observation naturally leads to another asset, procedures and procedure manuals, as well as documentation for systems, programs, equipment, and all else.

1.4.2 Physical and Environmental

Here, we are looking at physical assets besides such things as computer hardware, which is treated separately. A list of physical, tangible assets could include:

1.   Facilities
       Building, back-up storage area, equipment rooms, air conditioning rooms, office space
2.   Support
       Fire system, electricity, air conditioning, communications, fuel oil for backup power, water
3.   Supplies, Material, and Furniture
       Re-usable tapes, disks, diskettes, tape cartridges, expendable paper, forms, waste paper, blank checks, desks, chairs, containers, bookcases, filing cabinets

Physical, intangible assets do exist, despite the blanket comment earlier. A "prime location" such as Colorado Springs, Colorado, can make the job of attracting people to come to work with a company a much easier task. This would be an intangible asset, although the site location is clearly physical.

Of course, this list is nowhere near exhaustive and will vary depending on location. In Yellowknife, NWT (an isolated city of 10,000 in the Canadian Arctic), retail stores with computer-controlled cash registers have boxes between the machine and the power supply. Due to special problems with utility power reliability and "cleanness," some sort of filter is universal there. In Edmonton, Alberta, and most other major cities, such devices are rare since the power supply is quite dependable and "clean." Other major centers, especially in the United States Eastern Seaboard area, experience brownouts or other power supply problems; in those locations, the boxes between the machines and the wall plug are again common.

1.4.3 Communications

Communications was listed under "Physical and Environmental"; however, as computer and other technologies grow, communications is assuming an increasing part of a computer center's value and costs. Basic telephone is one thing; Local Area Networks, Distributed Data Processing, satellite communications and other capabilities are quite another. Physical tangible assets might include:

1. Front-end processors (specialized computers programmed to act as an interface between mainframe computers and communications channels)
2. Concentrators (a *concentrator* normally takes input from many low-speed channels and combines it into one high-speed channel leading to the front-end processor)
3. Terminals
4. Modems
5. Communication lines (coaxial cable or optical fibers, for example)
6. Data encryption hardware
7. Satellite uplinks and downlinks
8. Private Branch Exchange (PBX and PABX) equipment.

All of these assets could be included in a complex voice/data communications system for a transnational company; or a small company might use only telephone and public carriers. The details are not important for this text; in environments where they become important, there might even be a specialist to stay abreast of the exciting and fast-changing world of communications.

1.4.4 Hardware

The hardware area is the one most people associate immediately with the notion of a physical asset to be considered in an information system security program. It is probably the smallest, and probably also the area of the least total dollar investment. Hardware includes media such as paper, tapes, etc, both re-usable and expendable; these have been mentioned above. Equipment includes:

1. Processors
2. Disk drives
3. Tape drives
4. Printers
5. Terminals
6. Cabling
7. Spare parts.

The equipment probably varies as much as anything, except software and data, from place to place. Perhaps some installations still have card readers and card punches. Certainly some have mass storage devices.

1.4.5 Software

Software, particularly applications software, is different in each information system. (This is changing with the mass retail sale of identical copies of such programs as Lotus 1-2-3 and other proprietary software.) A list of common software would include:

1. Operating System (MS-DOS, UNIX, or whatever)
2. Utilities (sorts, editors, ...)
3. Compilers
4. Communications software
5. Database software (Cullinet's IDMS, IBM's ADABAS, Ashton-Tate's dBase II and III, ...)
6. Teleprocessing software (IBM's CICS and CMS, ...)
7. Application software
8. Catalogued Procedure libraries.

Each item has some value, if only in availability. Without the operating system, all other software is useless, even though the operating system may have been included "free" with the hardware.

1.4.6 Data and Information

The things which vary most from place to place naturally are data and information. It is somewhat pointless to attempt any sort of exhaustive listing of such variable items. Note, however, that data and information are assets of considerable value. Computer-readable data is worth *at least* as much as it would cost to re-enter it (that is, recapture or re-create it, if possible). Over time, this dominates the cost of hardware and software. Some types of data commonly found are:

1. Data bases (Nexis, for example, contains full text of numerous U. S. newspapers and would be enormously expensive to re-create, if it is even possible.)
2. Online files (whatever is more or less current)
3. Off-line files
4. Input files (alteration could leave an opening for fraud)
5. Output files

6. Audit trails and logs (Loss could make recovery, or fraud detection, impossible.)

7. Indexes (Just as a telephone book is more valuable with letter-of-the-alphabet tabs, most data are closer to usable information with a table of contents.)

8. Contents of memory (lost if power is lost and the data were not yet saved).

1.5 DETERMINING VALUES FOR ASSETS

1.5.1 Acquired and Intrinsic Values

In Section 1.3, the notions of intrinsic and acquired value were alluded to briefly. In determining asset values, it is necessary to be sure that these concepts are very clear, and that they are kept separate. For security purposes, protecting a blank diskette worth perhaps $2 is a very different problem from protecting a program on the diskette, which could be worth $100,000.

The *intrinsic* value of an asset is normally the cost of replacing the physical component, or what the physical component could be sold for. A diskette has an intrinsic value of perhaps $2. A five-year-old used computer may have a negative intrinsic value; you could have to pay for someone to take it away and dispose of it. The intrinsic value of a procedures manual may be $20 in copying and paper costs. However, intrinsic value is not the whole story. An asset also has an *acquired* value. When information is put onto that diskette, the diskette has an intrinsic value *plus* an acquired value. When people become used to new procedures and training programs are in place, the procedures manual has an intrinsic value and a very large acquired value as well. As an organization becomes used to one way of doing things, the system itself gains an acquired value. The first major step is when parallel testing is complete and the doubling of effort is stopped; the system then has no backup and a large acquired value component is added. As people get more and more comfortable with using the new system, the training, experience, and familiarity add further to the acquired value of the system. Sudden loss of availability after a few years can become catastrophic; the acquired value is thus extremely large. The five-year-old computer may still be in use to process the payroll; loss of availability at the wrong time could be catastrophic.

It helps ease the analysis process when standard forms are used; they are easier to combine in later stages, and they help ensure that things do not get overlooked. A form might contain:

Asset Valuation
Acquired Value Worksheet

Date Valued: _____

Revised: No._____
                     Date_____

Page __ of __

ASSET
Intrinsic Value:_____

ACQUIRED VALUES

1. Integrity
              VALUE:_____
Justification:

2. Availability
              VALUE:_____
Justification:

3. Confidentiality
              VALUE:_____
Justification:

1.5.2 Purpose of Assigning Value to Assets

Once the value of various services to the company has been determined, it is fairly straightforward to identify the assets involved in providing the services. The analysis of processing value was done without regard to the methods used to provide the service. When asset valuation is done, assets involved in providing the service as it is done now are identified, classified according to physical/logical and tangible/intangible categories, and by subcategory. It then is necessary to attach a value to each of the identified assets. Recall that the purpose of this exercise is to identify security exposures and the value of the assets which may be exposed, so that an intelligent security program can be designed. We are *not* trying to get an exact value of the business; in fact, it often is sufficient simply to know that one asset is worth more than another (you protect the more valuable one).

With this in mind, there are probably thousands of ways to ascribe a value to an asset. Some are difficult to use; some are expensive to use; some may not be possible or practical. The purpose of the valuation in security analysis is to rank assets and to get a reasonable idea of how much it is worth investing to protect them. The valuation process is part of the cost of the security system, and normally low cost outweighs greater precision. The ultimate result of all this work is to make sure that appropriate effort is invested to protect assets, but not so much that the cost of the security exceeds the cost of the effort.

Considering this purpose, four valuation methods will be outlined:

1.   Historical cost
2.   Replacement cost
3.   Cost of lost availability
4.   Estimated values

1.5.3 How to Measure Asset Values

With the purpose of asset valuation for security in mind, consider first, how to measure the value of an asset; that is, what units of measure to use. The traditional unit is dollars.

The arguments for using dollars as a measure are many and powerful. Firstly, it is a universal measure. A given number of dollars has the same value everywhere within a single economy. Reducing everything to this universal measure means it is easy to make comparisons. This is probably the most important argument for using dollars and cents. Secondly, using this measure forces people to expend more care on determining a value; therefore, the resulting values are more likely to be reasonably accurate. Thirdly, since a business's success or failure is measured in dollar terms, people are comfortable with thinking about assets in terms of dollars.

On the other hand, it can be very difficult to reduce some kinds of intangible assets to dollar values. It may be necessary to use statistical techniques or other methods involving estimation. Eventually, not only does the cost of estimating go up, but the final result comes to depend on very subjective assumptions and may not be any better than easier estimating methods.

Designing a security system involves accurate relative rankings. No system can protect everything perfectly; it is necessary to trade off cost against value and priority. Rather than expend extraordinary efforts to come up with dollar figures, it may be sufficient to use *scalar* measures. The most commonly proposed is simple orders of magnitude. An example is:

Scale for Asset Valuation in Dollars

Scalar Number	*Value in Dollars*
0	$1 or less
1	up to $10
2	$100
3	$1,000
4	$10,000
.	.
.	.
.	.
8	$100,000,000

In this scale, the number assigned is based on a power of ten ("order of magnitude"). If the asset has any value between, say, $10,000 and $100,000, it will get the scalar value 5. This is a very wide scale, but most people will be able to give a firm estimate within an order of magnitude. If more precision is needed, other power bases can be used. If the Naperian logarithm base e (2.7182818...) is used, we could construct a table like this:

Scale for Asset Valuation in Dollars

Scalar Number	Dollar Value
0	below $300
1	up to $700
2	up to $2,000
3	up to $5,000
4	$15,000
5	$40,000
6	$110,000
7	$300,000
8	$800,000
9	$2,200,000
.	.
.	.
.	.

In this table, each range limit grows by a factor of about 2.7183 rather than by a factor of 10. This allows people still to "guess" reliably, but gives smaller intervals and thus more precision.

Scales like this can be used in two ways. First, people can be asked to estimate a loss as "between 500 and 1000 dollars," or whatever interval is of interest. The guess is then recorded as a scalar (in this case, 3 or 1, depending on which of the above two tables were used). The scalars are then used in further calculations, which simplifies the arithmetic. A second way to use such a table is to ask people to rank exposures relative to a known exposure. If they ranked event B as "about 100 times as bad as event A," then (assuming powers of ten), if A were a $100,000 problem, B would be a $10,000,000 problem. Using this method, one arrives at (very conservative) dollar figures, which again are used in further calculation.

The main disadvantage of using scalars to get a relative ranking is that corporate management normally are conditioned and trained to think in dollars; the scalar rankings will not have the same impact as dollars would.

Dollar values are best, since they allow comparison and people are comfortable with them. If it is expensive or impractical to get exact dollars, scalar estimation methods are one way to convert "guesses" into dollar values. More sophisticated weighted entry table methods can also be used; these are beyond the scope needed here.

1.5.4 Asset Valuation: Standard Accounting

With the purpose of asset valuation in mind, and noting the possibility of using differing metrics, the easiest way to value assets relates to normal accounting practices. This will work only for tangible assets whose value is "on the books," that is, valued in the accounting records of the company according to Generally Accepted Accounting Principles (GAAP). Then the value of the asset simply can be looked up:

1.   Locate the book value of the asset.
2.   Locate the accumulated depreciation.

Add the two, and you have an idea of the loss. Depending on the depreciation method used, you may also have an idea of replacement cost.

1.5.5 Asset Valuation: Replacement Cost

Probably the main virtue of the previous method is that it is fast; for tangible assets, the numbers are already there, and there is little difficulty or cost in getting to them. Many accountants would caution that adding book value to depreciation does not necessarily give a good measure of replacement cost. There are accounting and other techniques which allow fairly good estimation of replacement costs. One which often works well at minimal cost is to call up a vendor and ask what the cost of asset A is today. For tangible assets, this works well for security purposes. Note that this issue is more complex in practice; one would not necessarily replace item A with an identical item today: the business may have changed, item A could be obsolete, etc. Accountants have devised ways to cope with this sort of problem. Recall again, that exact dollars are not usually needed in security analysis. Most estimates should be rounded to the nearest $1000 or even the nearest $10,000; don't spend too much time on small numbers.

1.5.6 Asset Valuation: Loss of Availability

Frequently, an asset with a relatively low cost ("intrinsic value") may be vital to the continued operation of the business. Loss of its availability represents a very large cost. The risk evaluation team should ensure that loss of availability is considered as a cost in each asset which is valued. Concerned personnel may be able to estimate these losses clearly; or estimating methods such as the scalars shown previously may be used.

1.5.8 Asset Value Recording Form

The procedures of identifying processing values, identifying assets, and valuing assets lead to a considerable amount of data. These data should be collected in a standardized format so they will be available for further calculation. Many sources show forms for this purpose. All of the forms are very similar, with entries for assets, intrinsic value, and the acquired value components of availability, integrity, and confidentiality. Such a layout is found in Figure 1.1.

General Value Analysis of System Assets

ASSET	INTRINSIC VALUE	ACQUIRED VALUE		
		AVAILA-BILITY	INTEGRITY	CONFIDEN-TIALITY

Figure 1.1

Filling in the asset, intrinsic value, and acquired value components columns will leave the data gathered in a format which is concise and useful for the fourth step in the risk management process, combining threat assessments with the asset valuation to calculate dollar exposures and priorities. Each asset is named in the first column. Then the intrinsic value is entered. The acquired values of integrity, availability, and confidentiality are filled in last. Repeat this for each asset.

As an example, a diskette (*asset*) may have an intrinsic value of $2. One possibility is a diskette with a word processor on it. (One also could list the intrinsic value as the cost of the software plus diskette, perhaps $450.) Its acquired values will vary from time to time. It has an acquired value of availability that might be equal to the down time incurred by the operator while a new diskette is obtained, say, $125. (If the diskette contains custom programmed macros, then the programming cost would be added to the availability.) The value of integrity in this case would be about the same -- if it doesn't retain integrity, the word processor won't work and the software has to be replaced. The acquired value of confidentiality in this case probably is zero.

1.6 USE OF ASSET ANALYSIS RESULTS

There are two primary uses for the results obtained from this asset analysis process:

1. A picture of the total investment by the firm is gained. Since much of the material has been reduced to dollars, senior management and others accustomed to thinking in dollar terms will get an appreciation (frequently, a *new* and *different* appreciation) of the amount at risk.

2. The figures derived are used as input to calculations leading to the final risk management assessment (described in Chapter 3).

The asset analysis could show that there are no really valuable assets to be protected, and thus it is a waste of resources to go further in the risk management process. More commonly, it alerts senior management to the fact that some very valuable parts of the business are exposed and need to be looked at very carefully. The total value of the assets related to information systems frequently comes as a great surprise to management, with a resulting desire to carry on in the process, at a rather high priority.

One such analysis involved the information system assets of a two-year technical training school specializing in training people to use computers. The obvious assets -- a minicomputer and associated equipment, and some hundreds of microcomputers -- turned out to be a very small part of the total. When one included the cost of retraining instructors to use different word processing software, the cost of re-creating student records (including all academic records and financial data), and the effect on the school of a loss of such records, the value jumped from a known $250,000 or so to a rather staggering figure over $1.5 million. Management instituted immediate measures to protect some assets which were not well protected, and allocated resources to continuing with the risk management process.

1.7 A COMMENT

In some form, the process of valuing services, identifying assets, and valuing assets must be undergone before one can plan a rational security system. However, for a smaller organization, often the basic data are unavailable. Statistical techniques which work well for large samples do not always work well for small samples. There is little actual difficulty in most of the asset identification and valuation process described previously; however, if done properly the result is a lot of data. The total risk assessment process does involve a substantial amount of arithmetic and detail work. It is probably impractical for a small organization to attempt a full-fledged risk analysis unless computer support is available.

It is important to avoid "paralysis by analysis" while still doing a thorough job of asset identification and valuation. Too much detail is as bad as too little:

1.   It is hard to value the "small stuff."
2.   The cost of the risk analysis rises.
3.   The result can be an overwhelming sea of numbers.

1.8 SUMMARY

In Chapter 1, the topic of risk management has been started. "Risk Management" has been defined as

A scientific, systematic approach to the quantitative analysis of security risks and the introduction of cost effective safeguards to reduce these risks.

The risk management process has six steps:

1.   Create a team of people to do the job.
2.   Identify the assets.
3.   Identify the threats.
4.   Determine the probabilities of the threats.
5.   Calculate the exposures.
6.   Introduce safeguards.
*   A "final step" is to review and refine this process based on the observed results.

Chapter 1 has examined some of the aspects of the first two steps, creating the risk management team and identifying assets. Chapter 2 goes into steps 3 and 4, threats, step 5, exposures, and step 6, safeguards.

In the first step, we saw that selecting a team involves getting at least the person in EDP with final responsibility for securing the system, and the owner(s) of assets from the user side. Other people, such as professionals to advise, may also be appropriate.

The second step, identifying assets, has been essentially the thrust of this chapter. We first defined "asset" to be, roughly, "anything of value to the business." Since that definition is not too useful, the process of processing valuation was examined, and three properties of assets relevant to systems security were identified:

1. Availability
2. Confidentiality
3. Integrity

Further definition of assets led to the two primary classifications used, tangible/intangible and physical/logical. For security purposes, tangible means that it is measurable in dollars, and intangible, that it is not. Physical means "of substance" ("the part you can kick" conveys the basic meaning, although the phrase is somewhat inaccurate); logical relates to how physical things are related to one another. Most physical assets are also tangible assets. More money invested in measurement often can convert an intangible asset into a tangible one.

The primary classifications were then used with several subclassifications to show how assets might be collected. Lists like those presented in Section 1.4 allow the risk analysis team to be reasonably sure that all things have been considered. Their main purpose is to be complete enough, to avoid duplication, and not to become excessively long.

Several kinds of values that assets may have, and ways of attributing those values, were presented next. The concepts of intrinsic and acquired values were defined, three metrics -- dollars and two types of scalars -- were examined. Assigning values to assets by means of examining accounting books, estimating replacement cost, estimating cost of loss of availability, and the Delphi class of estimating methods were looked at next. A format useful for recording the results of this analysis was the final presentation.

Risk management involves looking at what you need to protect, what you need to protect it from, and how to protect it. The asset valuation process answers the first need.

This Chapter closes with an observation drawn from involvement in a number of microcomputer installations. Using the breakdown of Hardware, Software, Data and Information, and People and Procedures, most new installations show a pattern over five years like:

Hardware	$10000 (stable by end of 1st year)
Software	$10000 (after about 18 months)

Data and Information $25000 (accumulates, but entry cost of
                                        $5000 per year is typical)
People and Procedures $55000

After the initial purchase, there is some more hardware cost (modem, better printer, more storage, etc.). During the first year to year and a half, most users spend a considerable amount on trying out software, then that settles down as well. Data entry continues and the value of the data keeps growing (eventually, the value levels off because older data loses value). People keep learning, the business itself changes to make use of the new capability, training programs are built, and so on; the people component never stops growing. This whole process is visually depicted by the familiar sort of pyramid shown in Figure 1.2. The point to be made here is that we are talking about acquiring and protecting a $100,000 asset when all the factors are added in. Asset identification and valuation shows this. Many managers think only about the tip of the pyramid, the $10-15,000 hardware and software cost the first year, and thus do not invest enough time in considering security and controls appropriate to a $100,000 asset. Some managers fail to see that there is more than a financial loss exposure as well. A major business disruption can result. For example, with fully utilized staff, there won't be a lot of spare time to re-create possibly several months' lost data; management may have to find and hire people to do this, and cope with the resulting disorganization and disruption.

There are two primary uses for the results obtained from this asset analysis process:

1. A picture of the total investment by the firm is gained.
2. The figures derived are used as input to risk management calculations.

The asset analysis could show that there are no really valuable assets to be protected; more commonly, the total value of the assets related to information systems comes as a great surprise to management, with a resulting desire to carry on with the risk management process, at a rather high priority.

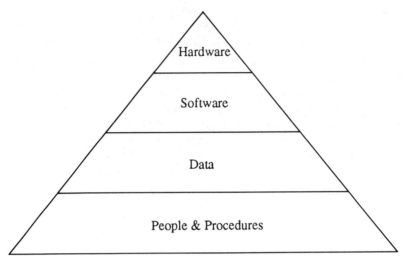

Figure 1.2

1.9 NEW TERMS;

New terms introduced in this chapter, or terms which may be used differently in risk analysis, are:

Acquired value
Asset
Availability property
Confidentiality property
Delphi methods of estimating
Intangible asset
Intrinsic value
Logical asset
Metric
Owner
Physical asset
Risk management
Tangible asset

1.10 QUESTIONS

1.1 processing value

Assume that you work in a major bank with a large, complex computer accounting system. The bank manager, Mr. I. Don Know, does not understand the importance of system asset availability, confidentiality and data integrity. He also does not know what the term"data integrity" means.

Required:

Explain to the bank manager the importance of system asset availability, confidentiality, and data integrity. Then give examples of problems that could be caused in a bank by loss of availability, loss of confidentiality and loss of integrity. (Give two examples for each one.) Then explain what "data integrity" means, in simple terms.

1.2 "acquired value

(This is taken from figure 1.1 in text.)

Fill in each space to rank its value as either high, medium or low.

1.3 "Value of a System"

In your new job at New York New Shoes Inc. you have designed a computer security system that would cost $30,000 to implement. This company is the world's largest shoe warehouse.

The company has 900 employees, $1,000,000 in accounts receivable, and 3,000 different types of shoes in inventory. $40,000 in checks are written in an average week. The applications software was custom written by a consultant and this took two years.

After spending five minutes reviewing your security plan (which took you five weeks to develop), the president tells you that, "We cannot afford your security system. It isn't worthwhile because our computer only cost $20,000."

Required:

Write a point form memo to the president, Mr. Nu U. Wood, giving a list of reasons why computer security in this company is important enough to justify a $30,000 expenditure.

1.4 Asset Valuation

Using the form outlined in Section 1.5.1, Asset Valuation: Acquired Value Worksheet, or the form specified by your instructor, indicate for your school or organization the acquired values in various categories of:

Data regarding student or other accounts receivable accumulated over the last three years

Data regarding student records, or sales records of some product, for the past two years

The "people cost" invested in training staff how to use the XYZ word processor (normally, staff take a two-day training course, then need another month of use at two hours per day to acquire real familiarity).

CHAPTER 2

THREAT AND EXPOSURE ASSESSMENT

INTRODUCTION

In Chapter 1, the risk management process was presented as consisting of a number of steps. The ones emphasized were:

1. Select a team.
2. Identify and set a value on assets.
3. Identify threats.
4. Assess the likelihood of the threats.
5. Calculate the exposure.
6. Introduce safeguards.
* Review the results and repeat the process as part of an ongoing process.

The first two of these steps were covered in Chapter 1. In Chapter 2, we look at steps 3, 4, and 5: identifying threats, associating a probability with each threat, and calculating the dollar value of the resulting exposures.

In the first subsection, some general comments are made about the types of things which must be considered in threat identification. The second subsection discusses analyzing threats by type of threat, by type of asset, and one way to combine these analyses. In Section 2.3, probability concepts used in this work are defined briefly. Section 2.4 looks at sources of threat information, and, in the process, begins to zero in on some more detailed methods which are likely to be of use in an actual risk management analysis. Section 2.5 presents a number of examples of threats, from the two perspectives examined in Section 2.2. In Section 2.6, the pieces considered to date -- asset identification and valuation and threat identification and likelihood -- are brought together in the exposure calculation.

2.1 THREATS, VULNERABILITIES, AND EXPOSURES

Many factors, some unique to EDP systems, which, singly and especially in combination, make computer systems particularly vulnerable to threats. A particular characteristic of EDP systems is the density of information. A problem which is not unique is what must be characterized simply as poor management. (See also Chapter 13 for comments on legislative efforts related to these factors.) There are six areas of special interest:

1.   Density of information
2.   Accessibility of systems
3.   Complexity
4.   Electronic vulnerability
5.   Media vulnerability
6.   Human factors

The first factor is density of information. A diskette contained in a package about 1/16" thick and about 3-1/2" square may contain the equivalent of 50 or 100 pages of textual information. It is easy for someone to slip several of these into a shirt pocket and carry out information and programs which may be worth hundreds or thousands of dollars. This exposure will increase with technological advances; optical storage, for example, permits densities much greater than presently achievable with the magnetic diskette described. In the near future, one diskette the size of a CD disk in audio use will be able to hold many thousands of pages of information. Similarly, anyone with access to this information from a computer has access to a great deal of information and can affect it very quickly. When a terminal may be connected from anywhere in the world where there is a telephone system, the problem of securing information is not in the same class as simply putting a lock on the file room door.

The second factor is that computer systems traditionally have been designed to be as accessible as possible to a wide range of people. As noted earlier, with communications included, the physical location of the people no longer matters very much. This accessibility means many exposures exist which were minimal or nonexistent in manual paper-based systems.

The third factor is complexity. It is not unusual to find operating systems or applications programs containing millions of instructions, far more than any single human being can comprehend as a whole. Worse, while it is simple to demonstrate that an error does exist, there is no universal way to prove that errors do *not* exist. Technically sophisticated people ("hackers") have taken advantage of errors to penetrate these complex, dense systems which are accessible from anywhere.

Computer systems function using electronic signals. These signals can be detected and interpreted from outside the systems. Outside sources such as radio transmitting towers or police radar in a speed trap can interfere with the internal working of unshielded computer systems.

The information-dense medium of magnetic disks mentioned previously is also subject to problems not commonly considered. For example, placing the diskette on top of a home television receiver, or beside a ringing telephone, may subject the information to corruption from unintended magnetic impulses. The fact that the information is not easily read by people without equipment can be a good thing -- it lessens the exposure to casual "eavesdropping." The same characteristic means, however, that people may have control over sensitive information without realizing it.

The sixth and final area where EDP systems are particularly vulnerable must be laid at the feet of DP management. As of 1986, most senior DP managers started in a technical position. Many have reached management positions with little or no proper training in management. It is not unusual to find a high degree of implicit trust and responsibility placed on personnel at junior levels without commensurate management control and accountability. This sort of human exposure is probably the greatest vulnerability associated with the EDP environment. It is essentially poor management (and here is a reason why this text is not greatly concerned with technical factors in system security, but spends so much time on non-computer areas such as procedures).

The word "threat" in casual conversation is used in relation to people with intent to do something bad to something else. In security and control analysis, this word has taken on a slightly different meaning. To the security specialist the word "threat" does not refer so much to a person, as to a *situation* where some (unknown and unspecified) person *could* do something undesirable.

To be precise:

A **threat** is an indication of an impending undesirable event.

The difference in usage is perhaps unfortunate, as it tends to cause management to consider security personnel to be paranoid when they refer to "threats." The word should be avoided (unless used with the more "standard" meaning) in reports to management.

The word "vulnerability," used as a noun in the context of security analysis, addresses the same area as "threat." The vulnerability is the exposure or weakness; the threat is the ability to take, or the act of taking, advantage of a vulnerability. This word will recur in the following text, for example when discussing possible exposures to threats from personnel as related to their normal job responsibilities.

The word "exposure" has a semi-technical meaning when used in a context such as "calculating exposures." In this context, we are talking about a dollar value which is assigned to the result of identifying an asset, a threat, and a likelihood and combining these three data. This dollar value serves two functions: to rank exposures, and to allow the risk manager to select security measures which control exposure without costing more than the exposure itself. In more casual discussion, "exposure" and "vulnerability" are more or less interchangeable.

2.2 METHODOLOGIES FOR THREAT ASSESSMENT

There is an almost infinite number of threats which can be of concern in an information systems risk management process. Obvious threats include such things as fire, power interruption, fraud, and accidental disclosure of personal data. Since the arena which must be considered in an information system extends outside the strict boundaries of the "EDP department," perhaps through telecommunications to anywhere in the world, the possible threats are many. There has been at least one report in the literature of a contingency plan for a United States federal government department in the case of an all-out nuclear strike. (Certainly some departments may need this, but the one in question likely would not be collecting excise taxes from businesses in nonexisting cities in the aftermath.) One of the first things which must be done in threat analysis is to decide on a way -- a methodology -- to select or eliminate potential threats from consideration.

In risk management, it is critical not to ignore threats, *however unlikely they seem.* A very small chance of an event which would kill the business still must be considered. Only if the likelihood is truly zero -- for instance, communications risk in a system with no communications capability -- is it valid to ignore the threat entirely. As was mentioned when discussing asset valuation, one of the goals of a methodology for selecting threats must be to be sufficiently complete without the analysis costing more than the exposure which might be avoided.

A starting point for a methodology is to consider either the properties of *threats* or the properties of *assets*. In the first case, what are the threats -- for example, earthquake, fire, nuclear disaster, or police radar. The exposed assets are then identified and the analysis proceeds. A second approach is to identify properties of assets, and then determine which potential threats relate to those properties. This approach is the basis chosen by the RCMP [RCMP 1982], and followed in this text.

Whichever approach is taken, the analysis must relate threats and assets to perform the exposure calculation; the two approaches thus converge in the end.

2.2.1 Properties of Threats

In taking the approach from the threat perspective, the attempt is to identify threats, then to relate these to assets which could be affected. Many lists of common threats have been created. One which is typical comes from Royal Fisher's **Information Systems Security** [Fisher 1984]:

Agent	Motive	Action
People		
Hardware		Disclose Data
Software	Accidentally	
Communications		Modify Data
Acts of God	Intentionally	
Procedure		Destroy Data

The purpose of this list, and generally of all such lists, is similar to that seen in asset analysis: to create a list which is

sufficient

not redundant

not too long

Of course, all possible combinations of such a list still lead to an enormous number of questions. A methodology remains necessary to select a reasonable and sufficient set from within the set generated by such a list. Fisher restricts his domain of interest primarily to EDP systems in the classical sense, and presents the IBM "SAFE" methodology of 11 control points as a means of accomplishing the selection. More detail of this particular tool is presented in Section 2.4.3 when specific means of getting threat information are examined.

2.2.2 Properties of Assets

A second approach to limiting the nearly infinite number of possible threats to be considered starts from the perspective of assets. Recall that in Chapter 1 assets were classified as tangible/intangible, physical/logical, and that they have properties:

Intrinsic Value, Acquired Value, Availability, Confidentiality, and Integrity

Using this as a basis, related threat classes can be defined as they affect the properties of assets:

Motive	Property Affected	Class of Threat
	Availability	1. Destruction
Accidental		
	Availability	2. Interruption
	Availability	3. Removal or loss
	Confidentiality	4. Disclosure
Intentional		
	Integrity	5. Corruption

There are now five classes of threat, doubled by the basic concepts of deliberate or accidental to ten, to consider. Here, we examine each asset already identified, then consider what threats (if any) will deliberately or accidentally lead to destruction, loss, disclosure, corruption, or interruption (of services). The methodology of the IBM SAFE study (see 2.4.3 in this Chapter) can be of use when this stage is reached, for assets may change as they pass control points. Using the control points also provides a useful second check on the asset and ownership identifications already done, as whenever an asset passes a control point it should change ownership, and may change its character as well.

2.2.3 Combining Properties: The Cost Exposure Matrix

Whatever starting point is chosen, threats and assets must be considered together in order to create a list of exposures for further progress in the risk management process. A tool which helps with the merging, suggested by the RCMP [RCMP 1982] and used in this text, is the "Cost Exposure Matrix" form. In this form, the data already gathered can be combined in a reasonably compact manner. The form is used twice: first, to identify the likelihood of a threat in one or more of the ten categories; then with the asset values to calculate the exposure represented by the threats identified. More detail on estimation of likelihood is given in Section 2.3.

Consider the form in Figure 2.1.

Column 1:   Asset

The assets have been identified and categorized according to a rule such as:

1.   Software

2.   Hardware

3.   Data and Information

4.   People and Procedures

5.   Communications

6.   Physical and Environmental.

Each asset is listed here. For this first time around, no dollar values are inserted.

Column 2:   Destruction

The total loss of the asset involved. Enter the likelihood of destruction (in this case, deliberate destruction) into this cell.

Column 3:   Disclosure

If the asset involved is such that it should or must not be disclosed, enter the likelihood of disclosure in this cell.

Column 4:   Removal

Enter the likelihood of removal of the asset in this cell. Note that removal implies that the asset still exists, but is (temporarily or otherwise) not available.

Column 5:   Corruption

Corruption refers to the unauthorized modification of software, data, or EDP equipment. Enter the likelihood of this threat in this cell.

Column 6:   Interruption

Interruption refers mainly to services. Enter the likelihood of an interruption here.

Note that some of these threat classes are not independent (more about that in Section 2.3). For example, destruction also implies removal and interruption. More than one entry may be in each row in this form.

Column 7 and 8: Accidental or Deliberate

Accidental and deliberate threats require quite different security measures for protection. Therefore, these columns are provided to give the full ten threat classes.

Use of a form such as the Cost Exposure Matrix Worksheet (Figure 2.2) will help in organizing the data to be summarized in the matrix.

COST EXPOSURE MATRIX

THREATS	**TOTAL COST EXPOSURE**				
	ACCIDENTAL ⑧	INTERRUPTION			
		CORRUPTION			
		REMOVAL			
		DISCLOSURE			
		DESTRUCTION			
	DELIBERATE ⑦	INTERRUPTION	⑥		
		CORRUPTION	⑤		
		REMOVAL	④		
		DISCLOSURE	③		
		DESTRUCTION	②		
ASSET			①		

Figure 2.1

Cost Exposure Matrix Worksheet

DATE: _____

REVISED: No. _____

Date _____

Page ____ of _____

ASSET Affected:

Basic Classification of Threat:

Accidental _____ Deliberate _____
Interruption _____
Corruption _____
Removal _____
Disclosure _____
Destruction _____

Nature of Threat:

Likelihood of Threat: _____ times per _____

Potential Loss:

Justification for Loss Calculation:

Description of Existing Control if any:

Figure 2.2

When this form has been filled in for all assets identified in the earlier steps in the risk management process, we have two pieces of data which can be combined to yield information: a complete list of assets to be protected, and a summary of the likelihood of each being affected by each of the ten threat classes considered. The remaining step to get to an exposure analysis is merely to multiply the likelihoods by the values of the assets. Before this is done, it will be worthwhile to examine some probability concepts as they relate to threat likelihoods and exposure calculations.

2.3 Probability Concepts

In essence, risk evaluation amounts to determining the value of an asset V (from the "General Values Analysis of System Assets" form, Figure 1.1) and the likelihood of loss L in some time period, and multiplying the two: $V * L$ gives the expected loss. One then designs safeguards which minimize this expected loss at the lowest practical cost. In the first two chapters, the assets have been assigned values (the V) and the threats have been assigned likelihoods (the L). Before exposure calculation is treated (the $V * L$), it is wise to look more carefully at what has been called "likelihood."

2.3.1 Definitions

Mathematically, the thing which has been called "likelihood" previously actually is related to a "probability." Precisely, it is a multiplier calculated by estimating the probability of one occurrence of an event and multiplying by the frequency with which the event occurs in a given time period. Whenever there is a "sample space" of events S, the chance that an event i will occur is expressed as $P(i)$; P is the "probability" function. If i *cannot* occur, the chance is nil and $P(i) = 0$. If i *must* occur, the chance is certain, and $P(i) = 1$. For example, in a sample space of comparisons of numbers:

> event i : 3 = 5 -- $P(i) = 0$
> event i : 2 = 2 -- $P(i) = 1$

All probabilities are between 0 and 1, by definition. If the sample space is created by flipping a fair coin with two sides, then two possible events are heads or tails (we ignore the chance of the coin balancing on edge).

> event i : heads -- $P(i) = 0.5$
> event i : tails -- $P(i) = 0.5$
>
> event i : either heads or tails -- $P(i) = 1.0$ (again assuming no edges)

The probability is simply a way to assign a numeric value to the likelihood. As it happens, this numeric probability is not a good measure to use in threat analysis: it turns out that people on the whole are very poor at estimating probabilities. (This is why casinos get rich.) A much better approach usually is to ask people how often something might happen. One may then use tables to relate "how often" to a probability so as to get a number for the likelihood and permit calculation of $V * L$ (see the tables and discussion in 2.3.2).

The concept of "independent events" needs to be introduced here. Mathematically, this can get somewhat involved; it is sufficient here to define two or more events as independent if they do not affect one another. In the coin-tossing example, any two coin tosses are independent of one another. (This is one reason people guess badly -- if five heads in a row have been thrown, the probability of a head next time is still 0.5.) In doing risk analysis, the end result involves adding together costs of various potential threats. This is mathematically valid *only* if the threats are independent. A fire or an earthquake may be unlikely, but are usually considered as though independent. However, earthquakes *cause* fires; if the earthquake happens first, the fire probably happens next. (The reverse of course is not true for fires and earthquakes.) The process of treating assets first, then examining the threats which may affect them, while following the objective of keeping lists complete and non-overlapping, maximizes independence of the threats identified. In filling out the Cost Exposure Matrix, some threats will wind up listed several times, as they affect each asset; one effect of this is to approximate the correct mathematical treatment for including non-independent events. Readers who wish to pursue the mathematics of probability further are referred to any standard introductory text in probability or statistics.

2.3.2 Tables of Probability Values

People generally can make fairly good estimates in terms of "how often should we expect this to happen?" Since most budgeting decisions are related to a yearly budget period, it is useful to create a table which relates "how many times per year" to a loss multiplier L. The final calculation of $V * L$ will then yield an expected loss per year, and one may easily compare this exposure to the cost per year of the proposed safeguard(s). One such table is given in Table 2.1. This table lists some subjective notions of "how often," then puts a fractional equivalent beside it, and in the third column what is in principle a probability figure. Using the "Cost/Loss Multiplier" from the table as a probability in the $V * L$ equation above can be easier than using more formal probabilities. If different intervals are appropriate in a specific situation, another table similar to this can be constructed easily with a calculator, as this one was.

Annualized Loss Multiplier Table

Subjective Frequency	Fractional Equivalent	Cost/Loss Multiplier
Never	--	0.0
Once in 300 Years	1/300	0.00333
Once in 200 years	1/200	0.005
Once in 100 years	1/100	0.01
Once in 50 years	1/50	0.02
Once in 25 years	1/25	0.04
Once in 5 years	1/5	0.20
Once in 2 years	1/2	0.50
Yearly	1/1	1.0
Twice a year	1/.5	2.0
Four times a year	1/.25	4.0
Once a month	12/1	12.0
Twice a month	12/.5	24.0
Once a week	52/1	52.0
Once a day	365/1	365.0
Twice a day	365/.5	730.0
Ten times a day	365/.1	3650.0
Hourly	8760/1	8760.0
Once a minute	525,600/1	525600.0

Table 2.1

As an example, consider a public timesharing system which has an average of 2000 users signed onto terminals (somewhere) at any given time. It may not be unreasonable to assume that there is a constant risk of exposure to at least one of those 2000 users (exposure to 1 of 2000 gives a probability $P = .0005$; L = number of users times probability of exposure $(2000 * P) = 1$ event per minute; if there were 4000 users, it might be 2 per minute). The multiplier of 500,000+ may be entirely appropriate in this case. That is, *if the system were entirely unprotected*, a loss might well occur every minute or so. Even a small loss, (say $V=\$0.50$ each time an event occurs) half a million times per year, adds up to a large exposure ($V * L$ = about \$250,000).

The recommendation which follows from the material presented in Section 2.3.1 and 2.3.2, is to estimate likelihood in terms of "how often per year"; then look up a multiplier and enter the multiplier in the appropriate likelihood cell in the Cost Exposure Matrix form. This would be roughly equivalent to estimating the probability, then multiplying by the frequency, to get a multiplier to enter into the form.

When this is done, the $V * L$ calculation can be done for the final step in risk analysis. In the next section, a number of ways to arrive at the "how often per year" are presented.

2.4 SOURCES OF THREAT INFORMATION

The general framework for doing the threat assessment is now in place. However, practical difficulties remain. Some have been alluded to already: people find it difficult to estimate probabilities accurately; more critically, there is, even with restrictions such as presented earlier, a near-infinite set of possible threats. Probably, no technique which will work everywhere is possible. In this section, six methods which have value in many cases are presented. Whatever the situation, one or more of these techniques, when combined with the risk assessment presented so far, will help in achieving a risk assessment without spending more for the assessment than the probable savings from avoiding the exposure.

2.4.1 Vulnerability Analysis

In some cases, there may not be any past history to refer to in estimating threats. Worse, the situation may be an entirely new one, and thus no other organization's experience (even if available) would give a good guide. One technique, especially applicable to the selection of administrative and personnel control measures, is analyzing the vulnerabilities of the new system with respect to the people who will work in the system. Briefly, one examines each job involved: the skills and training necessary to do the job, the access to the system necessary to do the job, the normal working conditions, and the assets which the job impacts, are analyzed. One typical result of such an analysis is given in Table 2.2, (updated for typical modern mainframe computer operations [*see* Figure 7.1] from Donn Parker's *Computer Security Management* [Parker 1981].)

Job Exposures

OCCUPATION	PHYS ICAL	OPERA TIONAL	PROGRAM MING	ELECT RONIC
User Transaction & data entry operator		X		
Computer operator	X	X	X	
Peripheral equipment operator	X	X		
Job set-up clerk	X	X	X	
Data entry & update clerk	X	X		
Tape librarian	X	X	X	
User tape librarian		X	X	
Systems programmer	X	X	X	
Application programmer	X	X	X	
User programmer		X	X	
Terminal engineer	X	X		X
Computer systems engineer	X	X	X	X
Communications eng. / operator	X	X		X
Facilities engineer	X			X
Operations manager	X	X		
Database administrator	X	X	X	
Programming manager	X	X	X	
Security specialist	X	X	X	X
EDP auditor	X	X	X	X

Table 2.2

Using this table, or a similar one developed for a specific organization, the probable exposures -- that is, if a person in this position wanted to do harm, in what areas could harm be done -- can be estimated. This identification could serve to guide the risk management effort to areas of greatest exposure. From the table, for instance, it is clear that only the EDP Auditor, Security Specialist, and Computer Systems Engineer can affect all areas considered. Further analysis will suggest that only the auditor and security person have the specialized knowledge actually to do anything significant. Thus, administrative and personnel controls should concentrate on the auditor and security specialist, both of whom know what to do to affect systems, know the safeguards in place, know how to hide acts, and have access to essentially everything.

It is important to examine such a table and ensure that it is customized for a specific situation. Some of the exposure categories may not exist, or may be different, depending on the way the organization manages its computer resources and what resources are available. In a distributed processing environment, for example, data entry personnel may not present any physical risk since their only access to the computer is by means of communication lines.

The degree of programming risk from a job setup clerk or tape librarian changes if these people have no programming knowledge.

This analysis can be carried further to a risk level by occupation. Since this is essentially non-quantitative, one should avoid too many categories. The following table shows a ranking by asset exposure, with the highest risk referring to people who have great capabilities and access and also can affect important assets.

Risk Level of Occupations Based on Asset Exposure

GREATEST Risk
    EDP Auditor
    Security Specialist

GREAT Risk
    Computer Operator
    Data Entry and Update Clerk
    Operations Manager
    Systems Programmer

MODERATE Risk
    Computer Systems Engineer
    Programming Manager

LIMITED Risk
    Application Programmer
    Communications Engineer/Operator
    Data Base Administrator
    Facilities Engineer
    Peripheral Equipment Operator
    Tape Librarian
    User Programmer
    User Transaction & Data Entry Operator

LOW Risk
    Terminal Engineer
    User Tape Librarian

Table 2.3

The security manager, for example, must have the skills, training, and access necessary to destroy the system in order to perform his or her work. This does *not* mean that the security manager *will* do this. Analyzing whether someone *could* do something is no guide as to whether they *will*. The exposure data available from this vulnerability analysis is most likely to be useful in designing administrative controls. (Perhaps dollar exposure figures could serve as a guide to how many dollars management should be willing to spend on having a "happy workplace," but this is at best a broad leap.) This analysis technique is useful mostly in identifying threats.

The vulnerability analysis presented here must be examined carefully for full applicability to any specific organization. In some contexts, for example national intelligence, risk levels will differ from those presented. A spy may be presumed to have capabilities which are not normally required for the job and which do not show on the resume. Particularly in small organizations, there may not be sufficient staff to separate duties as would be ideal, and some of the occupational classes noted in the table could be combined, leading to different exposures.

2.4.2 Scenarios

Another technique which is useful when solid data are not available is scenarios. One creates a scenario depicting what a specific threat might be. An example (somewhat elaborate in this case) is creating "penetration teams" whose job it is to simulate terrorists and attempt to penetrate a nuclear power station. A more scenario-like example could be considering what a terrorist *might* do to disrupt some event (for example, hijack a jet and crash it into a stadium).

The scenario technique is useful in visualizing what *might* happen when no real data are available. It is highly subjective, but nonetheless is valuable in identifying potential threats and vulnerabilities. A scenario may help managers to visualize something not clearly understood. However, scenarios are risky. In the first place, normally they should be *extremely confidential*: there is no value to be gained by publishing a plan for terrorists which they may not have thought of themselves. Also, scenarios may unnecessarily alarm employees or others if they become public. It is questionable whether the use of scenarios outweighs the risks involved. If used, their use should be cleared in advance with senior management, and means to ensure confidentiality should be in place from the start.

2.4.3 Control Points/Exposures

One tool which has considerable value at the detail level of identifying assets and threats, is "control point analysis." In this text, the overall security problem is examined, and only a summary of this particular detailed technique is appropriate.

In 1972, IBM and others participated in a major data security study known as "SAFE" (Security and Audit Field Evaluation)[IBM 1972, Krauss 1972]. One result of this study has been the identification of control points relating to data in any information system. While the technique is relatively limited to data in a classical sense, it is certainly a useful way to approach the necessity to limit the infinity of possible threats. The accounting profession, particularly in the Canadian Institute of Chartered Accountants *Computer Control Guidelines*, both the first and second editions [CICA 1986], has built on this technique, as well as updating recommended methods from time to time as technology has changed.

Briefly, eleven control points were identified in the SAFE study:

(The author's comments are *italicized.*)

CP1:   Data Gathering

The manual creating and transporting of data.

CP2:   Data Input Movement

The manual movement of source documents to the data entry area in which the source documents are converted to machine-readable form.

> *(NOTE: In more modern systems this and some other control points may not even exist--direct screen entry or machine scanning often supercedes source documents now, for instance. Trade publications report a dramatic decline in data entry positions in EDP departments between 1984 and 1987.)*

CP3:   Data Conversion

The physical conversion of initial source documents to machine-readable form.

CP4:   Data Communication (input)

The transmission of machine-readable data.

CP5:   Data Receipt

The receipt and storage of data via communications or manual facilities.

CP6:   Data Processing

The execution of application programs to perform intended computations and their results.

CP7:   Data Preparation (output)

The preparation of data output media such as cards, paper tape, disks, diskettes, and microfilm for dissemination to the users.

CP8:   Data Output Movement

The manual movement of computer-produced output, in various media forms, to the output area to await user pick-up.

CP9:   Data Communication (output)

The direct transmission and/or delivery of output to the user.

CP10:   Data Usage

The use of data by the recipient, including the storage or location of data while it is being used.

CP11:   Data Disposition

The disposition of data after the period of usage, including the methods and locations of storage, length of time for storage, and final disposal, as appropriate.

This is a detailed tool which may be used either in the "threat-based" approach described earlier, or the "asset-based" approach recommended by the RCMP and this text. It is necessary to use some caution in applying this control point analysis: many of the methods of data entry common today are materially different from those available in the early 1970's when the study was performed.

An alternate approach, which is similar in intent to the IBM "SAFE" approach, can be found in the Canadian Institute of Chartered Accountants' reviews of controls and auditing of data processing systems, noted above [CICA 1986]. This document is from the accounting standpoint, and covers areas beyond the "classical" view of data considered by the SAFE study.

As a comment on the use of the SAFE or CICA approaches: recall that the involvement of the user management has been identified as being critical to the success of the risk management process. Recall also that it is poor practice to spend more money analyzing or controlling exposures than could be lost if the exposure became actual. It probably is best to engage the services of a professional with expertise in security and/or EDP auditing in applying these exhaustive techniques. Detailed techniques tend to the direction of "overcontrol" referred to in Chapter 1, unless used intelligently. Experienced professionals should possess the background to know when it is appropriate to "break the rules" by applying less than total controls, and when the rules must be applied rigorously regardless of apparent cost-ineffectiveness.

2.4.4 Past History

Clearly, the best source of good data about security exposures is history: if losses have occurred in the past, usually it is simple to quantify them and thus to have exact data on what this type of exposure entails. The history need not be only of a single organization. The Stanford Research International group (SRI) at Stanford has compiled data about problems of organizations for a number of years. The *COMP-U-FAX* newsletter of the Data Processing Management Association has published data about computer security experience in organizations based on surveys of some 40,000 DPMA members in Canada and the United States.

Probably the greatest disadvantage of past history is that one hopes a problem will not have occurred previously; security is concerned first with *prevention*. Also, in a small organization, there may not be a very large data base.

2.4.5 Questionnaires

One way to get information from many sources is a questionnaire. Again, it probably is best to engage consultants expert in the use of questionnaires, unless the organization has its own capabilities; effective use of questionnaires is difficult and complex.

The objectives of a survey first must be defined, clearly and in writing. Then a sample must be chosen. Questions must be created; a pilot test is strongly advised to validate the questions; and considerations of time frame must be studied.

In summary, questionnaires probably are necessary to gather data from dispersed, varied sources. Their validity is suspect unless the designers have significant expertise in the design and administration of questionnaires. It is recommended that professionals be engaged if the questionnaire route is seen to be appropriate.

2.4.6 Outside Sources

Two outside sources already have been referred to: the SRI data bank, and the DPMA *COMP-U-FAX* newsletter. These may be unique in their presentation of information about actual problems in DP organizations. Any one organization is unlikely to be able to get good information about the security failures of any other organization, unless it is someone like DPMA or SRI who are demonstrably related to the profession rather than to, for example, potential competitors.

Other sources of specific data include:

1.   Insurance companies for loss data
2.   Statistics Canada for such things as fire loss data
3.   U. S. Geological Survey for earthquake risk areas
4.   National weather bureaus for weather risk data
5.   Federal Bureau of Investigation (FBI), RCMP or other police forces for criminal loss data
6.   U. S. Federal Information Processing Standards
7.   Electronic Data Processing Security Standards and Practices for Departments and Agencies of the Government of Canada (1986 update)
8.   Canadian Institute of Chartered Accountants Computer Audit & Control Guidelines, Second Edition
9.   Computer Security Institute publications
10.   Datapro Publications Computer Security Reference
11.   Data Processing Management Association Special Interest Group for Computer Security (SIG-CS) publications.

This list is not exhaustive. Unfortunately, the basic data needed often are not easily available, or even do not exist. This is why this section has concentrated on several techniques which help to get useful analysis in the absence of a database of basic information.

2.5 EXAMPLES OF THREATS

In Section 2.2, the notion of approaching the threat identification part of the risk management process was considered from the two standpoints of "what are the threats, and which assets do they affect?" and "what are the assets and from what should they be protected?" Throughout this chapter, we have seen that as the analysis progresses, the two approaches converge. As a further illustration of the kinds of things which are brought out for analysis from the two approaches, this subsection presents short lists of threats as derived from Royal Fisher's [Fisher 1984] and from the RCMP material already referenced [RCMP 1982].

2.5.1 Threats by Threat

Royal Fisher is concerned in his text primarily with the detail level of the control and movement of data within the information system. His starting point for threat analysis is to list various kinds of threats, then to limit the area of concern by examining agents, motives and actions, and then further to limit the area by using the 11-point SAFE methodology abstracted in Section 2.4.3. This approach -- "threat by threat" -- leads first to fairly general types of threats, then progressively narrows in to the specific threats relating to each control point. Its main virtue may be that the identification of very general threats in the first step minimizes the chance of overlooking something. The main problem is that it is difficult to narrow down to the very specific things which are of concern in a particular risk management study.

Fisher first proposes classes of threat (similar in fact to those of the RCMP described in Section 2.5.2):

Accidental or Deliberate

Disclosure, Modification, or Destruction.

Sample threats within these broad classes are:

Accidental Disclosure:

Output delivered to the wrong user

Sensitive material in the trash, uncontrolled

Leaving a terminal signed on and displaying sensitive data

Accidental Modification:

Editing the wrong version of a file

Spelling or transposition errors during entry

Hardware malfunction ("Dirty" communication lines, for example, can add or distort information *via* several types of interference; see Chapter 10.)

Accidental Destruction:

Deleting the wrong file during maintenance

Losing part of a printout due to printer jam

"Acts of God"-- earthquake, storm, and such

Intentional Disclosure:

Selling information

Breaking into a sensitive file

Intentional Modification:
Deleting records in files
Editing when unauthorized
Changing account balances

Intentional Destruction:
Deleting important records
Sabotage
Theft

This list is adapted from Fisher's. The difficulty is obvious: the classes generated are undirected and very broad. Fisher and others using this particular basic approach still must take the next step of narrowing down the examination somehow.

2.5.2 Threats by Asset

Other sources adopt the approach of defining assets to be protected first, then examining potential threats to see if they apply to these assets. As with the previous approach, classes of threats are defined. In the method recommended by the RCMP [RCMP 1982], the classes are similar to those seen previously:

Accidental or Deliberate
Destruction, Disclosure, Removal, Corruption, Interruption.

The most significant difference is that, having defined the assets to be protected first, one is searching among threats within these classes as they may affect those things of specific interest in this particular risk analysis. The advantage is that the universe of "all threats" is less likely to produce excessive data, since many threats can be ignored immediately as not applicable (tidal waves in Kansas, for instance). The main disadvantage is that possible threats may be overlooked, depending on how detailed the asset definition has been.

Examples of threats defined from this standpoint are more difficult to create, since by definition the threats are specific. The list given is not exhaustive, and the omission of a threat does *not* mean it does not apply in another situation. The categories of asset already seen are used:

Hardware
Software
Data and Information
People and Procedures
Communications

Physical and Environmental.

Examples of threats could include:

Hardware:

Disk crash accidentally destroys data

Printer fails causing accidental interruption

Memory fails causing program error (accidental interruption, perhaps also corruption).

Software:

This is probably the largest area of concern; everyone has encountered program bugs.

Error in length specification causes accidental corruption of data outside user area

"Trapdoor" causes deliberate disclosure of sensitive operating system tables

"Logic bomb" causes deliberate destruction of payroll files

Error in tax table causes too much withholding from final payment to departing employees

Data and Information:

Clerk deliberately corrupts invoice amount

Clerk transposes two numbers, causing accidental corruption

Hardware failure accidentally destroys database index tables, causing several exposures

Fire destroys disks containing company's accounts receivable.

Communications:

Spy taps a telephone line causing deliberate disclosure

Phone exchange cross-connects causing accidental disclosure

"Hacker" uses auto-dial modem to try to find computer lines and wakes up half a town at 5 AM

Post Office delivers to wrong address.

Physical and Environmental:

Power surge causes accidental interruption

Police radar at a speed trap causes CPU malfunction

Tornado destroys building causing several exposures

Unlocked door allows accidental disclosure.

As stated already, this list is nowhere nearly complete; it cannot be, except for a specific risk analysis.

2.6 Calculating Exposures

Once all the preliminary work has been done, the Cost Exposure Matrix, which now contains likelihoods expressed as loss multipliers, is combined with the General Value Analysis of System Assets form to yield exposures. The essence is simply a multiplication -- the "$V * L$" referred to in Section 2.3. If the preliminary work was done with a computerized spreadsheet, this step may be done with only a few commands to the software.

There is nothing "fancy" about this step; it amounts to simple arithmetic.

The result is a second version of the Cost Exposure Matrix, with dollar figures in each cell and assets along the side. It is now a simple procedure to examine the form, select the greatest dollar exposures, and decide where time and money is best invested in designing and applying safeguards. The obvious way is to start applying the cheapest safeguard which avoids the greatest exposure, and work down until the budget is exhausted. (In some risk situations, particularly where espionage is involved, measures other than dollars come into play; however, they should have been incorporated earlier in the asset valuation process.)

If the time and other resources are available, it is a good idea to perform a simple sensitivity analysis on the resulting form. With a computerized spreadsheet, it is easy to vary the values assigned to important assets by perhaps plus or minus 20%, or 50%, and examine the results. Usually, the relative ranking of the major exposures does not change when this is done, although small exposures may. If there is a material change in ranking among major exposures, more time should be spent on examining the assets involved to be sure that the best possible values have been obtained. Again, the risk analysis team must consider how much money to invest for better information; sensitivity analysis is *much* cheaper when it amounts to a few keystrokes in a computer than when it is done manually.

The approach just described can grow into a major analytical problem very quickly. Techniques such as "fuzzy metrics" (see, for example, [Schmucker 1984]), checklists presented by computer and sorted appropriately after filling in entries, and others have been developed to try to cope with the so-called "real world," in which very many things happen in complex patterns.

2.7 SUMMARY AND CONCLUSION

This chapter has presented the second side of risk analysis, the threat assessment and the final exposure calculation. First, "threat" and "vulnerability" were defined. In risk analysis, the word "threat" is used somewhat differently than it is in normal conversation, and it is wise to avoid this particular usage in management reports (unless the intended readers clearly understand the meaning intended).

Two ways to identify threats were explored:

1.   Identify threats and then see what assets they may affect.
2.   Identify assets and then see what threats may affect them.

As the analysis progresses, the two approaches converge to more or less the same final result. We recommend that the asset-based approach be used. The *best* approach for a specific risk analysis situation is the one which is most understandable to the risk team and to the management who will have to interpret and use the results. Using the recommended approach, the asset identification form presented in Chapter 1 and the Cost Exposure Matrix presented in this chapter combine to yield a useful way to organize data. The data must then be summarized for presentation to management; one way is to use bar graphs to show the greatest exposures.

The mathematical concept of probability was discussed briefly. This measure is a way to assign a number, between 0 and 1, to how likely some event is. Since people estimate probabilities poorly, other methods, particularly the "how often" approach, are recommended for risk analysis. The probability approach is ideal, if accurate data are available; however, sufficiently accurate data are not generally available. Estimating "how often" gives better results in most situations.

The issue of where and how to get threat information was addressed next. Six ways were covered:

1.   Analyze the vulnerability in terms of jobs, what skills they involve and what control over assets is needed to do the job.
2.   Create scenarios of "what could happen."

This method has problems, and must be used with care if at all. Normally, great confidentiality is needed to avoid unnecessary alarm and publishing of penetration plans to potential perpetrators.

3.   Use the IBM "SAFE" study results to analyze exposures at the 11 control points.

4.   Use past history, when available. The main problem here is that risk analysis really is trying to *prevent* problems which haven't occurred yet; there often is no past history to go by.

5.   Use questionnaires to gather data. This technique is tricky enough that professional help should be engaged.

6.   Get information from outside sources, such as insurance companies, professional association surveys, government loss data, professional accounting guidelines such as the CICA *Computer Control Guidelines*.

All of these methods have their place, as do others not covered in detail in this text. Since relative ranking is the primary goal, even approximate techniques usually work well enough. A number of examples of threat identification, from both major approaches, were presented as a guide. One method which may be appropriate is simply to be sure that your organization's security program is at least as comprehensive as those of others in your industry segment.

The final section deals with the actual calculation of exposures. If the asset identification and valuation, and the threat identification, were done carefully, the final arithmetic is straightforward. The General Value Analysis of System Assets and the Cost Exposure Matrix are designed to fit together to simplify this calculation.

The report to management needs to summarize the data assembled, and to be short and readable. Bar graphs, pie charts, and other graphic presentation methods are often of value in making a clear and understandable presentation. The exact form of the presentation naturally will vary depending on the people and situation involved.

2.8 NEW TERMS

New terms introduced or defined in this chapter include:

Accessibility of computer systems
Complexity of information systems
Control point
Corruption of data
Cost exposure matrix
Density of information
Destruction of assets
Disclosure of information
Electronic vulnerability of computer systems

Exposure
Independent events
Interruption of services
Likelihood
Loss multiplier
Media
Probability
Removal of assets
SAFE study
Scenario
Threat
Threat Analysis:
      Asset-based
      Threat-based
Vulnerability

2.9 QUESTIONS

2.1 Expected Loss

Assume that you are installing a $1900 microcomputer and a $200 modem in a beach front hotel that gets flooded once every 100 years on average.

(a)   Assuming that these are the only system assets, calculate the expected loss per year.

(b)   If the modem was unprotected, the hotel manager estimates that hackers would obtain access twice per week. What is the "cost/loss multiplier" in this situation?

(c)   What uses are made of the numbers resulting from an exposure calculation?

2.2 Explain the difference between doing a threat analysis by first identifying threats then assets exposed to them, *versus* first identifying assets and then determining threats to which the assets are exposed.

(a)   Give an example where each approach would be preferred.

(b)   Give an example illustrating the problem mentioned in the text which causes our recommendation to use the second approach.

SECTION II: SAFEGUARDS: SECURITY AND CONTROL MEASURES: ORGANIZATIONAL AND ADMINISTRATIVE

Having undertaken the first five steps of the risk management process, the analysis team has an understanding of what are the most expensive and most important exposures. Assets have been identified and given values. Threats to these assets have been identified and the likelihood of each threat for each asset has been assessed. As the final step prior to preparing a report, the dollar exposures have been identified and ranked. The report to management should have identified the most important threats in terms of what the exposure is, and thus how expensive the exposure could be and how important the exposure is. This report serves as a "blueprint" for implementing safeguards: the dollar identification suggests how much one should be willing to spend on a safeguard (that is, not more than the sum of the exposures avoided), and the ranking suggests where to look first in applying safeguards.

Section II begins a two-section overview of safeguards which may be applied, and some discussion of when and why to employ them. This is an *overview*; actually designing and implementing specific safeguards will require reference to more detailed treatments than there is room for in this text. Section II has the greater number of chapters: it deals with the organizational and administrative areas, which are the source of the greatest exposures and the most opportunities to limit exposure. Section III addresses technical safeguards -- such things as program controls and password access control.

In Section II, Chapter 3 opens Sections II and III with a broad look at safeguards. Basic types of controls, and basic design strategies, are examined. Each of the eight components of a security program identified in Section 3.4 of Chapter 3 is discussed briefly.

Chapter 3

OVERVIEW OF SAFEGUARDS

INTRODUCTION

Although the primary emphasis of this text is on information systems, the pre-ceding chapters on asset identification and valuation, and threat identification and exposure calculation, should have made it clear that any risk management program inevitably has impacts far beyond the nominal organizational limits of a so-called "data processing department." In fact, it turns out that *most* of the ef-fort, both in identifying and planning a security program and in implementing safeguards, usually is applied most appropriately outside these organizational limits. The best operating system controls possible will not prevent a dissatis-fied employee with authorization and training from compromising the system. Controls to help prevent or limit this kind of exposure lie in areas outside the computer. Chapter 3 takes a look at a way to approach the breadth needed in an effective risk management program.

The first topic is basic types of controls: protection, detection, and reaction. In Section 3.3, the "layers of protection" model proposed by the RCMP (and several other sources as well) is presented, both as a conceptual model for looking at organizations and as a specific one of the six primary safeguard de-sign strategies. Sections 3.4 and 3.5 present brief descriptions of each of the "rings of protection," or "layers of protection," of this model, organized into the administrative and technical components already mentioned.

Each of Chapters 4 through 8 addresses a specific topic area of protection in the realm of administrative and organizational security. Chapter 9 in Section III reviews Section II and addresses the topic areas noted as "technical" in Chapter 3.

3.1 COMMON SENSE

Attempting to choose from among a near-infinite number of possible controls for each asset and threat, and trying to determine to what extent each control will affect each exposure and asset, may be the most satisfying theoretical approach to security. In practice, however, the risk management team will rapidly get bogged down in detail. Not only do many controls affect in differing ways many different exposures and assets, but also controls affect each other. Trying to deal with all possible implications and complications is a good recipe for nervous breakdowns and ineffective, or uncoordinated, safeguards. (This sort of phenomenon is sometimes called "paralysis by analysis.") Some realistic starting point is needed.

We recommend a three-part strategy:

1.   Apply *common sense*.
2.   Consider *basic types* of controls.
3.   Consider *essential components* of any system of safeguards.

Common sense may be one of the rarer human virtues. From personal abuse such as drug use (smoking, alcohol), to refusal to use existing, obvious safety measures (seat belts in cars), people clearly use considerations other than common sense in their personal lives. Time after time, this phenomenon is observable in organizations and the work environment as well. People who are best suited to risk management often also are prone to "over-analyzing." The temptation to be perfect is strong. It is common to see literally months spent trying to devise sophisticated operating system safeguards -- when doors are not locked and people tape passwords and account numbers to terminals.

The first consideration in designing a security program must be *common sense*. Lock the doors. *Use* the security provided by the operating system designers. *Tell* employees that ethical behavior is a condition of employment and of tenure. *Don't hire* people without checking references. In planning to implement safeguards identified so far in the risk management process, look them over: are there simple, inexpensive measures which will be part of the final solution anyway? If so, implement them now. (Why leave a known, large, existing vulnerability while designing a perfect system which avoids nearly all vulnerabilities?)

Common sense, whatever that may be, seems to follow from considerable experience. A team approach to risk management combines the experience of several people. Engaging a consultant may bring to bear an independent view based on observation of many cases. Probably the best operational recommendation is to have the team stop after the analysis is done, "step back," look at the originally stated objectives, and search for simple inexpensive controls which can be implemented without further analysis. Such simple measures may form supportable, easily understandable recommendations in the report to management. Techniques such as brainstorming may help (as may the relaxed atmosphere at the local pub after work on Friday). The primary recommendation is to try to apply common sense.

3.2 TYPES OF CONTROLS: PROTECTION, DETECTION, REACTION

3.2.1 Basic Purposes of Controls

There are three basic purposes which all controls are intended to address:

1.   *Prevent* exposures.
2.   *Detect* attempted threats.
3.   *Correct* the causes of threats.

Many controls have elements of more than one of these basic purposes. The first thing the risk management team should consider is, for each identified exposure, how to prevent a problem, how to detect a problem if it happens, and what to do about making sure the problem will not recur. No asset is ever completely immune to harm, given enough will and resources on the part of threats. By setting up several layers of controls -- preventive, detective, and corrective -- the asset gets progressively safer. Keeping the basic purposes of controls in mind will help focus the risk management team.

3.2.2 Prevention

The first line of defense is protection, or prevention. Given that a problem is defined and may occur, risk management would include prevention of the known exposure. For example, it is known that without any controls, anyone could access a computer system and change someone else's data (if there is more than one person's data on the system). Therefore, some preventive measure is needed. One which has proven value is the use of account identification and password controls. Casual "potential threats" are deterred, and some prevention has been achieved.

Preventive controls generally have one or more of several characteristics:

1.   They are passive, and require no feedback:
        a fence
        a padlock
        a power-off switch

2.   They guide, or help things happen correctly:
        properly designed forms
        training programs
        employee awareness programs

3.   They are not impervious:
        "No Admittance" sign (this means *you*?)
        automatically closing door propped open
        password and account ID taped to terminal

4.   They reduce threat occurrence frequency:
        reference checks
        segregation of duties
        surprise audits (announced, but timing variable)

5.   They are transparent (people are not aware of them):
        fire-retardant materials
        anti-static mats and rugs
        shatterproof glass

6.   They are inexpensive:
        door lock
        employee identification badges
        signs (for example, speed limit)

The purpose of the protection, or preventive control, is to deter casual threats and slow down more determined threats. Several layers of preventive controls may add up to a rather effective protective mechanism.

However many layers of preventive controls there are, either sufficient determination or, more likely, unanticipated threats, can penetrate them. The frequency of occurrence should be much lower than for an uncontrolled situation, however.

3.2.3 Detection

Once the prevention is penetrated, the unwanted thing has occurred. The next step in controls is to detect this event. Detection systems indicate and/or verify an actual or attempted penetration. Examples include console printouts, alarms, video monitoring. Detective controls do one or more of the following:

1.   Trigger an alarm
    smoke detector
    radar in a speed trap
    oil pressure warning light

2.   Register the event
    console printout
    count errors in a batch
    photographs of intruders

3.   Stop further processing
    batch may not be processed with errors
    disconnect terminal after three unsuccessful logon attempts
    abort program on divide-by-zero

4.   Assess the situation
    reasonableness checks (sales of skis in July; 25 hours a day in a time
    sheet)
    range checks (voltage 100 to 130)
    expectations (sign-on Sunday at 0300)

5.   Alert people
    alarms
    warning lights
    error reports

6.   Test protection
    hash totals, check digits
    authorization tables
    batch balancing

According to the RCMP [RCMP 1981], a detection system normally has four primary components:

1.   Sensors to detect the activity

2.   Communications to relay the fact of the event

3.   Assessment system to evaluate the needs of the situation

4.   Reporting system to announce the situation to the appropriate response
    force(s).

As a simple example, a smoke detector has a *sensor* to detect smoke, and a light or buzzer (*communications*) to relay the occurrence of an event. The detection system includes a person noticing the detector's activity and deciding what to do (*assessment*), which may include calling the fire department and reporting to management (*reporting system*).

The last point in the list emphasizes again that no control is perfect, and also raises the point that detection is linked with correction. Protective controls can be bypassed. Once this happens, the event should be detected, or the security is compromised. Detection should be linked with correction: there is not much point in knowing that breaches have occurred if nothing is done about it.

3.2.4 Reaction or Correction

Once a threat has occurred and has been detected, something should be done about it. Doing nothing is also a decision: someone should have analyzed the situation and decided that it is cheaper not to correct the problem. The purpose of the communication and reporting components of a detection system is to ensure that someone does something -- reacts, or corrects the situation.

Some attributes of corrective controls are:

1.   They involve action to resolve a problem

automatic error correction (spelling checker)
call the police forces
review employment policies

2.   They are expensive

parallel operation
police forces
quality control group
change control group

Less can be said in general about corrective or reactive measures than about prevention and detection, as appropriate reactions vary according to the threat and assets, and the security policies of an organization.

Summary

There are three basic purposes of controls: prevention, detection, and correction. Some examples which should help to illustrate this are:

Given that people should not drive too fast:

Prevention: speed limit signs, speedometers required in cars

Detection: radar speed traps

Correction: flag down speeders and issue tickets; withdraw licenses if too many convictions

Another example:

An organization has a valuable list of names and addresses, which it sells to others (magazine subscriptions, motor vehicle licenses, catalogue lists, etc.). It wishes this list to remain confidential.

Prevention: label lists "confidential," restrict access

Detection: include "decoy addresses;" if mail is sent to these addresses, the security is penetrated

Reaction: determine who leaked the data and take action

A third example:

Given that unauthorized people should not use the computer system:

Prevention: require valid account numbers and passwords to access

Detection: system records signon attempts, prints on console log

Correction: disconnect terminal after three failures; print warning for system administrator

Looking at controls from the perspective of the three basic purposes will help the risk management team to design an intelligent security system.

3.3 DESIGN STRATEGIES

Another aid to the risk management team, in addition to the basic purposes of controls, is some set of tools -- basic strategies -- which the risk analysis team can "mix and match" in designing safeguards. Any security system may, as was noted with preventive controls previously, contain several "layers" (and indeed, layers of protection is one of the basic strategies). It is helpful to have several standard strategies to choose from, once assets and types of controls desired are gathered. At least six strategies have stood the test of time:

1.   Avoid the exposure.
2.   Split the target.
3.   Put the asset in a highly visible position.
4.   Hide the asset.
5.   Combine several assets.
6.   Use of multiple strategies: "Rings of Protection."

Sometimes, the easiest way to control an exposure is to *avoid* it. If there is a great concern that outsiders will intercept communications in the computer system, the problem can be avoided by not providing communications. If there is danger of legal problems from illicit copying of software, do not provide diskette drives so copies cannot be made or removed. Perhaps the most general expression of this is "don't ask for trouble." (A frequent example relates to walking in Central Park in New York at night.) This basic strategy can be useful; of course, it is not always appropriate (communications exposure may be impractical to avoid since communication is an important value-added part of many computer systems, and essential for electronic mail, for example).

The second basic strategy is to *split the asset.* A rifle is merely an expensive club without its bolt and ammunition; store the rifle, the bolt, and the ammunition in three places and the asset may be very well protected. Similarly, an encrypted file is useless without the key; store them separately. The disadvantage of this basic strategy is that separate security systems may be much more expensive than a single one. As well, *use* of the asset may be unreasonably difficult (storing rifles, bolts, and ammunition separately does not help fast response to a surprise attack, for example).

A third strategy is to *expose* the asset, in the sense that it is put into an area which is highly visible and under continuous normal surveillance. Convenience stores typically use several strategies: entrances and approaches are well lit, most money goes immediately into a safe and the safe is visible from the street, clerks are on a raised dais to have better vision and also to be psychologically more imposing. A portable computer in an occupied office is not in much danger of theft, as long as the office remains occupied.

The opposite of the third strategy is to *hide* the asset. There are two basic variations: the "purloined letter" method, and "invisibility." In the first case, a valuable asset is mixed in with many other valueless assets which are superficially similar. A potential threat agent would have to identify which one is worthwhile. In "invisibility," the asset is hidden, for instance at another location, or inside a building in a room without windows. There are many variations on either basic hidden-asset approach.

The fifth strategy is to *combine* assets. A disadvantage of splitting the target is that separate security systems can be expensive. By combining several assets in one place, better security can be provided at lower total cost.

The final strategy is *rings of protection,* or layers of protection, or the "onion skin" method. This has been referred to several times previously because it is an excellent basic strategy. Multiple layers of protection are provided, ideally with different strategies in each layer. In an operating system, the first layer might be account and password; the second layer, access control tables; a third layer, passwords on individual files; and a fourth layer perhaps a physical switch which must be thrown by an operator to permit access at all. Very few threats, accidental or deliberate, would penetrate four such layers, particularly since different methods are needed in layers 1, 2, and 4.

Summary of Design Strategies

The risk management team will find the task of designing safeguards easier if three ideas are kept in mind:

1.   common sense
2.   the basic purposes of controls
3.   basic, proven strategies for protection

There are three basic purposes of controls:

1.   Prevent occurrences of exposures.
2.   Detect events.
3.   Correct the situation to avoid repetition.

Six time-proven strategies should be understood fully (although other strategies have been tried, and some also work well):

1.   Avoid the risk in the first place.
2.   Split up the asset so several areas have to be penetrated to accomplish the exposure.
3.   Put the asset in a visible place so penetration attempts are obvious.
4.   Hide the asset, either literally or by the "purloined letter" method.
5.   Combine several assets to minimize costs of security.
6.   Utilize many layers of protection.

Keeping these principles in mind will help to minimize the risk of "paralysis by analysis."

3.4 COMPONENTS OF EDP SECURITY: ADMINISTRATIVE AND ORGANIZATIONAL CONTROLS

The chapters following deal with eight essential elements of information systems security:

General administrative and organizational controls

Personnel

Physical and environmental security

Communications and electronic exposure

Computer operations

Software

Hardware and encryption

The final category is not strictly part of the security, since it deals with what you do after the fact:

Contingency planning.

These have been re-ordered (to fit into the diagram) and listed in approximate order of layers of security from the external world to the asset, as depicted in Figure 3.1:

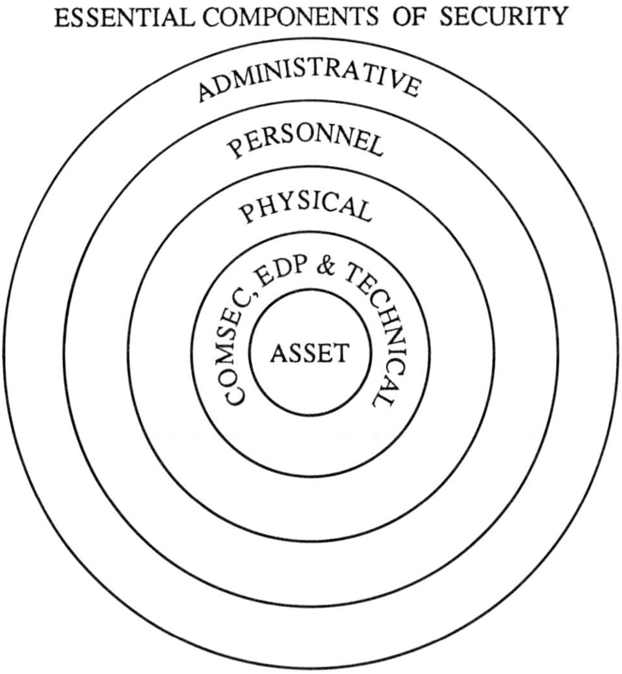

ESSENTIAL COMPONENTS OF SECURITY

Figure 3.1
(This variation of the diagram is from the RCMP "T" Directorate)

The "circle diagram" in Figure 3.1 is a useful theoretical picture of how the eight essential elements of information system security relate to a rings of protection basic strategy. For practical purposes, however, the risk management team at this point in the risk management process probably will be split into subgroups of people with specialized knowledge in areas such as personnel, accounting, computer systems, and so on. Therefore, the ordering in which the detailed safeguard areas will be examined is changed to emphasize the "Administrative and Organizational" and the "Technical" parts of the essential components.

Areas classed as organizational and administrative are:

1.   General administrative and organizational controls
2.   Personnel
3.   Physical and environmental security
4.   Computer operations
5.   Contingency planning.

Areas generally classed as technical are:

6.   Communications and electronic exposure
7.   Hardware and encryption
8.   Software.

The remainder of this chapter is a very brief description of what is meant by each of the eight categories, in the order in which they will be presented in the remainder of Section II and Section III.

3.4.1 Administrative and Organizational Controls

This area involves the development of an overall security policy and establishing procedures for its implementation. Such topics as corporate policies, organization structure and identification of responsibilities, training, employee awareness, and general working practices ("telecommuting," for example) will be addressed in Chapter 4.

3.4.2 Personnel

Chapter 5 presents some material on who commits crimes, and why they do so. (This is summarized and is strictly from an information systems standpoint. It is a very broad and complex topic without general agreement in many basic conceptual areas.) Employee selection, including standardized application forms, reference checks, and security clearances will be addressed next. An overview of existing professional certificates will be given here (this area is addressed in more detail in Chapter 14). The general working environment will be discussed. Finally, procedures recommended when employees leave (voluntarily or otherwise) will be considered.

3.4.3 Physical and Environmental Security

In Chapter 6, factors such as site location and physical protection will be discussed. The topics include:

1. Site location and construction
2. Physical access
3. Power supply
4. Air Conditioning
5. Fire prevention
6. Fire protection
7. Tape and other media libraries
8. Waste disposal
9. Off-site storage

While many of these things will be fixed for a given risk management team (cannot build a new building, for example), they should be included in the analysis, if only to be sure that consideration is given.

3.4.4 Computer Operations

The actual operations of an EDP or information systems department are examined briefly in Chapter 7. Typical organization structures for mainframe, minicomputer, and microcomputer/office automation establishments are shown. The security emphasis is on the actual physical computer room operations, but consideration is given also to analysts, programmers, and others involved. Separation of duties is a critical control measure (frequently neglected by EDP managers due to lack of training) and will be addressed. Interfaces between the information systems group and others will be looked at with a view to identifying control points for the implementation of safeguards. Controls on data storage media, backup procedures, and people will be explored.

3.4.5 Contingency Planning

Any information system provides a service to an organization. Contingency planning is the effort invested to determine how to cope with emergencies and other interruptions in service. What should be done if the data center is destroyed in a fire? What measures minimize problems from a power surge caused by lightning? The major emphasis of the treatment in Chapter 8 is on provision of backups for data, procedures, people, and hardware. Some consideration is given to catastrophe planning and to security in the backup site.

3.5 COMPONENTS OF EDP SECURITY: TECHNICAL

Several of the essential components of information systems security have been grouped under the rubric "technical." Because design and implementation of the technical controls normally requires specialized expertise, a separate Section III covers this area. Chapter 9 presents a recap of Section II and some material intended to provide perspective on the relative importance of technical versus administrative exposures (especially the "hot topic" of the mid-1980's, the so-called "hacker"). The three security elements which will be addressed are communications and electronic exposure; hardware and encryption; and software.

3.5.1 Communications and Electronic Exposures

Modern computer systems of any size normally have communications capabilities. Reasons vary all over the spectrum, but access to databases such as "the Source," "CompuServe," or "cansim," distributed processing, electronic mail, and other value-added communications features are worth so much that most organizations have communications if their data centers are of any significant size. Another area of communications is Local Area Networks, which offers different exposures and control measures.

Computers are electronic machines, and are subject to leakage and interference. This very technical topic will not be given much emphasis, but it must be addressed so that the risk management team will be aware that there may be a need to engage experts with the requisite skills and knowledge. Chapter 10 briefly explores the topic areas of communications and electronic exposures.

3.5.2 Hardware and Encryption

Much of the field of hardware security will have been touched on in Chapter 6 as a "Physical" aspect. The treatment in Chapter 11 relates mostly to power supplies and to special considerations relating to microcomputers, and to encryption.

Properly, encryption is primarily a communications-related matter (at least as it relates to information systems security). This is changing with the availability of low-cost DES chips and other technologies; encryption is now cost-effective in areas such as storing password tables and even data files. Since many hardware devices which provide "DES Encryption" are on the market, the field of encryption as it relates to current usage in EDP security is looked at. The treatment is *not* technical or mathematical, and is intended only to present some basic concepts and some rules useful in selecting encryption procedures and hardware.

3.5.3 Software

Popularly, the use of operating system design and programs to control EDP risk ("software" controls) is of great interest. Unfortunately, there are many important, fascinating, and complex problems in this area, and people with in-depth technical training frequently are seduced by the topic of software security controls. One purpose of this text is to emphasize that most of the security and control field has little to do with details of software or operating system design. It would be inappropriate, however, to ignore this truly intriguing area. Therefore, Chapter 12 presents material on the history of software controls in the area of operating systems, and some of the current standards in place. For completeness, a number of common penetration methods is listed; one would hope that they would not work, but with depressing frequency the same methods *do* succeed in one organization after another. Perhaps each organization is condemned to re-invent the wheel independently. The list is given since every security practitioner should be aware of, and prevent, these "tried and true" exposures. The major prevention techniques are looked at in Chapter 12, since they need to be considered during program development and during program maintenance.

3.6 NEW TERMS

New terms introduced or defined in this chapter include:

Control, corrective or reactive
Control, detective
Control, preventive
Invisibility
Onion skin
Purloined letter
Rings of protection ("layers of protection," "onion skin")
Target splitting (or asset splitting)

3.7 QUESTIONS

3.1.   (case) Basic Purposes of Controls

You are employed by a company that is planning to install a large mainframe computer system.

The President, Mr. I. Dunno, has asked you to comment on his proposed system. He has $50,000 to spend on controls and he plans to spend all of this on preventive controls. "This will make us completely sure that computer fraud will never happen."

Required:

Write your comments to Mr. Dunno.

3.2.   (case) Computer Security Evaluation

Evaluate the following security situations:

1.   Smoke detector. Its buzzer can fail when hot.

2.   After three unsuccessful logon attempts, the person must re-connect and try to log on again.

3.   Bank overdrafts are shown in the middle of a full screen of data; there is no automatic printout of bank overdrafts.

4.   If an employee's time sheet has over 24 hours for one day, the balance (over 24) is added on to the next day's hours.

5.   If batches don't balance, the difference is posted automatically by the system to the "suspense" account in the General Ledger.

6.   The payroll data entry is not proofread or checked because it is confidential data, and only one person can see all payroll data.

7.   The company requires all new employees to read and sign its policy relating to confidential data and trade secrets; all existing employees are required to read and sign the policy every six months.

8.   The bank manager is given a full report of all transaction details on all 100,000 bank accounts every day so that he will not miss any problem accounts.

Required:

Comment on each situation, highlighting which type of control is involved, what is wrong if anything, and suggesting one or more ways to fix the problem if any.

3.3.   (case) System Security -- Preventive Controls

Assume that you are the controller of Rich Oil Company, a new oil refinery that just started up at Richland Hills, Texas. The company was incorporated yesterday. You are installing a mainframe computer system and will have 5 programmers, 2 systems analysts, 1 computer operator, 2 data entry clerks, and 1 EDP auditor, all supervised by the systems manager. The office is new and there is still time to set up a specific area in the office for the computer staff (that is, you can renovate the area any way you wish).

The refinery has 500 plant workers and 50 office staff. Half of these already have been hired and half will be hired next month. None of the computer staff has been hired yet.

All employees will be given a weekly pay check. Plant workers are hourly pay, and others are monthly salary.

Required:

Prepare a short report (three pages or less) to the president, Mr. Richard Rich, describing only *prevention* controls that should be put into place in this company. You have a large (but not unlimited) budget for prevention controls.

Chapter 4

ORGANIZATIONAL AND ADMINISTRATIVE CONTROLS

INTRODUCTION

This chapter presents a brief overview of some specific security and control measures which fall into the area of administrative controls (organizational measures relating to security). This particular topic area in principle encompasses the entire spectrum of the organization; effectively anything can be considered an administrative or organizational feature. The emphasis in this text is on broad notions such as "organizational culture," policy statements, company policies defining assets such as trade secrets, elements in the organization responsible for security, and "how the company does business."

The types of assets which need protection at this broad level are what can be called "soft assets." By this we mean that they are intangible and generally hard to measure in dollar terms. At the level of detail we reach, it is difficult to separate control methods from assets. For example, the organization's "morale" is an important factor in security and control, and it is also an asset which is worth protecting; but it is very difficult to put a dollar value on morale. Most of the techniques mentioned in this chapter both support protection of the soft assets and enhance an environment in which control is much easier.

One asset has been mentioned: organization "morale." Are employees generally happy in their jobs, or is there an atmosphere of general mistrust and antagonism? The security problem clearly is different in "happy" and "unhappy" organizations. Similar soft assets are "how the business works" -- how does it go about its daily affairs (e. g., do people make extensive use of computers?); the normal functioning of the business (if disrupted, what costs are involved?); the "good name" of the business (how do customers perceive a bank if they cannot get money due to computer problems?). The basic organizational structure of the business is an asset: it has grown to meet needs and to match capabilities of people, and personnel changes or system problems represent costs. Reorganization can present very large costs (for example, the merger of Burroughs and Univac to create Unisys, with layoffs of duplicated headquarters staff, expenses for new logos, forms, new planning efforts, and so on). Training and experience of the employees, and their understanding of each other and how each goes about his or her job, are significant assets, difficult and expensive to re-create if changed or disrupted. The last group of representative assets here is the collection of data and information which support the organization's functioning: policies, procedures, manufacturing methods, patents, and the general knowledge base (customer lists and contacts, for instance).

The most basic of all control principles is that an organization which is "happy," which has knowledgeable and capable people, and which is committed to ethical and professional behavior as a culture, is usually a secure and controlled organization. Specific controls still are important to minimize temptations and ensure continued high morale and professionalism. In both information systems and organizations in general, committed people with appropriate skills can make lousy systems work somehow; incompetent or hostile people can and do cause supposedly well-designed systems to fail. Without top management direction on policy and commitment to professional and ethical behavior, the other two factors are directionless. If the organization fails in any of the three basic areas of morale, skilled and committed employees, or top management commitment, security must be imposed; imposed rules are inherently less efficient and effective than committed people.

The most basic control is segregation of duties, which essentially limits opportunity and temptation. Segregation of duties can be defined as "separating incompatible functions (giving these duties to two or more people) to strengthen internal control." The activities of a process are split among several people. Mistakes made by one person tend to be caught by the next person in the chain. Unauthorized activities require collusion of at least two people. Since this control is so basic, several variations and implications are presented in the next paragraphs.

In addition to the basic definition (and see also the "official" definition from various accounting and security-oriented texts, below), several elaborations are found in security material provided by computer people. These guidelines help to ensure good internal control and to define "incompatible functions," and include:

1.   No Access to Sensitive Combinations of Capabilities

The classic example is control of data about the inventory, and also of the physical inventory. Besides violating segregation of duties, this is an unnecessary temptation: an employee could steal from inventory, then alter the data so the theft is hidden.

2.   Prohibit Conversion and Concealment

Another violation of the segregation principle is to put people into a position where they are unsupervised and have access to assets. The lone operator of a night shift is a standard example. This person could copy ("convert") and sell customer lists. Instances have been reported of operators actually using the employer's computer to run a service bureau at night.

3.   Same person cannot both originate and approve transactions

Some of the most expensive frauds have occurred when the same person could enter an expense and also authorize it. An expense account is an obvious example. Often, corrections of transactions in error are entered without careful authorization; people have deliberately entered bad data, then re-entered their own corrections, and thus bypassed normal checks and balances.

All of these principles relate to separation of duties. Whether manual or electronic, systems should feature separation of duties and responsibilities. The exact definition of this principle comes from the professional accounting and auditing people (and is found in many security references such as Lobel, *Foiling the System Breakers* [Lobel 1986]):

This principle actually consists of two parts:
-No single individual must have responsibility for the complete processing of any transaction or group of transactions.
-The perpetration of a fraud must require the collusion of at least two individuals.

As has been noted previously, accounting professionals use a somewhat different meaning when they say "control" than computer people use. Accountants and auditors are concerned with protection of an organization's assets and ensuring that assets are used in accordance with the intentions of owners and managers. When an accountant or auditor says "control," it usually is linked with internal control, and relates to this use of assets and to prevention of *fraud*. People from a computer background typically use the word "control" to relate to the predictability, recovery capability, and quality of a *computer system*. The uses are not incompatible.

Above, principles from a perspective of computer professionals have been given, followed by the accountant's definition of segregation of duties. In the next paragraph, we list guidelines for segregation of duties from an accounting perspective.

Auditing: An Integrated Approach (Arens, Lobbecke, and Lemon, Prentice Hall, 1987) is a popular text used in accounting courses. Its treatment of segregation of duties includes four guidelines which should be compared to the three guidelines listed above (the *italicized* comments are the authors' comments comparing the previous treatment with this, not a restatement of this book's words):

1.   Separation of Custody of Assets from Accounting

     (Compare with "No access to sensitive combinations of capabilities.") This auditing text recommends that any person performing an accounting function be denied access to assets which can be converted to personal gain. Similar considerations apply to such EDP examples as programmers with access to master files containing valuable lists which could be sold, and to other EDP areas (see Chapter 7).

2.   Separation of the Authorization of Transactions from the Custody of Related Assets

     (Compare with "Same person cannot both originate and approve transactions.") The auditing text uses the example of a person authorizing payment of a vendor invoice and also signing the check for payment. The example under guideline 3 earlier relates to error correction, since it has been a favorite system penetration method in many EDP installations. The relation should be clear.

3.   Separation of Duties within the Accounting Function

     This manual accounting consideration has little direct *application to computers: typical EDP accounting systems deliberately* combine *as many accounting functions as possible. (This* combination *creates an exposure which needs controls. This exposure is controlled in a manual accounting system by having different people responsible for the journals and for recording in the subsidiary ledgers. This use of separate journals and ledgers involves repeated entry of the same data, which is inherently inefficient, in a tradeoff for greater control. Typical EDP accounting systems, especially microcomputer accounting packages, normally avoid the inefficiency by having* one *entry, with the computer automatically "posting" to "ledgers" and so on. Controls in such cases are an ongoing concern of EDP and internal auditors.)*

4.   Separation of Operational Responsibility from Record-keeping Responsibility

     (Compare with "Prohibit Conversion and Concealment," which is a special case.) Record keeping handled by a separate accounting department minimizes the temptation for individual departments to "fudge" data to make themselves look good. The Equity Funding in-

*surance scandal was possible in part because managers using comput-
ers were able to violate this guideline.*

Segregation of duties and responsibilities must be supplemented by systems
which feature:

1.   Integrity

The system does exactly what it should, no more and no less. For every input to the system, the output and response can be predicted.
Unidentified inputs should cause error messages and reports and should
not cause changes to data files.

2.   Auditability

It must be possible to trace what happened and who caused it to happen. The system should be able to point to a single individual who has
responsibility for any transaction. One way is to "time stamp" every
transaction with the date, time, and identification of the originator. A
detailed transaction list should be available. Note that good EDP system design, including "before and after" copies of records and transactions (intended mainly to allow recovery from a failure) will serve this
purpose, if the originator of the transaction is also identified.

3.   Controllability

The system must do what the managers responsible require of it, and
change as they require it to. A system should be broken into precise
"modules" for which one person can be held responsible.

The EDP principles of "structured design" and "structured programming" are
detail level applications of this controllability principle, and fit well with the
modularity need. The computer professional uses concepts of coupling and
cohesion to express the same logical concerns. "Cohesion" refers to the internal
unity of a program or system module; high cohesion corresponds to high granu-
larity. Coupling refers to interactions *between* modules and to control structures. Low coupling corresponds (approximately) to separation of duties.

There is a considerable literature on cohesion and coupling in system and
program design. The Yourdon Press publishers have a number of books, the
most recent of which reflect the latest thinking of the originators of cohesion
and coupling in computer system design, Ed Yourdon and Tom deMarco.
Lord's *CDP Review Manual: A Data Processing Handbook* [Lord 1986] has an
excellent summary; more can be found in Adams, Powers & Owles, *Computer
Information Systems Development: Design and Implementation* [Adams 1985],
and many other works on systems analysis. Those who need this specialized
detail should consult these and other specialized works for details.

The computer programmer usually is working at a detail level where people
interactions are not involved, or have been specified by the system designer.

Structured *analysis* and *design* should include considerations of people interactions.

Systems which have integrity, auditability, and controllability are the only ones which any professional should design, or allow.

The remainder of this chapter addresses five specific control areas:

1.   Trade secrets, employee agreements and conflict of interest (Section 4.1)
2.   Awareness and policy (Section 4.2)
3.   An organizational measure, the System Security Officer (Section 4.3)
4.   Training (Section 4.4); and
5.   Telecommuting (Section 4.5)

4.1 TRADE SECRETS, EMPLOYEE AGREEMENTS, CONFLICT OF INTEREST

Trade secrets relate to the ways a company does business, or to things unique to and of value to the company. There is a legal definition and a great number of legal decisions relating to trade secrets; these technicalities will be avoided here. (More detail on legal aspects is contained in Chapter 13.) For the purposes of this text, a trade secret is an asset which needs protecting. To have legal protection, it is necessary both that the asset is a trade secret, and that the company *treat* it as such. Specifically, employees must be made aware of the secrecy and the company and its employees must not publish it (in conversations over coffee at conferences, for instance).

A specific control measure which helps to protect trade secrets (computer programs, manufacturing techniques, or whatever) is to have

1.   A company policy regarding confidentiality
2.   Each employee sign both agreements to keep confidential things secret, and acknowledgments that he/she understands that "x" is a confidential trade secret

Without both elements, losses may not be recoverable through legal processes. In the Canadian case Regina v. Tannis (Dome Petroleum), a departing employee retained copies of programs. The company attempted to have the former employee held accountable for breach of trade secrets but was unable to establish that the employee knew the items in question were controlled, or that he knew they were trade secrets, or that the company had made any attempt to recover material on termination.

The acknowledgments should be read and signed both before employment and periodically while employed, and reviewed when the employee leaves.

Acknowledgments such as referred to here are one example of a detail item which would be part of employee awareness. More about the topic of awareness is found in Section 4.2.

Another example of a detailed supporting element of a policy, is conflict of interest rules. The company should have a policy which defines whether, for instance, spouses may work in the same department, or may report to one another. Both separation of duties and simple common sense come into play here. A married couple are not normally at "arms length" in a business sense; duties split between them may not be truly separated. If a spouse reports to another, could the company depend on performance appraisals? Again, rules should be made, communicated, and acknowledged by employees.

4.2 ORGANIZATIONAL AND EMPLOYEE AWARENESS, POLICY STATEMENT

As with most security considerations in this chapter, the overall climate of the organization, or its "culture," is crucial. Every organization will have unwritten rules that "x" is "simply not done," or that "y" is "done this way here." A key point in security and control is to make sure that the organizational culture includes norms which lead to professional behavior.

The methods used in working with organizational culture are many and varied (there is an entire field of study called "Organizational Development" which deals primarily in this area). Obvious ways culture is communicated include:

1.   Perception and observation

What does the boss do? If the owner regularly uses company funds for personal expenses, it is possible that secretaries may see nothing wrong with raiding petty cash.

2.   Employee Training

The initial orientation and subsequent "refreshers" should tell people what is considered acceptable.

The main point here is that employees must know what is expected of them. Rather than depending on more or less uncontrolled "osmosis," a security and control (and good management) principle is to *tell* people what you want. A secondary point also should be obvious: don't try to tell people things which they will observe for themselves are not true.

The lesson from these observations is that security and control first must consider the organization and its norms and expectations. The control program must be designed with this in mind, and it must be communicated: employee awareness must be generated.

These comments lead to the principle that security must come from the top. Employees must be able to recognize a clear top management commitment, or any security effort is likely to fail. The most workable way to meet this need is to have a clear policy of the company regarding security. This policy must be:

1.   Simple and clear

2.   Known to employees

3.   Supported and adhered to by top management

Exhibit 4.1 contains an example of a policy in an educational institution. It is short, clear, and "comes from the top." Managers have the responsibility to fill in details (such as trade secret agreements noted above) to ensure that the policy is carried out.

Note that this policy explicitly recognizes that in an educational environment people must be relatively free to experiment.

EXHIBIT 4.1   EDUCATIONAL INSTITUTION POLICY

Information Systems Security Policy

This organization is committed to conducting its affairs at all times in accordance with the law and the highest ethical standards. The reputation which we enjoy is based not on a list of detailed rules but on the example set by management and the character and good judgment of each employee and the reputation of our graduates. It is expected that employees at all levels will conduct themselves so that their actions will not embarrass themselves, their families or their organizations, and that students will conduct themselves in accordance with the student conduct guidelines. The following principles are stated to furnish general guidelines in a variety of situations relating to information systems:

> 1.   Integrity is an essential element of every business relationship; with our employees, with our students, with our suppliers, and with our shareholders and the general public.

> 2.   In the course of normal business operations, employees and students have access to the "XYZ" computer facilities and to privileged information. All employees and students are expected to avoid any actions which might harm the interests of any users of the computer facilities besides themselves. This includes, but is not limited to, affecting the

availability of the computer capabilities, integrity of data and information, disclosure of data or information not belonging to the student or employee, or any other action which is unlawful or harmful to others.

3.   No employee will knowingly fail to comply with all applicable laws and regulations of federal, state, and local governments in the conduct of the business.

4.   Detailed guidelines and standards regarding professional conduct and release of information about students will be adhered to strictly by all employees.

5.   Ethical business conduct is a condition of employment, and of continued employment, for all employees of this organization.

6.   As this is an educational institution and experimentation is part of the learning process, some student violations of the standards of conduct will be subject to warnings before actual suspension; however, deliberate damage to others, or disclosure of sensitive information for personal gain, will be cause for immediate expulsion from the academic program; knowing violations of federal, state, or local laws will also be grounds for immediate expulsion.

7.   It is the responsibility of the President and the Information Systems Manager to put in place systems and controls which will ensure minimal exposure of privileged information and the computer facilities, and of all employees and students to follow the relevant portions of those guidelines.

8.   It is the responsibility of the Director of Academics to put in place detailed standards of student conduct which will support this policy.

Computer uses, such as "playing games," which might be totally inappropriate in a secret government project, are condoned in this policy. Students are allowed to experiment, within the limits of not harming others or making the system unavailable to authorized users. Detailed guidelines, procedures, and stan-

dards involved in implementing this policy will include warnings prior to sus-
pensions; in other environments termination, or even police attention, might ac-
company the same rule violations.

Again, policies must be communicated; Section 4.4 on training addresses this
need.

4.3 RESPONSIBILITY AREAS, SYSTEM SECURITY OFFICER

4.3.1 Basic Role; Functional Matrix

One organizational measure which can be taken to implement security and control, is to create the position of System Security Officer (SSO). This position
has many alternate names, such as Data Security Administrator or Departmental
Security Officer (DSO); in very large organizations there may be several security people responsible for various aspects of security and control (separation of
duties). In small organizations, this function typically is part of the System
Manager's job. In every organization, some person must have responsibility
and be held accountable for security and control (excluding the element of control which is part of any manager's job responsibilities).

It is important to define carefully the responsibilities of the SSO. One way to
define responsibilities which has proven of value in many situations is to use a
"functional matrix." The risk management team or other management groups
can identify functions related to security (for example, "identify and classify
data;" "identify protective controls;" "monitor security and control incidents".)
The functions are listed along one side of a matrix. Positions in the organization
with responsibilities related to data and information systems are then identified
(for example, computer operator; systems manager; new project manager; operations manager; payroll manager). These positions are listed along a second
side of the matrix. The cells defined are then filled in with codes such as
"primary responsibility -- PR" or "not relevant -- N/A." The final result shows
who must do what, and who is held accountable. (In real organizations, this exercise usually leads to considerable negotiation the first time it is done, since
many managers will become aware that they have responsibilities they didn't
fully appreciate previously.)

Exhibit 4.2 shows a sample of part of a functional matrix. Notice that this
matrix resembles the job exposure matrix in Table 2.1; the logical tool created
by laying out functions and positions, then entering relations into cells, is useful
in many areas of security and other analyses. In Table 2.1, there was merely an
"X" or not, indicating existence of a vulnerability. Degrees of vulnerability,
rather than degrees of responsibility as in Exhibit 4.2, would have given a

matrix nearly identical to Table 2.1. (In this *partial* matrix, the abbreviated list of functions does not include areas for which anyone besides the SSO and, in one case, the systems development manager, holds primary responsibility.)

Sample: Partial Functional Responsibility Matrix

Position	Function			
	Identify Risks	Monitor Operators' Security Practices	Develop & Enforce Security Standards	Evaluate Effectiveness of Security Program
System Security Officer (SSO)	PR	MN	PR	PR
Top Managers	N/A	MN	MN N/A	MN
Systems Development Manager	MC	N/A	MN N/A	MN
Data Center Manager	MC	PR	MC	MN
User	MN N/A	N/A	MC	MN MC
Data Asset Owner	MC	N/A	MN N/A	MN MC

KEY: PR = Primary Responsibility   MN = Must be Notified
            MC = Must be Consulted   N/A = Not Applicable

EXHIBIT 4.2

4.3.2 Duties

The specific duties of the SSO, as revealed by this planning tool, normally will vary depending on the organization. The central duty is to be responsible for the security program of the organization's information systems.

A sample of these duties, as reported by Royal Fisher [Fisher 1984] is:

1.   Provide direct administrative support for installed security systems to ensure the secure use of all on-line and information systems.

2.   Set objectives for future development of security systems for evolving on-line and information systems.

3.   Determine special resource requirements such as manpower, training, and equipment and develop plans, schedules, and cost data relative to various security responsibilities.

4.   Negotiate with multiple levels of programming support management to assure integration of assigned security objectives with the long-range data processing strategy.

5.   Continually review and evaluate security alternatives to determine course of action based upon technical implications, knowledge of business objectives, and corporate asset protection policy, procedures, and requirements.

6.   Assure that assigned projects meet corporate security objectives and are completed according to schedule within committed costs; inform management as early as possible of problems that could materially affect objectives, schedules, and costs; recommend alternative solutions.

7.   Monitor the use of on-line and information systems to detect and act upon unauthorized access and use of proprietary business data.

8.   Interface and coordinate with legal, insurance, and security staff handling internal security investigations on a highly confidential basis.

9.   Conduct security audits, participate in security evaluations, and provide guidance and assistance, as requested, to facilitate the implementation of data processing asset protection programs.

10.   Supervise documentation efforts associated with internal security systems.

This list is a sample. Items 6 and 9 in particular may cause some problems: item 6 describes responsibilities normally assigned to a project manager, and item 9 covers many internal audit functions. The specific duties will vary among different organizations. The functional matrix, and the negotiations mentioned in the previous subsection, will help to define the System Security Officer position for any specific situation. Many large organizations have existing policies such as the Canadian Federal Government security policy manual, United States Federal Government manuals, Canadian and United States Department of Defense publications, and similar guides. All of the ones mentioned have very specific and detailed lists and descriptions of the duties of the SSO or equivalent person.

In performing these or similar duties, the SSO will have to interact with, and to understand and be aware of the activities of, many groups of people, both within and outside the organization. A sample list might include:

1.   Suppliers of services
2.   Users/owners
3.   Management
4.   Outsiders such as security guards
5.   Audit
6.   Suppliers of computer equipment
7.   Legal department.

In some organizations, this list would be expanded to include, for instance, suppliers of communications services (possibly within the company, possibly outside suppliers). The exact contents of such a list will vary depending on the organization and its normal activities.

4.3.3 Training and Skills for a System Security Officer

To understand and negotiate effectively with diverse groups such as outlined above, the System Security Officer needs a number of basic knowledge sets. Generally, they cover areas of accounting and audit, EDP and other systems, and business knowledge. More specifically, the knowledge sets normally include:

1.   Organizational knowledge: structure and behavioral
2.   Technical knowledge (EDP): computers, systems, tools
3.   Technical knowledge: manual procedures, systems, and tools
4.   Accounting and audit concepts
5.   Personnel administration matters
6.   Law and legislation
7.   Other business knowledge: strategic and tactical planning, the basic nature of the organization, labor and other negotiating strategies and tactics

Other knowledge sets also can be very useful: statistics is important in many types of analyses, for example. In working with physical and environmental security, knowledge of building construction and similar areas is an asset. A SSO in a communications environment may need in-depth knowledge of many communications specialties. In a manufacturing company, Material Requirements

Planning (MRP) may be needed. In retailing, marketing knowledge may be crucial.

In addition to the rather daunting range of needed knowledge, the SSO needs some specific personal characteristics:

1. Honesty
2. Tact and politeness
3. Oral and written communication skills
4. Professionalism and personal maturity

He or she is one of the primary risk exposures, since to do the job properly, virtually complete access is needed, and the training includes how to hide unauthorized events: unquestioned personal honesty becomes a critical characteristic. As noted in the comment about items 6 and 9 in the sample list of duties, many of the things a SSO does overlap with other managers: a considerable amount of tact and politeness also is needed. Much of the SSO's work involves communicating, either collecting information or being involved in awareness programs, reports to management, and similar presentations: superior abilities in written and spoken communication are essential. Last, but certainly not least, the individual selected for a SSO position must be highly professional and mature: not age, but possessing such characteristics as discretion, the ability to command respect, and leadership ability are the requisites here.

Combining all of the needed kinds of knowledge with the range of personal characteristics, a picture of some kind of "superman" or "superwoman" is generated. The requirements described above are ideals; probably, no single person could meet all of them. The knowledge sets alone, in the detail which a SSO needs, would require perhaps 24 years in university (by which time the first knowledge gained would be obsolete...). This presentation is to give an idea of the perfect situation. In the real world, one attempts to achieve perfection but must recognize its unattainability and work with available resources and make intelligent allowances for lacks.

4.4 TRAINING

There are two kinds of training which are significant from the security stand-point: orientation and skills. Orientation is training whose intent is to set a cli-mate, convey initial information about a situation, and so on. Employee orien-tation at the beginning of employment is of interest here. The second kind of training is specific skills training: courses of a few days or weeks' length which help employees upgrade their knowledge and capability or add new knowledge. From the security perspective, orientation relates to employee awareness and organizational culture; and skills training relates to reinforcement of the culture, and the critical need to have competent, knowledgeable people.

4.4.1 Orientation

Every employee hired should learn about the written components of the corpo-rate culture, such as policies, what is considered confidential, rules regarding conflict of interest, and so forth. More mundane knowledge is needed as well, of course: introduction to fellow workers, location of the washrooms and office facilities, formal reporting relationships, union rules and procedures if any, and so on. The initial employee training sessions should address these areas. A written employee orientation package, which is *kept current*, is highly recom-mended, and may be necessary to protect the organization in some kinds of legal disputes.

Employee agreement to such things as acknowledgments of "read and un-derstood" disclosure policies probably has little or no legal value unless it is *in-formed* agreement. The main thing the SSO needs to ensure is that discussion of just what the company's policies are in regard to security and control is included in the Personnel or Human Resources Department's standard orientation pro-grams, and that employees are asked to sign. Signing and acknowledgment should be a condition of hiring, and of continued employment.

It is highly recommended that employees review policies regarding confi-dentiality and security and sign new acknowledgments, each time there is a ma-terial change in employee duties and responsibilities, and in any case periodi-cally (perhaps each six months, or yearly).

Security and control principles include continual reinforcement. Tell em-ployees what is expected "up front," remind them periodically, and the factor of employee awareness will follow.

4.4.2 Skills

By far the most frequent cause of losses in any system is employee error. Even though a major part of the effort in any system design project is invested in making the system "bulletproof," people make mistakes. Properly trained people make fewer mistakes. Continued employee upgrading, and employee training before new tasks are attempted, are important for economic as well as security and control reasons. Training is not a primary responsibility of the security function; but ensuring that training is available and provided is part of the SSO's responsibility. This is a way to avoid many of the high-occurrence "accidental" threats identified in the risk assessment, as well as one way to help out in the employee morale area. The security people should ensure that training is available, and that new systems developments always include development of employee training programs. Security analyses may include data which will allow managers to assess the true value of training; training can be seen as strictly a cost, and thus avoidable during "lean times," without such data.

Basic control principles suggest that an organization with high morale, with knowledgeable and capable people, and which is committed to professional and ethical behavior, usually is a secure and well-controlled organization. Training both for specific skills and for orientation is an important component in two of the three basic needs.

4.5 TELECOMMUTING

This chapter on administrative and organizational aspects of security and control would be incomplete without mention of a phenomenon which is growing and may dominate some information industries in the future: "telecommuting." In something resembling in many ways a return to the cottage industry of the early Industrial Revolution, the communication capability of modern information systems, combined with the power of personal computers, has made it possible for people to work at home again. It no longer is necessary to fight traffic to reach the office. It no longer is necessary to have set hours; electronic mail can reach people wherever and whenever they "sign on." In 1988, it is possible to have complete communication with people (except physical contact) from anywhere there is access to two-way video and computer links. Less complete communication, voice and data but not video, is available from anywhere in the world with a telephone system.

All of this may sound, and may be, wonderful; since it is a new thing, the "jury is still out." From the security and control perspective, the company which experiments with telecommuting must take care to watch out for some potential new problem areas.

The corporation moving to telecommuting exposes itself to two major risks which may not have been there, or may have changed in character, with employees doing the same tasks in an office:

1.   Communications exposure

This is examined in more detail in Chapter 10. Here, it is enough to say that communicating is necessary to telecommute; the company incurs the exposures relating to information in public networks when it supports telecommuting.

2.   Asset Exposure

The assets -- data and information, personal computers, and so on -- used by the employee, will be in a home environment. Security usually is much looser in people's homes than in even fairly "loose" offices. If there were no other problem, there still will be many locations, rather than just one.

Sensitive company assets, both data and such costly physical assets as personal computers, will be exposed differently, and probably more, with telecommuting than in a single-office environment.

An exposure of the company which does not exist in single-location environments is changed employee relations. Offices serve purposes besides simply collecting people and equipment together; there are social and behavioral and interpersonal factors involved. Telecommuting supports many kinds of information exchange but not groups of people socializing on coffee breaks, for instance. There probably will be significant effects on employee morale for companies which encourage extensive telecommuting. The exact effects are not known for this new phenomenon; the security and control people need to monitor and watch out for morale problems.

Another potential morale problem is employee relations. Cottage industries in the early Industrial Revolution included piecework and other systems which developed into cruel abuse of employees. Although the technology is totally different, the people relation problems and exploitation of workers which prevailed then could recur. There is some evidence (lawsuits in California, for example) that such abuses are resurfacing in telecommuting. Successful examples of telecommuting clearly show that exploitation *need not* be a problem. Lawsuits show that it *may* be. The security and control functions must monitor the situation; not only is the "happy company" at jeopardy, but as well, there is greatly increased exposure.

A discussion of employee morale would be incomplete if it ignored management morale. One problem which occurs in telecommuting is that managers must be sufficiently secure to accept employees who are not subject to direct, exact controls. "Management by Walking Around (MBWA)" can be more than slightly difficult when staff could be located in several cities. With cellular telephones and laptop computers, it is entirely possible to work while sunning on the beach (although sand in diskettes could be annoying). Traditional managers may not find this easy to adapt to.

Telecommuting may be a benefit of technology which will free people from traffic, cities from gridlock, and work from the "9 to 5 drudgery." It may be a curse which will be used by unscrupulous employers to recreate the exploitation of the early Industrial Revolution. The author has considerable experience with using a world-wide network and combining people on different continents in the same project; the experience is exhilarating and one wonders how one ever managed without. Others have reported companies using telecommuting to separate workers, deny them interaction with fellows, and impose piecework and monitoring methods which amount to exploitation and invasion of privacy.

The jury is out; the security people must monitor the situation, as material effects on the risk assessment are certain.

4.6 NEW TERMS

New terms introduced or defined in this chapter include:

Auditability
Conflict of interest
Controllability
Data Security Administrator (also System Security Officer)
Employee awareness
Functional matrix
Integrity
Organizational culture
Organizational morale
Security policy statement
Separation of duties
Soft asset
System Security Officer (SSO) (also Data Security Administrator)
Telecommuting
Trade secret

4.7 QUESTIONS

4.1 Segregation of Duties

Consider these different companies:

A: A warehouse manager receives inventory, ships it, processes shipping invoices, does data entry for inventory ledger, and performs the inventory count alone at year end.

B: The accounts receivable manager opens mail (payment envelopes are always addressed to his attention) and enters these receipts in the computer general ledger and computer accounts receivable sub-ledger. All accounts receivable exception reports from the computer go to the accounts receivable manager. He also makes all the bank deposits and reconciles the bank statement.

C: A receptionist opens mail and gives checks to treasury department and remittance slips to the accounting department. The treasury department deposits cash in the bank daily.

Required:

For each case:

(1)   What frauds could be done? How? (Be specific.)

(2)   How could this fraud be covered up so that it might not be found?

(3)   What could be done to improve internal control?

4.2 Professional Behavior Norms

Provide at least two examples of a manager's behavior that would negatively impact professional behavior norms in a company.

Chapter 5

PERSONNEL CONSIDERATIONS

INTRODUCTION

After the general organizational climate and basic security and control measures at that level, the next "ring" of the security around information system assets, and where controls are needed to protect those assets, is personnel security. People, or personnel, are after all the entities who make an organization work, and whose purposes organizations serve. It is also people who protect, or try to penetrate, the organization. According to the RCMP in their "Security Information Publications" series [RCMP 1981]:

> Personnel security includes specifying security requirements in job descriptions, ensuring that incumbents meet these requirements and are provided with adequate security motivation and training. It involves supervising access to and control over system resources through appropriate personnel identification and authorization measures. It further requires attention to hiring and employment termination procedures.

Most organizations of any size have a "human resources department," or a "personnel department," or a group with a similar name. The primary responsibility for people concerns rests with this group. Chapter 5 looks at some specific things which, from the security and control perspective, should be included in those things which the Personnel Department does.

The assets involved in this section are the "people assets:" trained, experienced personnel. First, some of the results relating to why people can be a problem are reviewed. After that, we look at some specific recommendations for security controls which are appropriate in selecting personnel. Some topics related to working conditions -- again, from a security and control perspective -- will be the next focus, and finally recommendations on maintaining security and control when employees leave will be presented.

This chapter is not by any means a presentation of "all there is to personnel management." Its purpose is limited to identifying specific security and control measures which relate to personnel security.

5.1 HUMAN MOTIVES FOR CRIMINAL ACTION

It has been estimated that perhaps 85% of people are strictly honest: they would not commit crimes regardless of temptation and opportunity. Of the other 15%, perhaps 5% would engage in a dishonest act if they believed there was *no* chance of getting caught; another 5% might risk a small chance, and a final 5% might try even if there were a 50-50 chance of being caught. Regardless of the exact numbers (75%, 85%, 95%, or whatever), the point is that most people are honest, and some are not. The potentially or actually dishonest people are the security concern.

Criminal behavior involves three basic elements:

1.   Dishonesty
2.   Opportunity
3.   Motive.

If there is no reason to do something (motive), there is little risk. If there is no opportunity, there is little risk. If the person is one of the 85% who are strictly honest, there is little risk. Almost all of the controls examined so far have been basically preventive: aimed at reducing opportunity or motive. Personnel security in employee selection aims at not hiring dishonest people in the first place. Most of the administrative controls discussed in Chapter 4, and the material in Section 5.4 on Working Environment, are in the area of motive: reducing work-related incentives for people to cause problems. Since motives exist outside the workplace (large debts, gambling problems, and other non-work activities), other controls to be discussed later relate to prevention, detection, and reaction in areas of opportunity.

"Computer crime" probably is an inappropriate term. Crimes have been committed throughout human history, and there is no reason to expect differently of the future. Today, computers often are used in crime, and this is called "computer crime" as though the crime did not exist prior to computers. The actual fact seems to be that computers simply are a tool used by people because they are available. (Some specialized things noted in Chapter 1 may be new, and Chapter 13 discusses some legislative attempts to define "computer crime.") Most "computer crimes" have been perpetrated by the same sort of people who, for the same sort of reasons, committed crimes a thousand years ago using other tools. If computers have led to anything new, it is probably that more people have opportunity, and the motivational factor of money has increased due to information density and computer speeds.

The largest risk exposure remains employee error. Personnel security measures are aimed at hiring honest, capable employees.

5.2 EMPLOYEE SELECTION

The first step in hiring an employee is to create an accurate job description. It wastes time, both of applicants and of the people who must sift through resumes, if the nature of the job is not properly defined and communicated to applicants.

Given an accurate job description, the employee recruitment process will lead to many resumes, some interviews, and hopefully a successful placement. Most of this is the responsibility of the human resources group and the managers who actually will use the employees, rather than anything directly related to a security specialist's duties. There are some simple security and control pointers available to help the primary people to maintain security principles:

1. Application forms
2. Permissions for investigations
3. Reference and document checks
4. Security clearances and citizenship

We shall look briefly at each of these. First, there is an important point to make:

No measure will determine that any person is completely honest!

It may be possible to determine that a person previously was *not* honest (criminal record, for instance). There is no way to be sure that a person is now, and forever in the future will be, honest. The points presented in Sections 5.2.1 to 5.2.3 relate to minimizing the chance that dishonest people will be hired. The points in Section 5.4 relate to keeping them honest.

5.2.1 Application Forms

All applicants should be required to fill out an application form before being interviewed. The exact nature of the application will vary from position to position; the intent is that all applicants for a position should put relevant data into the same format. This aids in selection, and the information is verifiable. Some suggested components of an application form are:

1.   Names
       First, Middle, Last
       Nicknames used frequently
       Was name ever legally changed?
         If so, when, where, and what was the previous name?
2.   Date and place born
3.   Current address, and previous addresses (for a time period dependent on the type of job)
4.   Telephone numbers
5.   Employment history, most recent job first.

       *Note: **All** time since leaving school must be accounted for, including periods of unemployment. Gaps are serious warning signals.*

       -Company name, address
       -Date hired and terminated
       -Job title and nature of job
       -Salary or wage
       -Name and title of supervisor
       -Reason for leaving
6.   Education
       -School(s) name and address(es)
       -Dates attended
       -Major field(s) of study
       -Degree(s) obtained
7.   Health considerations relevant to job performance
8.   Credit references
9.   Criminal record if any

Some of these items may be inappropriate or unlawful in some jurisdictions. Questions about health, religion, racial background, criminal record, and so on may be violations of laws regarding privacy (such as the United States *Privacy Act 1975* or the Canadian *Privacy Act 1974*) or of human rights legislation (varies by province and state), or even of the United States *Bill of Rights* or the

Canadian *Charter of Rights and Freedoms.* The company should not put it itself in the position of violating the law in trying to hire honest employees.

The specific components of an application form will vary depending on the position in question. Having all applicants fill out a standard form helps in identifying obviously unsuitable candidates, and in comparing candidates when selecting some to interview.

These points are noted from a *security* perspective. A primary goal of the selection process is to evaluate qualifications, which is of course the responsibility of the manager(s) involved.

5.2.2 Permissions for Investigations

At the bottom of the standardized form there should be a paragraph like:

> I attest that the information provided above is true and complete to the best of my knowledge and belief. I understand that falsification or misrepresentation of any data provided in this application may be grounds for refusing or terminating employment. I authorize (company name) to check any data provided.

> Signed _____ Date _____

In addition to the blanket permission of such an acknowledgment, the applicant's permission should always be gained explicitly before checking with references, current employers, credit reporting agencies, educational institutions, or law enforcement agencies. Again, it is emphasized that legal advice is needed; some of these items or checks may be unlawful in some jurisdictions.

One way to avoid potential legal problems is to ask applicants to provide originals or certified copies of such things as birth and citizenship certificates, professional certifications, transcripts, and reference letters. This also may speed up the evaluation process.

The final point in this section is: check *everything.* It has been estimated that from 10% to 30% of resumes contain misrepresentations or actual falsehoods [Gibb-Clark 1988]. Inconsistencies in data provided (gaps in dates, unusual salaries in previous positions, many previous short jobs, unusual educational qualifications claimed, and similar things) are warning signs, and should be checked out in an interview or separate verification process.

5.2.3 Security Clearance and Citizenship

Many jobs involve work on government or other secret projects. Agencies responsible for the projects will have their own requirements; often such data as citizenship, previous or current clearances, and military service will be required. If it is lawful to ask, such information should be requested on the standard application for companies engaged in such projects: employees may be transferred, promoted, or otherwise moved from originally non-sensitive positions into sensitive ones.

Summary of Employee Selection

From a security perspective, all information should be checked. The purpose is to minimize the chance of hiring dishonest employees in the first place. Qualifications also must be checked, but this is the responsibility of the relevant management.

Specific items to watch are:

1. Gaps in employment history (Gaps are one of the most common areas of misrepresentation [Gibb-Clark 1988].)
2. Frequent job moves
3. Unusual previous salaries
4. Unusual educational background for previous jobs
5. Name changes (check under *all* names)

Items to confirm independently include:

1. References
2. Previous employment
3. Transcripts
4. Professional certifications
5. Credit record (large debts may indicate risk of blackmail or other pressure)
6. Criminal record

It is important to have the procedures and application forms reviewed by the Legal Department to be sure that the company is not violating laws regarding privacy, human rights, or discrimination.

5.3 PROFESSIONAL CERTIFICATES

One indicator of a potentially excellent employee is that of holding a professional designation. People who hold them have sworn themselves to codes of conduct and good practice, and may have higher commitment levels than others. They have proven by examination that they possess a defined level of knowledge. Certificates especially relevant to the computer field which are common in North America include the Certificate in Data Processing (CDP), Certified Systems Professional (CSP), Certified Information Systems Auditor (CISA), and various accounting designations such as CA, CPA, CGA, or CMA. Other certificates from outside North America, such as the British Computer Society's designations (FBCS and others), will be seen from time to time as well.

From the security and control perspective, claims of professional certification should be checked out with the certifying agency (as should university degrees and other "pieces of paper"). If the certificate or diploma is valid, the certifying agency or educational institution will be able to provide confirmation that it was issued, and that it is still valid. False claims about certificates and degrees are among the most common falsifications in resumes [Gibb-Clark 1988]. Chapter 14 contains more information regarding certificates, professionalism, and similar activities in North America and elsewhere in the information processing fields.

People with professional designations have a valuable asset (the certification) which they are very careful to protect. They normally are much less likely to take a chance at crime since the consequences of being caught can be severe. If convicted of a crime or of professionally inappropriate conduct, they can be debarred from their professional society and lose the designation which they have worked hard to obtain. (Some designations require seven years of education and job experience, in addition to examinations. All of those listed above require at least five years of education and job experience, in addition to success in demanding professional examinations.) As well, people working towards a professional certificate (such as articling students in an accounting program) are aware that being convicted of committing a crime may wipe out their chances of being admitted to the professional institute.

5.4 WORKING ENVIRONMENT

In Chapter 4, it was indicated that a "happy" company usually is also well controlled and reasonably secure, given reasonable control measures. In this section, we look at four components of the working environment important from the security perspective. Again, this is not a complete exposition; much of the responsibility rests with human resources, organization management, and management of specific areas within the organization. The four components which have proven to be especially significant from the security perspective are:

1.   Vacations and job rotation
2.   Employee-management relations
3.   Career path planning
4.   Remuneration (payment)

5.4.1 Vacations and Job Rotation

Vacations and job rotation are important from a security standpoint because they ensure that someone else checks up on employees' work. They have other characteristics as well: people need rest time, vacations often are part of the compensation package, and so on. The main concern from the security perspective is to ensure that employees *do take* vacations. The history is full of instances of dedicated employees who do not take vacations -- and are discovered later to have been maintaining frauds which needed continuous attention, or could not bear independent examination.

At least two consecutive weeks of vacation are desirable; ideally, the vacation period should include a month-end or quarter-end closing. Two needs are satisfied by this policy: first, someone besides a single person will be able to take over in an emergency; and second, the refresher aspect of a vacation often will result in an improved error rate and happier staff member.

Job rotation helps ensure backup capability and may also be a factor in improved employee morale; people are challenged to learn new things and to improve their own capabilities. From a security perspective, job rotation has many of the same virtues as vacations; in particular, a new person takes over and a fraud whose continuation requires constant attention might be uncovered quickly.

5.4.2 Employee-Management Relations

A "happy" organization works better and gives people fewer motives to engage in undesirable activities. Good employee relations are a function of the overall organizational climate and of individual managers. In some organizations, there may be union or other contracts which set the tone of the relations. The one rule which has been successful in the greatest number of places is that open communication between managers and employees works better. Good employees appreciate feedback; even negative feedback, properly delivered and combined with intelligent corrective measures, minimizes problems. The greatest problems occur when employees do not know what is required or how well they are doing. Perhaps the best single recommendation is "communicate." The security officer has a much easier job in an environment of open communication.

5.4.3 Career Path Planning

One element of personnel management is career planning. This primarily is the responsibility of the employee, his or her management, and the human resources department. The major involvement of the security position is to recommend that the company plan for continued upgrading of its employees; frustrated employees tend to leave or even to become a security exposure. This is another area in which the main duty of the security people is to be sure that organizational management are aware that there is an effect on security.

5.4.4 Remuneration

Money is not the most important element in Maslow's hierarchy of needs; however, adequate pay for the position, and appropriate raises for good performance, are proven motivators. Employees who feel they are reasonably well paid are less likely to try to "make up the difference" through unlawful activities. The company's pay scales should be on a par with other employers in similar organizations in the relevant area.

Once more, the security people should ensure that management is aware that poor pay, or pay out of line with competitors, can lead to motivational exposures. It is clearly outside the responsibility area of the security staff to set pay rates, but they should know whether material differences exist elsewhere, and keep an eye on employees who may consider themselves drastically under-compensated.

5.5 Employee Separation

In normal organizations, employees are hired, move through various positions, and leave. Not all terminations are voluntary. A few security and control principles are important in termination as well as in hiring.

First, any employee found to have falsified or misrepresented information when hired should be terminated. Employees guilty of serious violations of company policy regarding security and controls should be terminated. Employees guilty of unlawful acts should be *prosecuted* as well as terminated. Among other things, such action will provide a highly visible example for employees remaining, demonstrating that management takes security seriously.

Any termination should trigger certain steps, including:

1.   All company identification, including badges, ID's, business cards, and business-related materials should be collected.

2.   All keys, cards, signature plates, and other access tools or symbols of authority should be collected.

3.   All relevant locks, codes, passwords, and access codes must be changed immediately.

4.   All accounts should be settled (expense accounts, employee loans, etc.).

5.   Accounts over which the employee had control should be reconciled.

6.   Other members of the staff should be informed of the termination.

These considerations apply whether the termination is voluntary or involuntary. In addition, if the termination is involuntary, it is recommended that the employee be escorted from the premises and personal effects mailed or delivered later. In involuntary termination, it is critical to be *certain* that access to sensitive resources is denied *immediately* (to ensure that the unhappy former employee cannot sabotage systems, steal critical data or reports, or otherwise create a problem). Many companies use a "termination checklist," listing these and other significant matters; this is a good security practice and is recommended.

The principle of making sure that former employees no longer have access to sensitive resources is **important**. An amazing number of organizations do not do this. It is common to observe situations where, for example, passwords have not been changed, even though people who have not been employed for weeks -- or months -- previously know them. It should be remembered that employees have training in how to use systems and access which allows them to use the systems. If passwords and such are not changed, *former* employees still have the knowledge and access to do things. Not all former employees are necessarily happy with the organization or with their move; it simply is foolish to allow them to retain access privileges.

An "exit interview" or "exit review" is recommended in voluntary termination. Since morale is so important, it is important to know why people are leaving. Changes in practices may be appropriate. From a legal and security perspective, the exit interview should also include review of the acknowledgments regarding confidentiality, trade secrets, and similar agreements. At this time, the company should request explicitly that sensitive material be returned. Failure to take this step may make later legal recourse impossible or impractical.

SUMMARY

In closing this chapter, it is important to note that the personnel controls mentioned are from a *security* perspective. They should not be viewed or implemented in isolation; the purpose is not to generate paranoia but to indicate measures specifically security and control related that should supplement good management in personnel matters.

In hiring, data provided by applicants should be checked after permission is obtained. In working, vacations should be taken, adequate compensation should be given, open communication should be encouraged, and career planning aid offered. When employees leave, the company should take immediate steps to ensure that they no longer have access to sensitive resources, and that other employees are aware of the separation.

Legal or personnel advice should be obtained regarding hiring, management, and separation practices. There are many pitfalls, and the company does its image no good if it is itself violating human rights laws in its practices.

5.6 NEW TERMS

New terms introduced or defined in this chapter include:

Charter of Rights and Freedoms
Dishonesty factor
Exit interview
Exit review
Human Rights Act
Motivation
Opportunity
Privacy Act, 1974
Standard application form

5.7 QUESTIONS

5.1 Vacations

From a security standpoint, why should a company not allow employees to go for several years without a vacation?

5.2 Job Rotation

What is "job rotation?" In the context of information systems security, how does it provide extra protection over and above that provided by regular vacations?

5.3 Why is it important for a company to have a "termination checklist?"

5.4 (case) The New Hire

Mr. Sec U. R. T. Gaap was hired by XYZ Inc. on December 24th. His boss, Mr. I. M. Smart, described the job as follows:

"We need to hire you because the Systems Manager and the Controller both quit yesterday. All of the rest of us are going on Christmas vacation as soon as we give you your orientation, consisting of giving you a password and showing you where the blank checks are stored, and where the washrooms are. While we are gone, please do the computerized accounting run, handle the Accounts Receivable, and run the December 29 payroll.

"Don't try to do anything foolish because our auditors (a CPA firm) will be in soon after the June 30 year end to check up on you.

"By the way, thanks for the photocopied reference letter. You saved me the time phoning. I'm a busy man, so please write down some job performance objectives for yourself when you have the time between doing the controller's job and the system manager duties.

"Remember, we're a security-conscious company," said the boss as he walked into the computer room sipping his coffee, waving his cigarette at an operator using the computer to play games.

Required:

Describe the security weaknesses in this case.

Chapter 6

PHYSICAL AND ENVIRONMENTAL SECURITY

INTRODUCTION

Physical and environmental security probably is the thing most familiar to most people: everyone has seen fences and other obvious forms of physical security. In Chapter 6, we concentrate on nine elements of physical security: site location and building construction; physical access control; power supplies; air conditioning; fire prevention; fire protection; tape and other media libraries; waste disposal; and security and control concerns in using off-site storage.

As in previous chapters, the first thing to be done is to identify the assets -- the "what must be protected." Four physical components are identified here:

1.   Facility -- Building, rooms, work space, back-up storage area
2.   Support -- Air conditioning, fire systems, electricity, communications, water, fuel supplies, etc.
3.   Physical and Components -- Hardware: CPU, printers, disk drives, terminals; desks, chairs, containers, and similar objects
4.   Supplies, Materials -- tapes, disks, paper supplies, waste material, and so on.

Note that some of these assets also appear elsewhere. In particular, Chapter 10 deals in more depth with communications, and Chapter 11 with computer hardware.

The table following, reproduced from a RCMP presentation, indicates a number of specific protective measures and to which of the asset classes identified above each applies.

Physical & Environmental Security
Preventive Techniques/ Countermeasures

	Facility	Support	Supplies, Material & Furn.
Site location	X	X	X
Perimeter security	X	X	X
Construction standards	X	X	
Security containers			X
Drainage water detection	X	X	X
Access control procedures	X	X	X
Doors	X	X	X
Locks, keys, cards	X	X	X
Recognition badges	X	X	X
Access control logs	X	X	X
Maintenance logs		X	
Transportation	X		
Fire protection	X	X	X
Off-site facilities	X	X	X
Waste disposal			X

Table 6.1

The primary vulnerabilities of the classes identified here are:

1.   Facility

Destruction
    Accidental (fire, flood, earthquake, wind, snow, construction faults)
    Deliberate (vandalism, sabotage, arson)

2.   Support

Destruction
    Accidental (same as above)
    Deliberate (same as above)

Removal
    Accidental (equipment failure, public utility outage, fire, flood, earthquake, wind, snow, construction faults)
    Deliberate (sabotage, vandalism, arson)

Interruption
    Accidental and Deliberate same as above lists.

3.   Supplies, Material, Furniture

Destruction
    Accidental (fire, flood, earthquake, wind, snow, etc.)
    Deliberate (arson, vandalism)

Removal or Disclosure
    Accidental (carelessness)
    Deliberate (theft)

Interruption
    Accidental (fire, flood, etc)
    Deliberate (sabotage, arson, vandalism)

At this point it is appropriate to review the "rings of protection" concept, and to define three types of security: perimeter, area, and point.

Previously, we have looked at "rings of protection," or the "onion skin" approach, to security. Use of this concept is particularly clear in the case of physical security. The obvious example would be several fences, one inside the other. Less obviously, there might be a fence, then locked doors, then video observation. Each of these three "rings" would require a different penetration method, further slowing down intentional penetrators. Multiply backed-up power supplies could be another example.

Now let us define three types of security: perimeter, area, and point.

Perimeter security concentrates on keeping threats outside some defined area. A fence or the locked doors in the previous example would be perimeter security measures. The video observation camera is also perimeter security, unless the cameras scan the entire interior.

Once a threat penetrates the perimeter, area and point security come into play. In a home situation, locked doors and lighted yards are forms of perimeter security measures. Once inside the house, the homeowner might have an infrared system which detects body heat, or ultrasonic systems detecting motion. Such systems are **area** security measures.

Point security might be a last line of defense. An intruder could get into the house, and perhaps evade the detectors, but still be unable to open a safe and reach the valuables. Point security is, in principle, an "included" perimeter security: a very secure installation might define areas within an overall perimeter, each of which areas would itself form a perimeter for further measures inside. A specially constructed computer room inside a building could be an instance of point security. It illustrates the ring concept as well since the special room would include its own rings of security.

6.1 SITE LOCATION AND CONSTRUCTION

Where the building is, and how it is built, are measures which significantly affect the level of vulnerability to threats. If the security team has the luxury of considering the location and construction of a new (or remodelling a different) building, the following need to be looked at:

Vulnerability to crime, riots, and demonstrations

Is the area in a high-crime part of a city? Are you planning to construct a nuclear power plant on the San Andreas Fault? Will your staff be comfortable and safe leaving after hours in a dimly lit warehousing district? Is an unlit parking lot hazardous to night staff? These and similar questions need to be asked. Nearby police and fire stations also could be factors.

Adjacent buildings and/or businesses

Does a nearby business attract types of attention you don't want directed towards your information systems facility? If there is an adjacent building, can someone get from it into yours and, if so, is its security as strong as your own? A weak point in many homes is an attached garage; it often is less secure than the house and provides cover and tools for an intruder to spend time getting into the house proper. The same principle applies to adjacent buildings.

Emergency support response

This already has been referred to: nearness of fire stations affects how great your fire risk is, for example.

Vulnerability to natural disasters

Is the proposed location susceptible to earthquake? tornados or hurricanes? located below a dam? in the approach path to an airport? All these and other factors need to be considered. Government statistics from groups such as the United States National Weather Bureau help in assessing such threats as weather and other natural phenomena. Flood plain maps, earthquake risk maps, and similar data are available as well. It may be wise to consult an engineer or architect if more detailed information is needed; unless the security person is also qualified in such areas, risks may be missed.

General Building Construction

Building construction is a major topic in itself. Obvious points include such things as: can the structure withstand hurricane-force winds (if relevant)? is it earthquake-resistant? how many doors does it have, and how strong are they? will the roof withstand expected snow loading?

Computer center construction

In 1969, a computer center at Sir George Williams University in Montreal (now Concordia University), which was "on display" behind large glass windows as was popular then, was destroyed by gasoline bombs during a student demonstration. The computer center should be a further protected (point security) area within the building.

Even in an existing building, a computer center can be made fairly secure with little change to the existing structure. Full-height fireproof walls (to close off access through a false ceiling and some fire exposure) often are not especially expensive. Shatterproof glass and good locks on doors are other fairly inexpensive preventive security measures.

If alternatives are available, location of a new building and its construction should be considered in the risk analysis and control program. Even if a new building is out of the question, secure areas for information systems, within existing buildings, usually can be added at a reasonable cost.

6.2 PHYSICAL ACCESS

Some areas, such as computer rooms and rooms where computer media or data are stored, should have restricted access. Such areas need to be identified and marked. "No Admittance" signs do deter many people and are very inexpensive. For greater exposures and potential losses, more expensive measures may be appropriate.

Passive measures include doors and locks. The doors should be of solid construction; making them fireproof may be a good idea as they will then also be solidly constructed. Reasonably secure locks are fairly inexpensive and often are not provided unless specifically requested. Alarms to indicate that doors are open may be reasonable measures, if someone is monitoring.

More active measures basically require people, or in some cases expensive automated measures such as a computer-controlled card access system. The people could be guards or receptionists. In either case, persons wanting to enter restricted areas should be pre-authorized, or accompanied by someone who is authorized. Some system of identification cards or badges normally is required to identify authorized personnel, unless the company is so small that everyone knows everyone else. Disaster planning should consider personnel access as well; many security procedures break down completely for janitors, and are completely useless in stressful situations requiring access by emergency response personnel.

One thing which guards or receptionists should do is ensure that access logs are maintained. Anyone (authorized or not) entering a restricted area should log in and out. Closed circuit TV inside (an "area" control) may be appropriate to detect unwanted inhabitants.

What has been discussed so far are essentially preventive and some detective controls. Reactive or corrective controls also should be included; as mentioned previously, a log of who is inside and when they are inside is not much good unless someone reviews it from time to time. Procedures defining what receptionists should do if someone unauthorized is discovered, should be defined as well.

6.3 POWER

Computers need electrical power to work. This section looks briefly at some considerations relating to power supplies. This area is a technical one in which detailed examinations require specific technical training, and an expert should be involved in the design process.

The first level of expert is the manufacturer of the computer(s). Pay attention to what type of power the maker says should be supplied.

Most computers are sensitive to "dirty power." For example, some electric typewriters generate a fairly powerful short surge when the carriage return is engaged; this surge does computer equipment attached to the same power line no good; protection is needed. The first rule of computer power usually is "isolation" -- the computer should be on a different line than other office equipment. This rule applies to personal computers as much as to mainframes. (Practically, manufacturers have made personal computers relatively insensitive to this sort of power fluctuation; otherwise no one could use them at home).

The power supply conditions should be monitored. Many automatic devices are available which will keep a record of usage and similar items. From a security perspective, it is wise to consider the building electrical room as well; penetration here could stop the computer as surely as penetration into the computer room itself. Relatively cheap surge protectors and filters can protect from most dirty power problems; a power supply monitor allows the designer to know what sort of filtering is needed.

One way to minimize problems with power is to install a "UPS," or Uninterruptible Power Supply. The level of UPS needed can range from batteries which will support the system for a few seconds so that it can "fail soft" (i. e., shut itself down controllably), to elaborate systems including backup generators for systems which must continue to function regardless (air traffic control, or hospital systems, for example). UPSs can cost from one or two hundred dollars (for a small system which will run a personal computer for long enough to finish copying files onto a diskette) to a hundred thousand dollars or more, for elaborate battery systems with automatic backup generators.

6.4 AIR CONDITIONING

Most large computers require special air conditioning to continue to function properly. This may extend to smaller systems as well; it is not unusual to see someone begin to experience copier problems when a copier is enclosed in an improperly air-conditioned room.

Again, the manufacturer is the first line of expert advice. The maker should specify cooling requirements, and the user should heed the specifications.

As with power, the air conditioning for a computer should be for the computer only. It makes no sense to try to share the load with other, unrelated areas and risk expensive computer hardware.

Air conditioning units require supplies of air and (usually) water. Fire prevention includes making sure the fire won't find a ready entry to the computer through the air conditioner. Water supplies must be controlled to be sure that burst pipes won't destroy the hardware. As electricity-consuming equipment, the air conditioning needs its own power, separate again from the computer. Often, a second cooling unit is appropriate, to be sure that if one fails all cooling is not lost, and the system can continue to function.

Automatic humidity and temperature monitoring devices should be installed in climate-controlled computer rooms; the records should be examined regularly to be sure that the climate control is functioning properly.

As solid state technology continues to improve, the amount of heat generated by computers and the resulting air conditioning need is decreasing. Most personal computers require no more "comfort" than people, and this is also true of many minicomputers and some mainframes. In fact, the primary air conditioning problem found in offices with many microcomputers, is uncomfortable people. A lot of computers collectively generate a considerable amount of heat, as do copiers and even typewriters; offices not designed to handle the load can get to be very uncomfortable workplaces. This does nothing good for productivity; to help keep a "happy company" the risk management team needs to consider cooling the people as well as the computers.

6.5 FIRE PREVENTION

Fire prevention is not the same as fire protection. *Protection* refers to detecting fire and minimizing damage to people and equipment when it happens. *Prevention* is avoiding the problem in the first place and usually is much less costly and rather more effective in minimizing damage.

Most jurisdictions have fire codes, which will specify legal requirements for minimum fire prevention measures. Expert advice should be sought to ensure that the information systems activities conform to applicable fire code regulations.

Four elements of prevention are reviewed in this chapter:

1.   Computer room construction
2.   Employee training
3.   Testing
4.   Smoking.

1.   Construction

The materials used in a computer room should be as fireproof as practical. Combustible material (stacks of paper, for example) should not be stored in computer rooms, or indeed around any other electrical equipment. False ceilings should not be flammable. Rugs, unless specially designed for the purpose, do not belong with computers (for reasons of static electricity as well as flammability).

2.   Fire regulations should be known to, and observed by, all employees.

Employees should be given training in fire prevention as well as in what to do when a fire does occur. The training should include instructions about exits, extinguishing equipment available, emergency power and other shutoffs.

3.   Fire procedures should be tested periodically with fire drills.

(This normally will be required by local regulations as well as being simple common sense.) There is a risk here: too few fire drills will not maintain familiarity with procedures, too many will create a "boy who cried wolf" situation where real alarms may be ignored.

4.   "No smoking"

For fire risk and other reasons, smoking should not be allowed around computers. This also applies to personal computers -- the lifetime of diskettes in environments with cigarette smoke can be very short indeed as the smoke particles adhere to the media via static and other charges and cause read errors. Smoking also provides a source of ignition. Everyone probably has seen the "worm tracks" in carpets where cigarette smoking is common and ashes fall to the rug; a cigarette dropped into a waste paper box could cause a very destructive fire.

6.6 FIRE PROTECTION

If prevention does not work, fire protection becomes the issue. The first thing is to detect the fire, preferably while it is still small and controllable.

Fire detection systems are common and inexpensive. Ionization type smoke detectors react quickly to the charged particles in smoke (remember what charged particles in cigarette smoke can do to oxide surfaces on diskettes). Photoelectric detectors react to light blockage caused by smoke. Heat detectors react to the heat of a fire. Combinations of these detectors can detect a fire very quickly, and often before there is a serious problem. Most local fire codes now require smoke detectors in residences; the mass production of them has brought the costs down drastically. Effective smoke detection, including both ionization and photoelectric detectors, can be had for under $75.

The first rule after a fire is detected (either by smoke, heat, or other means) is: *get the people out.* People are the most important asset and are difficult for an organization to replace, as well as having high intrinsic value. Only after all personnel are safe and accounted for is it appropriate to attempt to put out a fire, and then only after calling the fire department.

Many fire extinguishing systems are available. Portable fire extinguishers always should be available near any electrical equipment, including computers. These extinguishers must be examined periodically to be sure they remain useful. For computers, type ABC extinguishers are appropriate, since combustible solids (class A), combustible liquids (class B), and electricity (class C) all are common in computer room fires. Get the people out *first*, then an attempt may be made to extinguish a small fire using portable or other extinguishers. The primary purpose of extinguishers is to make sure that an escape route can be cleared; the fire department always should be called and the people evacuated before any extinguishing attempts are undertaken.

Fixed systems include carbon dioxide extinguishers, with or without directing hoses. The entire computer room may be flooded with carbon dioxide to put out most fires by depriving them of oxygen to support combustion; with hoses, the gas may be directed at specific fire sites. Such systems are expensive and should not be automatic: they deprive people (such as computer operators) of oxygen, as well as fires. Installation of such systems definitely is a job for professional advice and services.

A fire protection system that is safer for people and which extinguishes fires without irreparably damaging computer equipment uses Halon 1301 gas. This gas has the convenient property of smothering fires without being quickly fatal to people, so automatic systems can kill the fire while allowing people enough time to get out. Halon systems are definitely installations requiring specialized expertise. Professionals should be engaged. Halon systems also are expensive as are tests of the system (a refill can cost over $1000). Such elaborate fire systems probably are appropriate mainly in mainframe installations. Portable Halon units containing Halon 1301 and Halon 1211 are available and may be appropriate in spite of greater cost (standard fire extinguishers usually will seriously damage equipment they are directed near, while Halon does not). [Halon

1301 and Halon 1211 are trademarks of chemical compounds, owned by Great Lakes Chemical Company Inc. The details of their composition are not relevant in this text and are not public information in any case. Halon 1301 is not self-pressurizing and requires expensive pressure systems for a fire installation; Halon 1211 *is* self-pressurizing, and can be put into a portable extinguisher, either alone or mixed with Halon 1211. Such portable extinguishers recently have become available as normal retail items.]

It is a good idea to avoid water in computer room fires; automatic sprinkler systems normally use water. First, computer fires usually involve electricity; water conducts electricity. Second, water is likely to damage computer equipment seriously, and may do more damage than small fires. The fact remains however, that water is an excellent way to extinguish fires -- one reason it is used by fire departments. The main lesson from a security perspective is that computer room fire protection should be carbon dioxide or halon, not the building's sprinkler system.

A special problem often overlooked in using water to extinguish fires is how long the water has been "sitting around" in the building's pressurized system. Since fires often disrupt electrical power, building sprinkler systems must have separate water supplies, not dependent on electricity. One common way to do this is to have a reservoir somewhere high and separate pipes which are always filled. (This is called a "wet standpipe" system.) Such reservoirs tend to be filled once, then checked for level periodically; it is rare to see checks for purity as well as level. The statement made above that water conducts electricity is not strictly true: *distilled* water is not a conductor under normal circumstances. However, *tap water*, and especially water which has resided in a reservoir for an unknown time, is *not* distilled. Some of it can be decidedly contaminated.

6.7 TAPE AND MEDIA LIBRARIES

Computers work with data, and the data, and information into which the data are processed, generally need to be stored. This is the job of magnetic tape, diskettes, and other "media." The list of media is long already, and grows daily. (It also shrinks: punched cards are no longer very common.) Different media have different characteristics and different capacities. All media contain data, and the data on the media are just as valuable and just as sensitive in movable form as when being used by the computer. Removable media, by definition, also are at least somewhat portable. This presents a security and control risk. It usually is recommended that there be a tape/media library for storing such things.

Depending on the installation, the media library may range in size from a small cabinet up to a rather large warehouse-sized space. Whatever the size, the media storage area should be:

1.   Restricted

It needs *at least* as careful control as the area in which the data are used. Many computers are not especially portable; removable media are. The equivalent of a small book can fit onto a 3-1/2" diskette which will fit easily into a shirt pocket. If the "book" (e. g., the corporate budget) is sensitive, careful protection is needed. All of the access control recommended for any other restricted area also is needed in the media storage area.

2.   Controlled

Someone should have specific responsibility for keeping records of media entering the library and leaving, and for conducting frequent inventory of the contents. Any discrepancies should be followed up immediately.

3.   Locked

This is elementary, but frequently ignored. Some form of automatic locking mechanism is preferable, so carelessness cannot lead to a large exposure.

4.   Protected from fire

Media contain, as an acquired value, information which may be expensive or impossible to replace, and which may be valuable to others as well. The storage area should be separate from the rest of the computer resource and should have its own independent fire protection. This could be elaborate in a large installation, to fairly simple in a small shop.

No general rules on fire and access protection are practical as media vary too much in their characteristics. Punched cards were flammable and had to be kept in humidity-controlled areas to prevent warping, which can cause feed jams. Magnetic tapes are sensitive to heat and burn fiercely but are not especially easy to ignite. Optical storage media are extremely long-lasting and are not fragile (but have very high capacities and may need more careful protection because of the sheer volume of information they hold).

A minimum rule is that any sensitive data should have at least two backups, at least one stored in a different building than all others. There is more on this topic in Chapter 8.

6.8 WASTE DISPOSAL

One of the "classic" computer crimes reported in the literature involved a person gaining accounts and passwords to get into a computer system, and instructions on how to compromise it, by going through a telephone company's waste bins. The security and control principle here is that discarded listings, media, and anything else containing data or information, remain sensitive (if they were in the first place). Control on disposal is needed.

Classified wastes should be:

1.   Stored in separate containers
2.   Collected frequently, by security cleared personnel
3.   Retained in a secure area
4.   Destroyed by cleared personnel, using an approved and effective method (shredding, incineration, etc.)

Note that the cleaning staff must be cleared, or kept out of areas containing sensitive assets.

Some points should be kept in mind here:

1.   Most personal computers actually do not *erase* data files when the operator says "erase" or "delete;" they set a flag indicating the file is "deleted." The flag can be reset, and fragments of data may still exist (a lot of applications software is like this too: for example, many data base products don't delete items until the database is "packed"). In fact, programs exist specifically for the purpose of recovering "deleted" files. Degaussing (a degausser generates a strong, varying magnetic field which randomizes the magnetic bits used to store data on magnetic media) is needed to be sure of erasure.

2.   Data stored on commercially available optical media cannot, at the present state of the technology (1988), be erased; the medium must be destroyed thoroughly. (Read/write optical systems do exist and will be common soon. Read/write optical media are erasable.)

3.   "Core dumps" generated during program development are sensitive waste. They contain a great deal of information which can be read by trained personnel, sometimes from areas outside the specific program's authorized accesses. Listings must be controlled as classified waste.

4.   Some kinds of computer memory stay "live" for a long time (up to years) even with the power turned off. An unauthorized user turning on the machine might get access to sensitive information unless the memory is actually written over with zeroes, or some similar destruction method is used.

5.	As above, data on magnetic media usually are non-volatile. If you put a customer list on a fixed disk, then sell or trade in the computer, format the disk before it leaves your premises.

"Degaussing" is a coined word relating to removing magnetism (a "gauss" is a measure of the strength of a magnetic field). Earlier, we cautioned against leaning diskettes against a telephone; we could add "don't put a diskette on top of a television or audio speaker." A "degausser" is merely something with a strong magnetic field, preferably a "moving" field, which field is not the same as the patterns on storage media. (In computer terms; properly, degaussing *removes* magnetism, and the discussion here is merely of *changing*.) The magnet which rings a telephone bell, or moves the cone in a speaker, or controls the picture tube in a television, induces a magnetic field which is not at all like data on a diskette. Magnetic media are designed to capture and retain imposed fields; the media don't care what the patterns are. (The computer decidedly *does* care.) Most firms which deal with magnetic tape have bulk tape erasers (it's much faster than doing it with a tape drive, and tape drives have rather more valuable uses). A recent edition of a commercial catalog lists a "Magnetic Bulk Tape/Floppy Disk Eraser" for $34.95. If sensitive material is stored on magnetic media, a degausser can be very cheap insurance, if it is used regularly.

Security personnel should recall that data stored on *optical* media have a very different, non-magnetic, means of recording, and magnetic fields (and degaussers) are irrelevant. Except for future read/write optical media (and some current, very expensive, systems as well), optical disks *cannot be erased*. Even considerable *physical* damage may not destroy the data. One favorite demonstration of optical-disk sales people has been to pour coffee, or cream, or some such, on a disk, then wipe it off and proceed to read it. (This works better with black coffee; you need to use soap and water to remove sugar and other sticky stuff.) To dispose of an optical disk, *physical destruction* is necessary -- breaking it into pieces or melting it works best. (See point 2 above.)

6.9 OFF-SITE STORAGE

This topic is considered in somewhat more detail in Chapter 8. For this section, we note that data (or whatever) stored off-site (somewhere outside the normal computer center) must have a level of security and control at least as good as the computer center has. Extremely tight security in the computer center does little good if backup copies of the same data and information are unsupervised in a warehouse without adequate fire or access control. The same considerations apply while media are being transported.

6.10 NEW TERMS

New terms introduced or defined in this chapter include:

ABC Fire Extinguisher
Area protection, area security
Degausser, degaussing
Facility (physical asset for protection)
Fire Prevention
Fire Protection
Halon 1301
Halon 1211
Media
Off-site
Point protection or security
Perimeter protection or security
Supplies and materials (physical asset to be protected)
Support (physical asset to be protected)
UPS (Uninterruptible Power Supply)

6.11 QUESTIONS

6.1 Matching

Match each of the three examples below to the correct type of security:

1 ____ Area	(a) Locked door at office entrance
2 ____ Point	(b) Motion detectors
3 ____ Perimeter	(c) Lock on Computer Room door

6.2 Computer Room

Describe security considerations in computer room location and construction.

6.3 Multiple Choice

A. If you were not concerned about cost, which one of the following would be the best way to put out computer room fires, while protecting staff and equipment?

(1) Carbon dioxide extinguishers
(2) Gasoline
(3) Halon gas
(4) Automatic sprinklers

B. Write out the reasons for your choice.

6.4 Backup Security

Should a company spend money on security for its backup and storage areas? Why, or why not?

Chapter 7

COMPUTER OPERATIONS

INTRODUCTION

The actual operation of the computer center is an area in which careful attention needs to be paid to security and control. Many aspects of the security need already have been addressed in Chapter 6; more about .i.physical; security is presented in Chapter 11 under "hardware." Chapter 7 looks primarily at various procedural means for ensuring security and control. The emphasis is on control: organizational aspects, input and output controls, and similar considerations.

Computer operations can be organized in many ways. There are three major ways to organize operations, based essentially on three different kinds of technology. "Mainframe" computers, or large minicomputer installations, tend to have a particular kind of organization based on size of the operation and the kinds of things which normally are done. Smaller minicomputer installations usually are organized somewhat differently since they don't require the same staff, and the smaller machines generally are not used for the same purposes as the larger centers. A third main branch is the "office automation" type of organization. The use of personal computers, linked into a network or separate, has created a need for a new kind of information systems organization, the "information center." The first section of Chapter 7 looks briefly at each of these three ways to organize.

Once the organization's structure and positions are identified, it is appropriate to take a closer look at some specific things which can be done to improve control, or to avoid security and control exposures. These include separation of duties (Section 7.2); controls at the interfaces (that is, where things move into or out of the "operations room," Section 7.3); control on media such as tapes and diskettes (Section 7.4); a brief introduction to backup procedures (Section 7.5); and "people controls" (Section 7.6).

We try to give examples of each control component in each of the three environments described in Section 7.1. It is important to understand, however, that no two computer operations are organized quite alike. Further, the "office automation" area is so new that the best ways to organize it still are open to debate. The control principles presented here must be applied with careful consideration of each individual operations environment. A good place to start is in the *Computer Control Guidelines* [CICA 1986] which are summarized in Section V of this text. Other sources of material useful in this area include information from books intended for CDP candidates' study: Lord's *CDP Review Manual, A Data Processing Manual and Handbook* [Lord 1986]; and the *Review Course Text for CDP Candidates*, from the Data Processing Management Association [Cromer 1987]. Each of these contains coverage, at an introductory or review level, of the needs encountered in managing a data processing operation.

7.1 ORGANIZATION OF COMPUTER OPERATIONS

7.1.1 Mainframes

Mainframes, and some minicomputers as well (so-called "superminis" in particular), can be large computers, both physically and in terms of the amount of work they can handle. They are found in environments where there is a great deal to do, and they handle a very great amount of information. Today, "mainframe" computers also may be quite small; the technology, and the meaning of what a mainframe is, are changing very rapidly. Regardless of the size of the machine, the mainframe is a complex environment. There is far too much work within this environment for a single individual or even a small group of individuals. "Computer operations" in this area means several groups of people who do things like:

1.   Enter data into computer-readable form
2.   Deliver output to users
3.   Check input for obvious errors
4.   Check output for obvious errors
5.   Mount tapes and disk packs and run production jobs
6.   Put paper into printers, change ribbons, and other maintenance jobs
7.   Monitor the functioning of communications links

8.   Decollate and burst multiple-copy forms produced during the run

9.   Order supplies such as paper

10.   Schedule operators and jobs

This list is not exhaustive (nor unchanging: the data entry function is being replaced by automated scanning and departmental computing very rapidly). The point is that this environment is complex. There well may be hundreds or even thousands of users and great numbers of batch and on-line jobs, some of which may take up so much computer capability that special scheduling is needed. To make cost-effective use of what may be several millions of dollars invested in hardware, it is common to schedule operations for three shifts to service users any time they need the machine (and often from anywhere in the world they may be located as well). The organization of such an operation reflects the complexity of what is being done.

An organization chart is presented in Figure 7.1, that identifies many positions which have been found to be needed in the sort of environment typical of mainframes and large minicomputers.

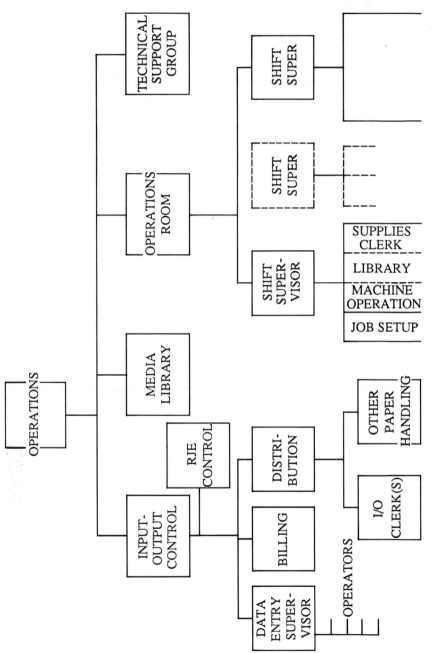

Figure 7.1

Basically, the operation is split into three components: input-output control, actual operations, and support functions such as technical support and the media library.

Input-output control includes people who are responsible for data entry from manual forms into computer-readable form, and people who are responsible for distributing the resulting output. In some cases, more direct connections may bypass the usual data entry function (for example, entry of purchases from terminals rather than filling out a form manually). Distribution of bills to users for use of computer resources may be included within this group as well, since the distribution function already has the necessary channels set up. Many mainframes support remote job entry (RJE); this function likely also would be found in I/O control.

The actual operation of the equipment -- mounting tapes and disks, putting paper into printers and removing reports, controlling scheduling of batch jobs, and general "trouble-shooting" -- falls under the operations room group. There may be two or three shifts with identical staffing, or there may be variations in staffing due to differences in workload for different shifts.

A mainframe normally includes a large collection of machines which requires a special room or rooms. With many machines depending partly on mechanical processes, some break. Frequently, there will be a technical support group either on call or actually in the operations area at all times, to fix problems. A second support group is those people in charge of the media library. There may be thousands of magnetic tapes, and the media librarian(s) record who signs them out, for what purpose, and their return. The media library also would be responsible for such things as erasing tapes at the end of the retention period.

This whole process is complex, and many people are needed to accomplish all the work. However, the critical principle of separation of duties is enforced by having large jobs split up into several small jobs. More on separation of duties will come to light in Section 7.2.

In the near future, this sort of organization will change very dramatically as more and more functions of the operation of the computer are automated. There has been little use of automation in the actual operation of the computer (perhaps partly because the job of computer operator has been seen as an entry-level position leading to "better things"). In the late 1980s, the increasing speed and capability of mainframe computers, the shrinkage in their sizes, and changes in characteristics of what is done, have led to experimentation with automating many of the things traditionally done by an operator. Often, the results have been significant improvements in operations effectiveness. This is particularly evident in an on-line communications-oriented environment.

7.1.2 Minicomputers

Discounting the special-purpose machine (minicomputers often are responsible for process control such as petroleum refineries, for example), a minicomputer operation is pretty much the same as a mainframe -- but not as large. The same functions need to be performed, but a mini normally has far fewer users (perhaps only a dozen or two), so fewer people are required. As well, minicomputers have fewer things to go wrong, so less technical and operator attention is required. The functions of librarian, output control, and operator well may be combined into one person.

Adequate separation of duties for control purposes can be difficult to achieve with the smaller number of people.

A sample organization of a minicomputer installation is shown in Figure 7.2. This shop had two HP-3000 minicomputers, with a number of terminals scattered among several buildings and about a hundred users. The output control function was small enough that only one person, during a day shift, was needed; the technical support was handled on an "on-call" basis (from a city 600 air miles away). Data entry was a separate functional group. There was one operator at a time, with limited technical support capabilities as part of this person's function.

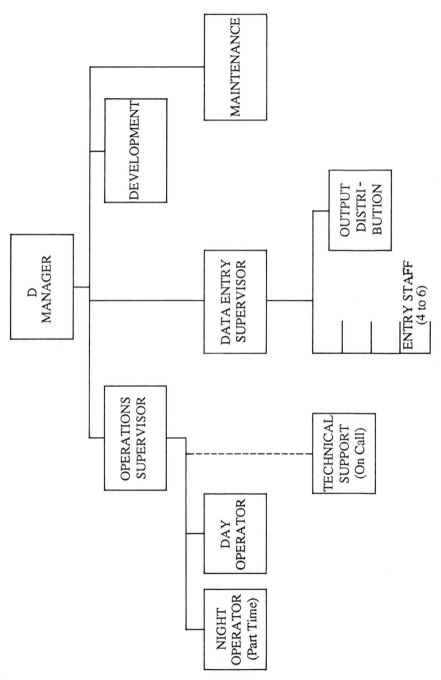

Figure 7.2

7.1.3 Microcomputer/Office Automation

By definition, an organization includes more than one person working together. A microcomputer is also called a "personal computer" and, in business, has a major use as an approach to a "manager's work station"[1]; if only one person is using it, there is no organization. All functions -- data entry, operations, output control and so on -- still need to be handled; however this usually is done by one person (with, obviously, no separation of duties at all).

Microcomputers are far more reliable than mainframes have been. Operators and technical support functions are not needed on a regular or frequent basis. For example, mean time between failures in one organization is 2-1/2 weeks, with 128 micros, for an expected value per micro of 320 weeks of continuous (24 hour) operation. This reliability difference is related to complexity and to certain other technical factors, and the difference is decreasing as the size of mainframes decreases.

This lack of need for several people to run the computer raises a number of security and control problems; microcomputers today easily may have more complex data and programs than many mainframes of 1966, and *some* control is appropriate. There is no way to determine how much time is lost due to, for example, inadequate backup, but it certainly must be considerable.

When many microcomputers are in use in an organization, the control problem can become extraordinarily difficult. Managers may each produce impressive looking printouts in meetings, based on different data -- with disastrous effects on productive meeting time usage. These and other problems -- of compatibility both of different brands of equipment and of data bases; of a need to help users learn to use packaged programs; and similar issues -- have led to some reasonably common and workable solutions. (Denying purchase of micros is not a workable solution: managers have been known to list them as "electronic typewriters" to sneak into an uncontrolled budget category. When the denial does work, the organization in the longer term loses out to competitors who have the benefit of micros.)

There are four fundamental issues in using microcomputers in large organizations:

1.   Deployment (who gets them)
2.   Role of the existing data processing center
3.   Design responsibility (who ensures proper, cost-effective use of the tools?)
4.   Limits of centralized responsibility

A number of other problems arise in various circumstances; Thomas Madron's *Microcomputers in Large Organizations*, (Prentice-Hall, 1983) addresses these issues in some detail. Computer technology is changing rapidly and there are no universal solutions for all problems. Most of these other problems really do not fall into the area of "security and control;" use of information centers and "in-house computer stores" does in that it helps to address the issues of coordination, support, and responsibility to use the tools in a cost-effective manner.

Two solutions to standard microcomputer problems in organizations are the "information center" and what may be called "in-house stores."

The information center is staffed with people who have business knowledge as well as knowledge of how to use micros and packages. Users often may buy "non standard" computers -- but they will not get support from the information center staff. The basic purpose here is to allow people to use micros effectively while keeping some sort of control of equipment and data. An example of this organization is illustrated in Figure 7.3. Linking the micros into a network can help to add some control to the problem of differing data bases mentioned earlier (and raises its own problems; complex networks have organizational needs for support staff similar to mainframes).

Another proven way to minimize some of the problems with microcomputers is to establish an "internal store" which "sells" microcomputers and software. A variation of this approach is an "approved supplier" list. This technique has proven useful in very large organizations: potential users of the computers have a fairly good selection to choose from, at reasonable prices since the supplier knows many will be purchased and gives discounts, and all the choices are supported by information center staff.

Control problems and the four fundamental issues apply in large organizations. There are no universal solutions and we must leave the details of existing attempts at security and control solutions for another text. In smaller organizations, the problems are of a different nature and generally simpler; following hints given in this text will result in reasonable levels of security and control.

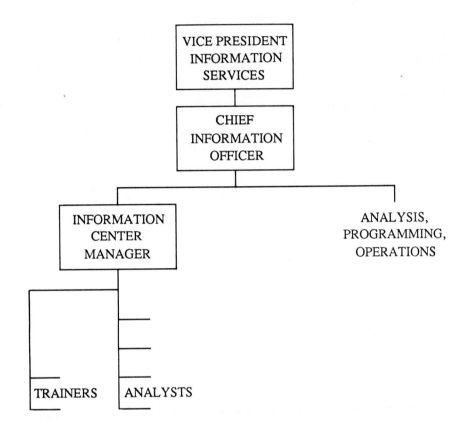

Figure 7.3

Office Automation Organization Example

7.2 SEPARATION OF DUTIES

Probably the most fundamental principle of security and control is separation of duties Because of its importance, we repeat the two parts of the principle here (see Chapter 4 for more details):

No single individual must have responsibility for the complete processing of any transaction or group of transactions

The perpetration of a fraud must require the collusion of at least two individuals.

From this principle comes the important rule that the functions of computer operation and programming should be divided between two or more individuals. If both these duties were performed by one individual, he or she would have the ability to revise production programs and run these programs on live data to perpetrate or conceal a fraud.

The ideal type of person to hire as an operator should not have programming aptitude or knowledge (but see the comment at the end of this section about reality *versus* ideals.) He or she will be using production programs and data files, and a lack of programming knowledge and aptitude, plus lack of access to detailed documentation, will keep the operator from altering programs fraudulently.

Since programmers have a detailed understanding of the application programs and data, they could alter these easily if allowed to perform operations functions. Keeping the programmers out of the computer room will be a solution in a batch, off-line system. However, when there is on-line programming, additional controls are required. For example, password control mechanisms should allow programmers to access only *test* programs and data, not production programs or live data. Some large organizations go to the length of having development done on separate computers, with no connection whatever to production machines or data.

In addition to separating system design and programming from operations, it is desirable to have an independent data control group and a separate media library. Sensitive media (such as payroll files) should be released from the library only to the operators, and only at the time scheduled for a particular run (for example, payroll check printing). This would reduce opportunities for unauthorized changes.

The data control group, also known as the "input-output control group," reconciles control totals, record counts and hash totals (see Section 7.3 for more detail on hash totals), and follows up any errors or discrepancies. This serves as an independent check on processing and thus the control group must be separate from the operator.

A favorite way to penetrate systems in the past, has been in the handling of rejected transactions. One way which has been used frequently to defraud systems (manual as well as computerized) is to enter deliberately erroneous transactions. These are rejected; the perpetrator (who usually has responsibility for handling these "rejects" -- for example, a night operator) then replaces them with seemingly correct transactions -- but with, for example, the "pay to" account number changed. The batch totals and record counts stay the same, but the wrong person gets the money. In analyzing separation of functions, special care should be taken to ensure that this sort of intentional distortion cannot be perpetrated by one individual: corrections also need approvals.

The sheer amount of work and appropriate specialization tends towards adequate separation of duties in large organizations. Smaller organizations tend not to have so much work, nor to be able to afford the number of people necessary to separate all functions as would be desirable. At the limit, if only one person is using a microcomputer, there is no separation at all. Perhaps there is no need for separation here -- but what if the person is preparing a budget which will be used to make critical decisions? Is there no need for an independent check on the results? (Lack of such an independent check in a situation very similar to this budget scenario led to a company losing millions in one of the reported computer supported frauds.)

In companies with poor or no segregation (such as the microcomputer example above), there should be increased supervision and careful analysis of output by management.

Section V contains a summary of the recently revised *Computer Control Guidelines, Second Edition* [CICA 1986], from the accounting profession. These guidelines have details of recommended separation of duties in many circumstances.

Many of the specific comments above violate what has been said in Chapter 4 about training: operators are denied a career path into programming which has been traditional, for instance. The extreme of doing development on a separate machine, even when combined with use of that machine as a hot site backup, is an expensive practice. Other costs, in personnel and management time as well as in dollars, arise from ideal separation of duties. Company management, supported by the risk analysis, must decide what to implement when.

Separation of duties is an ideal, to which any accountant or auditor will subscribe. The reality is a need for effective management of a tradeoff between risk of fraud and cost of the controls (extra people, for example). The risk analysis process described in Chapters 1 to 3 should have identified and valued assets which are exposed; consideration of separating functions can be costed out, and the cost compared to the potential loss.

7.3 CONTROLS AT INTERFACES

Computer and other information systems deal with data entered into them, and produce some form of information as output. The points where things enter a system or leave it are called "interfaces." If the analysis is at a general level, interfaces include such entities as the data entry clerk, or the output clerk, or a terminal connected to a system. At a more in-depth level of analysis, each program could be a "system," where the interface is the point at which a data file from another program is accepted. An example at the detailed level might be an "integrated" accounting system which passes transaction files between programs, or the edited transaction file from an entry program going on to the master file update program. (Another term for these interfaces is "control points." This phrase can be confusing since accounting professionals use it in one sense and computer professionals often intend a slightly different meaning; "interface" will be used in this text.)

Controls at *all* interfaces to systems are crucial to a secure and controlled environment. If someone can alter the file of "edited data" mentioned in the previous paragraph, system security and control checks may be bypassed. This is the "integrity" property of data defined in Chapter 1.

Data entering systems must be complete and accurate, and integrity must be maintained, to ensure control. *Complete* means that *all* data crossing an interface must be recorded and must successfully cross the boundary. None may be lost, and none may be added; otherwise, security and control may be breached. Ways to ensure completeness include many very sophisticated techniques; however, one very simple means is available and effective: count how many transactions there are (record counts). At every interface, transaction counts on each side need to be maintained to ensure proper control and completeness. Procedures to use this (detective) control include having people or programs ensure that record counts are consistent. Results of processing offer opportunities here as well: the number of entries in the old master, added to the number of new entries, less the number deleted, must be the total in the new master. Similar basic counts need to be established at every interface.

On-line systems pose more complex problems in ensuring completeness. Since transactions across interfaces happen at random rather than in neat batches, batch totals and batch record counts are not appropriate. Probably the only method which will ensure completeness in an on-line system is to record *every* transaction in the system and "time-stamp" it. The transaction is copied, and the originator and timing recorded; thus, "who did it when" is available, and recovery from "system crashes" is feasible. More elaborate schemes involve copying "old" and "new" versions of every data element changed as well. Combining all of these can ensure that completeness is maintained, and that auditability in the sense of identifying "who, what, where, when" also is maintained. (Auditability in the sense used by public auditors may not be maintained, and there remains the risk of sophisticated criminals altering the records of their fraudulent transactions.) Using such an elaborate mechanism also adds considerably to system development and operating costs; intelligent management will compare such increased costs with the exposures identified in the risk analysis before making decisions.

The second characteristic which data must possess is *accuracy*. Since this is dependent on individual systems' needs, no universal rules can be given, save one: editing routines must check *every data element entered in every transaction*. *Nothing* can be assumed; experience clearly shows that ***all*** data must be checked. Reasonableness checks and others are part of the standard elements in programmed checking.

Once accuracy is determined, it must be maintained: this is the *integrity* part of data across interfaces. Every program must check every data input to ensure that it has not been changed in an unauthorized manner while "between programs." Every batch transferred from one person to another must be checked. Detective controls include recording and checking record counts, batch totals, hash totals, check digits on numbers, and others. In computer operations, the emphasis is on detecting changes in data while it is not under the control of the system and ensuring that no bad data gets across interfaces without detection and appropriate action.

Hash totals involve adding things like account numbers to get some number which should not change. For example, the sum of the employee numbers in a payroll run could be calculated, and recalculated at each control point. If an employee number is altered between control points (for instance, to pay the wrong person), the *sum* of the employee numbers will change even though the number of transactions and perhaps the total dollars stay the same.

Check digits are arithmetic relations built into numbers; if an employee number with a check digit were altered, the new number would have to have a correct check digit or it would be caught immediately. Credit card numbers, Social Insurance numbers and Social Security numbers, and bank account numbers contain check digits for this reason.

One operational method of helping to ensure completeness, accuracy, and integrity is the Input-Output Control Group mentioned earlier. Integrity *inside* the computer is the responsibility of good systems and programs. Data entering is counted, entered, and edited. It then goes into the computer as a "black box." Once the computer is finished, reports are generated; these reports should include printing of the appropriate control totals, and the output clerk would compare with the input counts and totals. Output then is directed to the appropriate recipients.

Specific recommendations to ensure that output reaches the proper people include the following:

1.   Restricting access to the printed output storage areas
2.   Printing heading and trailing banners with recipients' names and
         locations
3.   Requiring signed receipt acknowledgments before releasing output
4.   Printing "no output," with banners, when the report is empty

The I/O clerk also should check that control totals and record counts are appropriate, and inform management of discrepancies.

Note that the effect of these recommendations is to ensure separation of duties, and to ensure that different people check, as part of their normal job responsibilities, interface controls. Again, we emphasize that in a small shop, this level of separation may not be practical; management must be aware of the risks and security and control issues involved, and make an intelligent decision: is a high level of control worth the cost? The risk analysis should indicate the potential loss, making the cost comparison simple: do not spend more to avoid a problem than the problem would cost if it occurred.

7.4 MEDIA CONTROLS

Tapes, removable disks, diskettes, and even punched cards and paper backup copies of original transactions, are a valuable data and information resource in any organization. In computer operations in any reasonably sized organization, there will be a tape and/or disk or diskette library. These "media" -- magnetic tape, magnetic disk, diskette, perhaps optical disks or other storage media -- need some specific controls in a good operation.

First, volume labels are an absolute requirement before any other control measure can be effective. Every volume (reel of tape, disk pack, diskette, optical disk, or whatever, containing data stored on media) must be labeled, both in human-readable form and in machine-readable form. Both labels should indicate:

1.   Date created
2.   Date to be destroyed (or retention period)
3.   Who created it
4.   What the name of the volume/file(s) is(are)
5.   Version of the volume/file(s)

Many other items, such as length of files, may also be appropriate. Periodic checks should be made to ensure that human-readable labels on the outside of the volume match the machine-readable labels on the media themselves. Any discrepancies naturally must be reported and followed up.

An interesting variation sometimes found, is to use color-coded media. Diskettes and tapes can be purchased with containers in different colors. If a coding scheme is used, such as "black for backup, red for production files, no yellow or blue media in this shop," then inappropriate uses can be detected very rapidly by sight.

Data volumes need to be stored somewhere. While the "somewhere" may be different for a 3-1/2" diskette or a 2400-foot reel of magnetic tape, any data relating to a computer needs to be stored in an identified place, with characteristics appropriate for safe storage of the media which will go into the storage area. Ideally, there should be logs of entry, removal, replacement (another interface, really). The locations of all storage areas should be included in operations and backup and contingency planning documentation.

There is a different level of need in small organizations than in an organization storing perhaps hundreds of thousands of magnetic tapes; security needs will vary as well. The key is to *have* a defined storage area ("library"), and to apply appropriate controls to ensure that what is stored there is labelled, and that it is possible to trace who "checked it out" when.

It is especially important to emphasize the need for careful labeling and for control of media in an office automation or personal computer environment. Many people using microcomputers do not have a data processing background and may not be aware of the value of the data on their diskettes, nor of the methods developed by computer professionals to minimize problems. One of the virtues of a risk analysis procedure is that the value of the data on diskettes should be identified. People who may not have been aware of the actual value previously often will initiate their own controls once they realize what their data assets are worth and how much disruption could be caused in case of loss. The control techniques recommended above are neither new nor especially sophisticated; they do work, *if* they are used.

7.5 BACKUP PROCEDURES

This section is inserted here mainly to emphasize that backups should be done. Details of how often to do backups and other procedures are covered in Chapter 8 as part of contingency planning.

In the office automation environment, people may not realize how important it is to keep current backups. Diskettes are sensitive: leave one leaning on a telephone when it rings, and the magnetic fields created in ringing the bell may make the diskette unreadable. Data on diskettes are valuable. The risk analysis identifies how valuable. Backup procedures are included here simply to emphasize that backup is important.

Three (or more) copies of every file are recommended. One would be the original, in use. A second copy would be of the original, stored away from the computer, but on-site. The third copy should not even be in the same building. (A fourth copy is needed for complete safety while transporting the second and third backups, so there is no risk of losing the only two backups while in the same vehicle, and also losing the original due to some computer problem.)

7.6 PEOPLE CONTROLS

Computer operations rooms contain expensive, sensitive equipment. In some cases, data and information in the room is even more valuable than the hardware. Controls on the people inside computer rooms are needed. The level of control depends on the specific environment: a personal computer at someone's desk is not at much risk of anything (except being picked up and carried away) if the diskettes with software and data are locked up (and there is no hard disk included). A minicomputer will be larger physically and may be in a separate, climate-controlled room; more control is needed here. A mainframe computer typically has a secure and climate-controlled room with very restricted access. If national secret projects are under way in the computer, very stringent controls indeed may be needed, even for personal computers. There are no universal detailed rules.

There are two general principles which will apply nearly anywhere, though:

1.   Hire competent people.
2.   Restrict access to people who actually need it.

The first principle applies everywhere in any organization. Incompetent people are an obvious security and control problem anywhere. Chapter 5 detailed a number of principles and specific controls in personnel areas, which if followed should minimize problems in computer operations.

Computers, and any other valuable or sensitive assets, should be accessible to, and used by, only people who actually have a valid reason. For mainframe computers with special rooms, this translates to careful access controls such as locked doors, no-admittance signs, receptionists and even guards. The same would apply to sensitive or large minicomputer installations. Every person other than regular staff who enters or leaves the computer area should be recorded: who, why, when in, when out. In large or very sensitive operations, such things can be done automatically with (expensive) computer-controlled card-lock systems. Less expensive is a system with a receptionist who in addition to secretarial duties ensures people use sign-in logs appropriately. In any case, each person should have an identification card, with his or her photograph and access permissions attached; use and display of this card should be required in sensitive areas.

Separation of duties also is a "people control." Another is alertness on the part of supervisors and fellow employees. Any large change in someone's behavior may indicate problems which could lead to security and control exposures. (Of course, in any case it is good management practice to be sensitive to personal problems of employees.) Such things should be checked out.

The basic principles of controlling people in computer operations are simply to have competent staff and to keep unauthorized people out. Many ways to accomplish these objectives are available.

7.7 NEW TERMS

New terms introduced or defined in this chapter include:

Control total
Hash total
Information center
"In-house computer store"
I-O Control Group (Input-Output Control Group)
Interface
Record count
RJE (Remote Job Entry)
Volume label

FOOTNOTE

[1] The technology and capabilities of so-called "microcomputers" are changing at an enormous rate. While it is not clear just what the future usage of microcomputers will be in business, it is abundantly obvious that multi-user work stations, and other capabilities presently considered to be minicomputer or mainframe computer capabilities, will be commonplace. The security professional must pay close attention to the usage of personal and other computers in whatever manner his or her own organization has chosen to follow. Allowance for rapid change and frequent review will be of utmost importance in any realistic security program involving personal computers.

7.8 QUESTIONS

7.1 Explain "hash totals." Give an example from your own organization.

7.2 What is the difference between an external file label and an internal file label?

7.3 What is an "information center" and what are its functions?

7.4 (case) Segregation of Duties

You are a consultant advising Maxwell Headcrash Inc. about separation of duties. The president of the company, Mr. Bigcheese, is concerned because his former accountant, Mr. Thickglasses, has recently issued an income statement printed in red ink.

Mr. Bigcheese tells you that "due to hard times, we will have to lay off our operator, Miss Cue, and our programmer, Miss Code. The only staff left will be Miss Take, who will do all our accounting on a microcomputer. We had to sell our minicomputer to pay our legal bills, which we received from Mr. Clause Encounter for the third time this month. Our new accountant, Mr. Chip A. Countant, has been hired today to start slashing costs. However, Chip's first recommendation was to hire additional staff to improve segregation of duties."

Required:

Explain how Mr. Chip A. Countant can improve control without hiring additional staff.

7.5 (case) Controls *(Adapted with permission from the Institute of Chartered Accountants of Alberta)*

You have been asked by ABC Inc. to review their computer environment in the area of computer operations and to report to them on strengths and weaknesses that you encounter. You have also been asked to explain the exposures that exist because of weaknesses and to make recommendations for improvements where you encounter significant weaknesses.

Following your initial examination of the client's facility, you have summarized your observations as follows:

The client's system consists of an IBM 4341 mainframe computer to which are attached 50 remote terminals. All significant accounting applications are processed on this system. I examined the computer site and the systems development areas and reviewed procedures with the computer operations manager and systems supervisor.

The computer room is fully enclosed and is accessible via one door with a combination lock. The combination is known only to the operations personnel and certain user department personnel who were previously employed by computer operations.

Inside the room, temperature and humidity are controlled. There are smoke and heat detectors and a Halon system controls any potential threat of fire. The operations supervisor made a comment about computer down-time due to an unreliable power source but I have not explored this further.

A customer of the client has similar hardware and has offered to provide a backup site. The operations manager says that although he hasn't visited the customer's site, he feels this backup arrangement is an ideal situation.

The computer uses the IBM operating system VM/CMS. The operating system checks internal file labels and monitors all hardware and software activity. The operating system also generates an activity log and a console log. The operator on the morning shift prints these reports for the previous day and files them by date.

The computer runs for three eight-hour shifts each day. The morning and afternoon shifts are supervised. For the night shift, no supervisor is on duty although one is always on call. All operators rotate shifts regularly. Operators' manuals are used although a review indicated that they may not all be up-to-date. However, the operators seem to understand what is to be done. Most operators are taking programming courses in an attempt to graduate to systems development.

Because of the nature of the system, most live files are on-line all the time. However, a librarian is used to control any files that are demounted. She is also responsible for controlling backup files and doing production scheduling. All master and transaction files are backed up regularly and a copy is stored in a fire-proof vault remote from the computer room. No backup is currently done for the operating systems or program libraries.

The operations manager indicates that if the system goes down for any reason, the operators are instructed to call him. There are no written procedures for reconstruction of files or in the event of other emergencies but he is familiar with the steps required and does not feel additional documentation would serve any useful purpose.

Systems development uses on-line programming capability, that is, programmers do system development through terminals which are on-line to the main computer. Each programmer is assigned an area of the computer system to do his development and testing. These areas are entered via a password and are separate from areas where production files are stored. The password to access production areas is known to all programming staff. However, written systems development standards prohibit programmers from working in these production areas, either to test programs or catalog them without approval. Programming standards are also written and are strictly adhered to by programming staff.

The systems supervisor indicates that all new programs and program changes must be tested by the programmer before they are catalogued for production. If a major change is involved, the systems supervisor determines if user testing should also be done. The supervisor indicated that he trusts programmers to have the proper user testing completed where required and as a result the supervisor does not require written user approvals.

He feels that the cataloguing and documentation procedures are very tight. A documentation check-list must be completed before any new programs are catalogued. The supervisor reviews the documentation package before authorizing the programmer to catalog the new program. No similar review is conducted for major program changes. The computer libraries are controlled by a librarian system which monitors all changes to the libraries. Reports are produced daily of these changes. The reports go first to the programmers so that they can check that up-dates were completed and then to the systems supervisor who checks that all changes were authorized.

Documentation is stored in an open hanging file in systems development. Operations personnel also have access to this area. There is no duplicate copy of documentation since the supervisor wants to keep systems as confidential as possible.

Required:

Prepare your initial outline of the report requested by ABC Inc. Organize your answer under the following headings:

I. Computer Operations Controls Review

    A. Control Strengths

    B. Control Weaknesses

    C. Exposures and Recommended Improvements

Remember to concentrate on *computer operations controls*; other weaknesses/strengths are for other Chapters (see Question 8.4 in Chapter 8 and Question 12.7 in Chapter 12).

Chapter 8

CONTINGENCY PLANNING

INTRODUCTION

Webster defines "contingency" as

A possible or not unlikely event or condition

Another possible definition (Shakespeare) could be

The slings and arrows of outrageous fortune

From the standpoint of information systems security, a "contingency" is something which might happen, which requires a response, and which thus should be planned for. The quotation from Shakespeare suggests the proper planning: assume things will go wrong, and have a "contingency plan" in place to guide in how to cope. Perhaps the key point in contingency planning is to *have* a contingency plan. After one is in the middle of an emergency situation, whether merely annoying or a real disaster, there is never enough time to cope with immediate needs, much less to reconstruct what should have been in place previously.

The risk analysis process outlined in the first part of this book will have led to identifying many contingencies, things that are "possible or not unlikely." At some point in the carrying out of his or her responsibilities, the Security Officer should have gathered data enabling an assessment of how likely various contingencies are and thus how much time to spend on preparing for them. This will help in deciding how much money to spend: remember the familiar notion that one should not spend more than the expected loss to avoid the loss.

In this section, several aspects of contingency planning are looked at. There is no effort to be exhaustive; specialized material is available on the topic if needed. What has been done here is to try to cover the things which, in the authors' experience, are most likely not to have been thought of. In order of probable importance, these are:

1.   Backups and procedures

Backups of data files and other material need to be kept. Procedures for making backups must be defined and controlled. A description of deciding how often to make backups, and how many backups to make, is given in Section 8.1. Some elementary comments about precautions involving equipment are presented as well.

2.   Catastrophe planning

Catastrophe, or disasterdisaster, planning looks like a waste of money and time to a lot of managers who haven't given the topic enough thought. After all, catastrophes are rare and hard to plan for. An amazing number of organizations have no disaster plan at all; they tend to make up the one-third or so of businesses who go *out* of business after a problem. Some hints are presented in Section 8.2.

3.   Security in backup operations

It is common for organizations to be reasonably well-controlled in normal operations but to have normal controls break down completely or be ignored in backup operations and during problems. Some advice regarding controls is in Section 8.3.

One topic which is not covered in this book is insurance. As well, other forms of pre-arranged backup are not more than mentioned. These are specialized topics which vary from place to place and from time to time and thus are outside the scope of this treatment. Insurance coverage, arrangements with others to use their computer when yours is down, arrangements for rapid response from suppliers, and similar things definitely should be considered and in place.

8.1 BACKUPS AND PROCEDURES

8.1.1 Data

Magazine advertisements, articles, books such as this, and computer manuals, all emphasize that data files should be backed up. This means that in addition to the copy in use at any given time, at least one other copy should be available in case something goes wrong. Exactly what to back up, and exactly how often, vary enormously. Backing up files costs time, media, and money. An on-line database system may require easily as much (or more) computer resources keeping audit trail and backup copies as it does actually processing.

How often should backups be made? There is no easy or universal answer to this question. In the days of sequential systems using magnetic tapes, the "grandfather, father, son" file management procedure was a standard and nearly universal. It is not so easy now. The "volatility" of the file -- how often it is changed and how fragile it is -- must be considered, as well as the value and the size of the file.

Using the risk analysis results gathered as recommended in the first part of this book, the value of the data should be fairly clear. For any given situation, the costs of producing backups can be calculated exactly. The probability of loss will have been estimated. A rough rule of thumb is that the probability of loss P, times the cost of recreating lost data V, is an upper limit for how much to spend ($\$$) on backups: ($\$ < P * V$). Some examples follow, using common situations, which may serve as a guide.

One thing that is very common is entering data into a file. This may be a programmer typing a program, a word processor operator entering a document, someone entering accounting data, or any of many other similar activities. It is a good idea to save files frequently. If anything happens to the power, even for a fraction of a second, or if the communication line used "drops," or *anything* that interrupts whatever is under way occurs, whatever hasn't been saved will be lost. Usually, it takes only seconds to tell the program to save the file. The file representing this chapter of the book has just been saved; it is about 37,000 characters and took 5 seconds to save on a personal computer. If the power were to go down, only this and the previous sentence would have to be re-entered; over 1/2 hour of time would be saved. Random Access Memory (RAM) is very volatile indeed, and the disk to which the file was saved doesn't lose data when the power "blips." (Some personal computers use "nonvolatile" memory and this paragraph doesn't apply, but they are special purpose units today.)

The disk containing this chapter is non-volatile -- that is, if the power is turned off, the data still will be there. However, some kinds of power problems can destroy disks. Various system "bugs" can cause data on disks to be lost. At least daily, data on a disk in a computer should be copied onto a *removable* storage medium; in the case of this personal computer, a diskette. If this is done, and the diskette is stored in another room, the computer could be destroyed and only one day of work would be lost. Such destruction is very rare, but it can and does occur.

Diskettes themselves can be destroyed. It is a good idea to keep two or more copies. The second copy might as well be in a different location; then a fire in the office or home will not result in loss of all the data. In one example, the backup procedure was to save at least hourly, copy onto diskette daily, and make a second backup weekly. The second copy was stored in another building. Once, a hardware problem caused the internal disk to "crash" *at the same time a daily backup was being made*. The copy in RAM, the copy on the internal disk, and the copy being made on the diskette all were lost. Until things were returned to normal, there was only *one* copy of data which would have taken at least a week to recreate. The backup procedure was changed to require a third copy, so that there would never be a time when only one copy existed.

In a larger installation, a more formal backup procedure should exist, probably involving transport of significant volumes of material to a site away from the computer center. While the grandfather/father/son rotation leads to two backups, perhaps with some other "family member" being a third backup off site, there still is a reason to have yet another backup: the transport process itself. While unlikely, it is possible that some computer problem could destroy the current (son) and most recent backup (father) files, at the same time the oldest backup (grandfather) is being destroyed in a traffic accident. If a fourth backup is stored at the off site facility, recovery is still possible.

This discussion has presented some very common situations as examples, with reasons for maintaining as many as three copies in addition to the one currently in use. Note that there is an implied catastrophe plan in keeping one copy in a separate location (see Sections 8.2 and 8.3); even total destruction of the computer does not mean total loss of data. A new computer can be brought in, and processing continued with minimum problems.

At the other end of the scale, an on-line database, in use 24 hours a day, cannot be backed up as simply. It is impractical to stop everything, take a copy (which may cost hours of time), and restart. What is done in most cases is to keep a "running" copy, with duplicates of every transaction and the before image of the affected records; thus, in case of a problem, the effects of the transaction can be reproduced. The recovery process can get very complex, to the point that a modern on-line data base *cannot* have complete backup protection (it would take more time and resources to ensure backup than it takes to do the work). One scheme sometimes used, to minimize the amount of information which has to be stored and processed to be able to do a backup, is a program (part of the database management system) which "browses" through the database, and makes a copy of everything which has been changed since the last "look" (or perhaps, in the last hour, or some other rule). This limits the loss to data changed since the program last copied it, and thus limits the cost of recovery.

In really critical situations, duplicate computers may be used, both doing the same work; if one fails, the other takes up the load while the first is repaired. In extreme situations there may be more than two: the Space Shuttle uses *three* main computers; if anything goes wrong with one, there still is a backup. Obviously, this is very expensive, but the consequences of total failure include billions of dollars and loss of human life. Similar considerations apply in hospitals and medical applications, air traffic control, and other situations where lives are at stake.

The principles are that backups need to be made; the cost of backups should not exceed the probable cost of replacing data; files (or in some systems, pieces of files) changed often need to be backed up often as do files which are important or exposed to high risk.

8.1.2 Manuals and Documentation

Many programs and systems are practically useless without the manuals which tell people how to use them. Any system which needs to be maintained -- and that is all systems -- will be almost impossible to alter without the *documentation* relating to programs, systems, operating procedures, and so on. Consider the effects on a computer operation if the copies of the manual in use, containing handwritten and undocumented notes, and the operator who wrote the notes, are both lost in a disaster, and the backup copies are six months out of date. Contingency plans must include keeping backup copies of the *manuals*. If the manuals contain sensitive information, then the same security controls which apply to the originals must also be applied to the copies (see Section 8.3).

Procedures must be set up to ensure that the backup copies of manuals are updated to stay current with the copies in use. This is especially important for the Security Officer to look into: in very many organizations, the copies *in use*, especially system and program documentation, are not kept very current, much less *backup* copies. Outdated manuals can be literally worse than useless. The Security Officer can do the organization a favor, not only in the unlikely case of a real disaster, but in saving personnel training time, by helping to ensure that manuals exist, are current, and have current backup copies.

8.1.3 Equipment

8.1.3.1 Air Conditioning

"Air conditioning," for most people, means "cooling." For computers, it might be better to speak of "environmental control," as heating and humidity control may be needed as well. Much of this is a normal responsibility of operations management, who will work with manufacturers in setting up a reasonable environment for the equipment. Some security involvement is advisable, however.

Some computers require no special cooling equipment. Some require a great deal of cooling. Personal computers normally require only "room temperature," with no special considerations. This is becoming true of more and more computer equipment; however, large mainframes have required many tons of air conditioning capacity in the past, and some still do. Some supercomputers rely on liquefied gases, such as nitrogen, to function at all. The consequences of loss of air conditioning capability differ as well, from "basically, none" to destruction of sensitive equipment.

Details of need for, and appropriate supply of, air conditioning capability will be specified by the manufacturer, and should be adhered to. The Security Officer should be involved in the process, at least to ensure that someone has asked, "What happens if the air conditioning goes down?" Some computers may be able to function without cooling at least long enough to be shut down "gracefully." Some can be damaged very quickly. Security considerations include being sure what the behavior of the organization's computer is, and planning accordingly. Backup power supply for the cooling may be advisable and may be necessary for computers which *must* continue to run. An uninterruptible power supply (Section 8.1.3.2) is not much use if there is no power for air conditioning, and it is not a good idea to assume that the cooling will continue to run unless explicit backup power has been provided for.

One idea which can provide enough cooling capacity to allow a graceful shutdown, is simply to use two or more cooling units. That way, if one fails, or needs maintenance, the other provides at least partial capacity. Whether both (or all) units should be capable separately of providing all needed cooling, or whether the separate units should be smaller and both (or all) run at the same time, is a matter for technical specifications of specific situations.

"Air conditioning" includes heating as well. In some climates, loss of power can lead to very quick cooling of buildings, and things like frozen and burst pipes can become a problem. Also, most computers have a *lower* limit on operating temperature as well as an upper limit.

Humidity control is needed as well. In some climates, low humidity, especially in winter, can present considerable static electricity exposure.

Security personnel should ensure that these and other similar environmental control items have been addressed.

8.1.3.2 Uninterruptible Power Supply

Computers are sensitive to the quality of the power supplied. Low voltages ("brownouts"), sudden, short-term high voltages ("spikes"), and loss of power can be very disruptive to computer equipment. Spikes can cause burnt out chips; brownouts can cause destroyed disks and motors; loss of power means *at least* that whatever is being worked on at the time is lost; sometimes data files can be affected as well. Computers work at speeds much faster than people; by the time a human being notices a problem with power, it's all over for the computer. One solution to this exposure is an "uninterruptible power supply (UPS).

One aspect of power supply already has been mentioned: try to supply the computer with a separate source. Large motors, or powerful small motors such as the carriage return in some typewriters, first *drop* the voltage as the motor comes on, then *increase* the voltage as the line readjusts to the sudden change in load. Many computers will react unfavorably to such a surge. While a UPS will avoid this, putting the equipment on a separate power line also avoids the problem, and it may be free or very low in cost.

An uninterruptible power supply can be anything from a short-term backup to allow the computer to "fail soft" (that is, to save files and shut itself off "gracefully," without causing further problems), to a massive installation which will continue to run the computer for a long time.

A common example of a UPS with minimal capability is a battery backup in a clock. Depending on the type of clock, such a backup may hold the correct time for up to many days. Computers use more power than a clock, naturally, but personal computer users can obtain battery-powered UPSs which will run the computer for 1/2 hour or so. This time should be long enough to finish what was underway and save files, then to shut the machine off until main power returns. A half-hour backup capability can cost as little as about $125, depending on how much power is needed and how long continued operation is required.

The range of UPS equipment can be very wide. Next up from the minimal battery backup mentioned would include a "spike protector," and probably simple filtering provisions too. A spike protector can be a very simple arrangement attached to a "power bar" (low cost), or a more elaborate device capable of handling larger spikes such as lightning surges. A spike protector in a power bar, which is little more than a *fast* fuse, is quite cheap and readily available from retail suppliers. Spike protectors up to the level of handling nearby (not direct!) lightning strikes are common on farms and cost in the under-to-low-hundreds of dollars (one type is called a "ground fault interrupter," for those who want to look it up). For a personal computer installation, a battery UPS with a spike protector would be all that is normally advisable.

A computer which is monitoring an ongoing process, or which maintains medical equipment in a hospital, or which maintains air traffic control, or which is involved in an on-line banking operation, needs something more elaborate. The exposure in such cases can be anything from large monetary losses to loss of life: the computers *must keep running*. (There is, in fact, a significant industry supplying dual, or "tandem," computers so that computer capability remains even if one machine is destroyed; this level of complexity is outside the scope of this book.) A UPS that ensures proper power supply to continue normal operation is more elaborate than a simple fail-soft unit for a personal computer. Large battery packs are common. If long outages are a possibility, the battery pack will be supported by an independent generator: when main power dies, the battery pack takes over until the generator is started, then the generator substitutes for the main source until the main source returns. In such an installation, the computer normally runs from batteries; the batteries are charged either from main power or from the generator, and there is no "blip" from a changeover. Facilities such as this can be very elaborate and may cost well over $50,000. An installation which needs this sort of backup must also be sure that things such as heating and air conditioning are backed up if necessary.

Professional engineering help, and advice from the manufacturer, would be appropriate if an elaborate system such as described above were under consideration. One thing in which the Security Officer should be involved is ensuring that ongoing procedures include regular maintenance and tests. If the backup power is inoperable during an outage, the money spent for protection was wasted.

This section has had little detail; the variance of power requirements is too wide to be easy to summarize. The basic principle of assessing the assets, the exposures, and the risks should be followed. For example, personal computers, at least the better ones, usually are not exceptionally sensitive to brownouts or spikes; they have some built-in protection. Many people do entirely without power supply protection and never have a problem. A simple backup-plus-spike protection is relatively cheap insurance, and is advisable if the location is rural or the main power may have known problems.

In Yellowknife, Northwest Territories (a city of about 10,000 in the Canadian Arctic), the city's power supply also powers a large gold mine; when the mine's crusher goes on, the whole town experiences a short brownout. In Yellowknife, even electronic cash registers normally have some form of UPS and spike protection. In Edmonton, Alberta, a city of over 700,000 a few hundred miles south, even some relatively large installations have no backup protection, as the city power supply is very reliable (and in the cited cases, the consequences of a power outage are not life-threatening nor very expensive). Very large installations, and those in places such as hospitals and petroleum refinery complexes, very definitely *do* have backups.

Brownouts -- significant periods when the demand on power utilities exceeds their generation capability and voltage drops -- have been reported with some frequency, especially in cities on the United States Eastern Seaboard. If your installation is in one of these locations, a fairly sophisticated UPS may be needed.

8.2 CATASTROPHE PLANNING

At seven minutes after three in the afternoon of a Friday before a holiday week-end in July 1987, Environment Canada issued a tornado warning for Edmonton, Alberta. Most people's reaction was disbelief: Edmonton doesn't *get* tornadoes! By three-thirty, 25 people were dead and hundreds had injuries, some fatal. Hundreds of people were homeless, and dozens of businesses simply were not there any more. The city was totally unprepared for an unprecedented phe-nomenon (it *did* have a disaster plan which operated quickly and well and man-aged to learn to cope very quickly).

In Houston, a snowstorm paralyzed the city, bringing down power lines, snarling traffic, and destroying buildings. (That snowstorm would barely have been noticed in Edmonton, which *does* expect winter.) Mudslides in Montreal have severed connections and brought down banking computers. Explosions in utility transformers have crippled downtown Toronto. Floods are common in many river systems. Many places are subject to earthquakes. Florida has hurri-canes, California has mudslides, Oklahoma and Kansas have tornadoes, and so on. Catastrophes happen, even though they may be rare.

This emphasis on major disasters should not blind the reader to the fact that small disasters occur much more frequently. While they may not make the news, incidents like a cup of coffee spilled in the wrong place at the wrong time could impact a business almost as much as a major problem like a fire.

Did you know that, if your microcomputer has a hard disk and uses MS-DOS, removing the file "COMMAND.COM" from the *root directory* will make it impossible to start up the system unless you have a backup copy of the sys-tem, of the correct version, on diskette? Even if "COMMAND.COM" still ex-ists in another directory, a copy of a recent version of MS-DOS on a diskette is needed before *anything* on the hard disk can be accessed.

Of course, all employees know that one should not FORMAT a hard disk -- don't they? What is the contingency plan for that occurrence -- it *has* happened.

Because catastrophes *do* happen, contingency planning needs to consider them. If it is a business, backups in separate buildings should exist. Off-site backups across town, or even in another city, may be good insurance. Arrangements for backup computer facilities can be made in advance. As noted in the previous section, sometimes even duplicated computers are appropriate. Every location has its own exposures to natural and other risks; the contingency plan should use data such as government weather records, flood plain data, earthquake history, and so on to decide what to prepare for. Sometimes this won't help; tornadoes *never* happen in Edmonton -- but one did. Thus a catastrophe plan needs to be in place. During or after a disaster is the wrong time to try to come up with a plan.

Things to consider include priorities of activities. For example, probably budget work for next year is lower priority than getting out the payroll at the end of the week. Data and equipment need to be available in places removed from the main computer operation. Some businesses, such as banks or refineries, can be out of business in days without computer capability. The Security Officer should be, or become, aware of common types of catastrophes, especially those common to his or her specific area, and should work with management on creating some catastrophe plan.

Who gets called? Lists of emergency contacts, people and phone numbers, will be needed.

An organization coping with a disaster has priorities other than maintaining good security principles and separation of duties. Nevertheless, these issues must be considered. If your data are too sensitive to let janitorial staff look at them during normal operations, should they be exposed to unscreened and unknown people during a problem? What level of contingency still allows what level of controls? (This topic has very different emphases if one is considering *intentional* penetration of a system; a spy may *cause* a catastrophe in order to bypass controls. Such considerations are outside the scope of this book.) It may be that nothing can be done in many instances; still, the instances should be identified as far as possible. *Most* problems are not catastrophic, yet a very common occurrence is breakdown of many security and accounting controls (for example, during a labor dispute).

The catastrophe plan needs several basic elements, and there are some things which can be done in advance, such as data file, program, and documentation backups. Several stages are common to any disaster, and associated advance preparation is obvious:

1.   The event itself

It probably will be unexpected; at best preparation time is likely to be short. The activities will be dictated by the nature of the problem, and saving human life should be first priority. At this point, anything done in the way of planning has to have happened already; it's too late now.

2.   The first response

After the immediate event is over -- the tornado is past, the earthquake stops, the fire is out, or whatever -- the disaster plan becomes operative. It should include an emergency response team, damage assessment, notification procedures identifying responsible people with names and contacts (frequently updated), and outlines of what to do.

3.   Impact assessment

People identify what has been lost, which gives an idea of what can be recovered immediately, what may take longer, and what may not be recoverable. By now, surviving responsible management should be in action, and the response team should be functioning. The response team must include people who can make decisions, and people who can cope with unstructured tense situations.

4.   Startup

If the disaster plan was done well, it should serve as a guide; levels of damage should have been identified in the plan, and lists of such things as the location(s) of backup data and manuals, whom to contact for replacement equipment, what activities need to be restarted in what order, and similar things should be guiding the operation. Startup may be as simple as rebooting a system, or as complex as flying in replacement equipment and recreating data lost between the last surviving backup copies and the catastrophe. In a small business, it may be necessary to create interim manual systems which will "bridge" until full operation can be restored.

5.   The final stage is full recovery

Hopefully, this will be possible. Certainly, it will have been made faster and far easier if a disaster plan existed and data were properly backed up and equipment replacement arrangements were in place, *before* the problem occurred.

With the stages of a disaster in mind, a disaster plan can be formulated. A good disaster plan should include at least the following features:

1.   A secure site needs to be in use for storage purposes
2.   Offsite storage needs to include *everything* needed to restart after a disaster
3.   Items stored off-site must be kept up-to-date
4.   The data files stored off-site must include current backups
5.   Arrangements for back-up hardware must be made, must be *tested* periodically, and must be kept up-to-date
6.   Disaster plans must be tested

7.   Insurance and other coverage should be reviewed.

The final point is overlooked in many cases. Even if there is adequate insurance, the money will not come to the company until after adjustors and others decide on the loss. The company's need is not money several weeks or months later; it is for replacement equipment *now*. An arrangement for an emergency line of credit can be made with a bank in advance of any problems; this line of credit would bridge the time between a loss and the insurance payment.

Some manufacturers offer plans involving replacement of equipment, or other variations of contingency arrangements. Such alternatives should be explored during consideration of the disaster recovery plan.

Part of the contingency planning process should include at least an outline of what to do if the information center is totally destroyed. During a disaster and the recovery, immediate reaction is necessary.

At some time, and preferably periodically, backup and contingency plans need to be *tested*. The time to find out that critical phone numbers are not available is *before* an actual emergency when the error can be corrected. Some kinds of plans such as fire evacuation *must* be tested by law; all contingency plans *should* be tested as a matter of professional responsibility and common sense.

The single most important thing about a catastrophe plan is *existence*.

In addition to the characteristics noted above, the disaster plan must be *communicated* to staff. In the tornado incident in Canada, one provider of ambulance services had just completed an excellent disaster plan -- but staff did not know what was in it, or where to find it! Being capable people, they developed, in real time under emergency conditions, many of the elements of the plan. However, the plan itself was wasted effort without communication. The training mentioned in Chapter 4 should include things like contingency plans, and the testing recommended in this chapter will supplement and reinforce such training, as well as lead to improvements.

8.3 SECURITY AND CONTROLS IN OFF-SITE BACKUP AND FACILITIES

Any data which were sensitive inside the computer center remain sensitive, at least for some time period, while they are stored outside the center as backup data files, programs, manuals, or in any other form. There are two fundamental control points:

> When backup material is being transferred to the site
> While backup material is stored at the site

An example could be transfer of cash: guards watch while the transfer is made to an armored vehicle; the vehicle is armored and its route and timing will not be publicized; guards watch while the cash is transferred to a storage area; the storage area itself will be monitored and subject to many rings of protection. The same sort of considerations apply to information systems. It doesn't make much sense to be very careful about disclosure of data in use in the computer, then transfer backup tapes in a van to an unsupervised warehouse.

The backup site itself may need even better protection than the computer center. Data in the backup site are likely not to be used very often, certainly not as often as the computer itself. Problems could go undetected for a long time. More than one company has experienced a problem with a dissatisfied programmer sabotaging the system in use, only to discover that no one checked and the backup tapes are blank.

These and similar considerations often mean that it is cheaper and more effective to contract someone to handle backup storage. The "someone" will be in the business, will be able to spread the cost of expensive security systems over many clients, and probably has a very solid and well-protected storage area which is monitored continuously. These things can be costly for one company to do on its own.

SUMMARY

A contingency plan is a plan for things which might happen, that could affect an information system unfavorably. The single most important thing about a contingency plan is to *have one*. Once a problem occurs, whether it is a "contingency," which is short-term and merely annoying, or whether it is a true disaster, there is no time left to plan; reaction is necessary.

The contingency plan should specify a number of "insurance" things such as backups of data and manuals. The frequency of backups, and what is to be backed up, need to be considered and defined. Issues such as environment control and power supply backup are important. Actual insurance, arrangements with other companies and suppliers for provision of emergency computer capability, and other similar things, can and should be done before there is a real need. Lists of people responsible for various activities, and where they can be reached, are important. The location of backup material, and procedures, authorizations, and means for retrieving it and using it to restore full operation, are needed.

Somewhere in the contingency plan, catastrophe planning is needed. While disasters are rare, they do occur; it has been estimated that 1/3 of businesses involved in a disaster do not recover. The existence of a disaster plan makes recovery much more likely. At a minimum, the catastrophe plan should consider what to do if the computer center is totally destroyed, by whatever means. If backups and lists of who should do what are available, recovery can be comparatively simple; without backups recovery may be impossible. At the minimum level, it is not necessary to specify what kind of disaster -- fire, flood, weather, sabotage or whatever -- may happen, but only to consider total destruction of the center. A larger firm, or a firm expecting known types of disaster (such as a company in a hurricane zone), may go into much more detail in planning for specific things.

One security issue which can be overlooked is that controls are needed in backup arrangements as well as in the operating center. Data and other material are exposed during transport to and from the backup site, and the backup site itself needs to be secured.

As a final point, contingency plans need to exist, need to consider disasters, and also need to be tested periodically and revised based on test results: fire drills are one example.

8.4 NEW TERMS

New terms introduced or defined in this chapter include:

Backing up
Before image
Brownout
Contingency
Contingency plan
Catastrophe planning
Environmental control
Spike
Spike protector
Stages common to any disaster
Uninterruptible power supply (UPS)

8.5 QUESTIONS

8.1 What is a contingency? Why is it necessary to plan for contingencies even though they are rare? Give several examples of contingencies which should be in a plan, and indicate how likely they are in your organization.

8.2 Power Supply Protection

(a) In your area, what are the main risks associated with power supply?

(b) Recommend, for the risks identified in 8.2 (a), solutions for one microcomputer with a hard drive; for a top-end microcomputer with hard drives, a laser printer, and four terminals; for a mainframe. List where the needed items can be obtained and their costs.

8.3 All surge protectors are not equal. Compare the surge protection available from a retail store, built into a power bar (typically around $30 to $40), with the filtering and surge protection available from a special box designed for computer power supply filtering (typically around $100 to $150). (*Hint*: Look carefully at actual electrical specifications, particularly how fast the protector operates and how much energy it can dissipate before the protector goes up in smoke and passes the surge along to your computer. These specifications may not be printed with the advertising on the outside of a box but should be included inside.)

8.4 (case) Contingency Planning and Controls

Using the case material in Chapter 7, Question 7.5, comment on the client's situation from the standpoint of *contingency planning*.

Required:

Prepare your initial outline of the report requested by ABC Inc.

Organize your answer under the following headings:

I. Contingency Planning Review

   A. Strengths

   B. Weaknesses

   C. Exposures and Recommended Improvements

Remember that you should concentrate on *contingency planning*; other weaknesses/strengths are for other chapters.

SECTION III: SAFEGUARDS: SECURITY AND CONTROL MEASURES, TECHNICAL

Chapter 9

REVIEW OF ORGANIZATIONAL SAFEGUARDS

INTRODUCTION

Section III of this book deals with some fairly technical issues related to communications, encryption, operating system security, and software quality. These sections should follow coverage of the first three chapters, to give a framework into which to put technical issues. To help provide this framework, this chapter reviews Chapter 3. For perspective, the second section of this chapter looks at the commonly perceived threat of "hackers;" media have convinced many people that so-called hackers are the real threat in computer security. Many of the technical issues in Section III are related to deterring hackers, but the perspective is important: hackers are really a very small part of the problem of information systems security.

9.1 REVIEW OF CHAPTER 3

Chapter 3 is a review of the overall components of information systems security. Some of this material is repeated here, in a more condensed form, for those who are interested mainly in the more technical security measures and may have skipped the first part of the text. It is important to retain an overall perspective: treating only technical issues often leads to omission of much more effective, and often cheaper, organizational controls. The idea is not to miss the forest while pruning trees.

9.1.1 Basic Strategy

A three-part strategy is recommended for designing any security program:

1.   Apply *common sense.*
2.   Consider *basic types* of controls.
3.   Consider *essential components* of any system of safeguards.

9.1.1.1 Common Sense

The first consideration in designing a security program must be common sense. *Lock* the doors. *Use* the security provided by the operating system designers. *Tell* employees that ethical behavior is a condition of employment and of tenure. *Don't hire* people without checking references. In planning to implement safeguards identified so far in the risk management process, look them over: are there simple, inexpensive measures which will be part of the final solution anyway? If so, implement them now. (Why leave a known large, existing vulnerability while designing a perfect system which avoids nearly all vulnerabilities?)

9.1.1.2 Basic Purposes of Controls

There are three basic purposes which all controls are intended to address:

1.   *Prevent* exposures.
2.   *Detect* attempted threats.
3.   *Correct* the causes of threats.

Many controls have elements of more than one of these basic purposes. For each identified exposure, the first things the risk management team should consider are: how to prevent a problem; how to detect a problem if it happens; and what to do about making sure the problem will not recur. No asset is ever completely immune to harm, given enough will and resources on the part of

threats, or simply an accident.   By setting up several layers of controls --
preventive, detective, and corrective -- the asset gets progressively safer.
Keeping the basic purposes of controls in mind will help focus the risk
management team.

9.1.1.3 Prevention

The first line of defense is protection, or *prevention*. Given that a problem is defined and may occur, good risk management would include prevention of the
known exposure. For example, it is known that without any controls, anyone
could access a computer system and change someone else's data (if there is
more than one person's data on the system). Therefore, some preventive measure is needed.   One which has proven of value is the use of account
identification and password controls. Casual "potential threats" are deterred,
and some prevention has been achieved.

9.1.1.4 Detection

Once the preventive control is penetrated, the unwanted thing has occurred. The
next step in controls is to *detect* this event. Detection systems indicate and/or
verify an actual or attempted penetration. Examples include console printouts,
alarms, and video monitoring.

According to the RCMP [RCMP 1981], a detection system normally has four
primary components:

1.   Sensors to detect the activity
2.   Communications to relay the fact of the event
3.   Assessment system to evaluate the needs of the situation
4.   Reporting system to announce the situation to the appropriate response
        force(s)

9.1.1.5 Correction

Once a threat has occurred and has been detected, something should be done
about it. Doing nothing is also a decision: someone should have analyzed the
situation and decided that it is cheaper not to correct the problem. The purpose
of the communication and reporting components of a detection system is to ensure that someone does something -- reacts to, or *corrects*, the situation.

Corrective controls:

1.   Take action to resolve a problem, for example:

        automatic error correction (spelling checker)

call the police forces
review employment policies

2.   Are expensive, for example:

parallel operation
police forces
quality control group
change control group

The risk management team will find the task of designing safeguards easier if three ideas are kept in mind:

1.   Common sense
2.   The basic purposes of controls
3.   Basic, proven strategies for protection

9.1.2 Basic Strategies

Six time-proven strategies should be understood fully (although other strategies have been tried, and some also work well):

1.   *Avoid* the risk in the first place.
2.   *Split* up the asset so several areas have to be penetrated to accomplish the exposure.
3.   Put the asset in a *visible* place so penetration attempts are obvious.
4.   *Hide* the asset, either literally or by the "purloined letter" method.
5.   *Combine* several assets to minimize costs of security.
6.   Utilize many *layers of protection.*

Keeping these principles in mind will help to minimize the risk of "paralysis by analysis."

The final strategy is "rings of protection," or layers of protection, or the "onion-skin" method. This has been referred to several times in the book, because it is an excellent basic strategy. Several layers of protection are provided, ideally with different characteristics in each layer. In an operating system, the first layer might be account and password; the second layer, access control tables; a third layer, passwords on individual files; and a fourth layer perhaps a physical switch which must be thrown by an operator to permit access at all. Very few threats, accidental or deliberate, would penetrate four such layers, particularly since different methods are needed in layers 1, 2, and 4.

9.1.3 Essential Elements of Information Systems Security

There are eight essential elements of information systems security:

1.   General administrative and organizational practices

   This involves the development of an overall security policy and establishing procedures for its implementation. Such topics as corporate policies, organization structure and identification of responsibilities, training, employee awareness, and general working practices (telecommuting, for example) were addressed in Chapter 4.

2.   Personnel

   Chapter 5 presented some material on who commits crimes, and why they do so (summarized, and strictly from an information systems standpoint; this is a very broad and complex topic without general agreement in many basic conceptual areas). Employee selection, including standardized application forms, reference checks, and security clearances were addressed next. An overview of existing professional certificates was presented (this area is addressed in more detail in Chapter 14). The general working environment was discussed. Finally, procedures recommended when employees leave (voluntarily or otherwise) were considered.

3.   Physical and Environmental

In Chapter 6, factors such as site location and physical protection were discussed. The topics included:

Site location and construction
Physical access
Power supply
Air Conditioning
Fire prevention
Fire protection
Tape and other media libraries
Waste disposal
Off-site storage.

While many of these things will be fixed for a given risk management team (cannot build a new building, for example), they should be included in the analysis, if only to be sure that consideration is given.

4.   Communications and Electronic Exposures

Chapter 10 addresses communications and electronic exposures. Most organizations have some form of data communication, and it needs protection. Since computers are electronic machines, certain electronic exposures exist, and some guidelines relating to these will be given.

5.   Computer Operations

The area of actually running an information system was discussed in Chapter 7. Typical organizations were presented, and some control principles were covered.

6.   Software

Programs and other software need protection and must be designed properly to support a secure and reliable information system. Since this topic overlaps with operating system security, it has been included along with some consideration of the history of operating systems security, and some of the basic principles involved, in Chapter 12.

7.   Hardware and Encryption

Any discussion of communication security inevitably very quickly reaches consideration of encryption. Since this is a very technical topic and mathematics is involved, it cannot be covered in detail in this text; however, some simple principles and examples, and some information about the Data Encryption Standard (DES), are presented in Chapter 11.

8.   Contingency Planning

Contingency planning has been addressed in outline in Chapter 8. Some of the details backing up elements discussed in Chapter 8 are found in the following chapters. These include further discussion of controls in the systems development area and operating system area, among others.

9.2 "HACKERS" AND REALITY

In July 1987, several newspapers reported the activities of a group of "hackers" caught by the United States authorities. The group included people, mostly juveniles, in several states and some other countries, who were accused of stealing telephone time, obtaining goods through use of credit card information, and a number of other crimes. The crimes were committed using personal computers and modems. This type of activity is reported fairly frequently in the popular press. Certainly many organizations remain vulnerable to sophisticated agents such as juveniles who know a lot about computers and have access to micro-computers and modems. Indeed, many organizations are totally vulnerable: 41% of organizations surveyed in a 1987 Data Processing Management Association study reported that they had *no security at all*. (Checking up on this somewhat unbelievable finding has elicited comments such as, "The survey was wildly optimistic."[!])

There are books, some in the reference list for this text, on the topic of "hackers." There are even motion pictures and occasional television programs which depict people penetrating military systems and nearly causing wars.

"Hacker" once meant "the kind of computer specialist who gets totally involved and works until all hours of the night." Today, it has come to be a label identifying sophisticated people who commit crimes using computers. The media regularly report on hacking activities, and the public seems to have a perception that they are a severe threat to computer systems. As noted above, hackers *can be* a threat; as will be clear from some comments in the following chapters, nearly all hackers can be kept out by quite simple methods The astounding percentage of organizations reporting no security to the survey noted in the preceding paragraph certainly would face a severe threat should a hacker become interested in their systems.

The actual loss in the case reported in July 1987 is almost certainly under $1 million. At the same time, a bank in California (as reported in the *Risk Digest* electronic newsletter) was experiencing problems with implementing a new on-line banking system; they have lost *at least* $23 million to date, and possibly much more. No one has yet added up the bank's loss in customers who have left or will not deal with the bank. In March 1988, a major telephone switching computer suffered a component failure; in about eight hours, some 950,000 long distance calls could not be placed or received. If the average charge per call is about $1.00, nearly a million dollars was lost. There was no backup computer. These cases, and many similar ones, are far more representative of the kind of information system security problem which commonly occurs.

It has been estimated that hackers and, for that matter, unlawful activities in general, account for less than 5% of problems with information systems (probably less than .5%). The greatest loss is due to error: bad data, badly programmed systems, poorly trained employees, and so on. Hackers, except for the *very* sophisticated ones with complex equipment, can be kept out of most systems cheaply and easily. Even a simple procedure such as requiring account identifications with passwords, and disconnecting and notifying a security officer of the attempt after three unsuccessful signon tries, will keep out nearly all hackers. More sophisticated measures such as discussed in Chapters 10, 11, and 12 will deter all but the most capable "hackers."

On the other hand, employees have access quite legitimately; if they make a mistake the cost can be very large. (An insurance company employee in 1987 wrote "$93,000" instead of "$93,000,000;" the company may lose $92,907,000 because of this error. The issue is before the courts; whatever the outcome, this error has cost the company legal fees at least.) An employee who is fired but whose access privileges are not removed is a dangerous exposure: he or she has access and training, probably knows just how to hurt the system in addition, and may have a powerful motive to "get even."

In studying the technical safeguard material in Section III, it is a good idea to keep the hacker in perspective. He or she is a significant threat only to companies who do not use known, cheap, and simple preventive controls. The real problem is addressed with controls, training, and organization morale, not with technical fixes.

9.3 NEW TERMS

Many terms are used in this chapter which have been defined previously and thus technically are not "new terms". Readers who have not studied the first part of the book at least should study Chapter 3.
hacker

9.4 QUESTIONS

9.1 Using references such as your organization's library, or the local newspaper's files, identify at least five incidents involving "hackers" that occurred in your area in the past two years.

(a) Write up, in as much detail as available, the precise methods used to perpetrate the offense.

(b) Using the material in Chapters 1 to 8, indicate which, if any, of the methods so far studied would have prevented the problems.

(c) If possible, indicate which methods *did* work at least to *detect* each incident so that it could be reported.

(d) Indicate which incidents could *not* have been prevented by any of the methods in Chapters 1 to 8.

(e) Retain the lists you have created so that you can identify technical measures which *would* have prevented the problems, as you study the following chapters.

Chapter 10

COMMUNICATIONS AND ELECTRONIC EXPOSURES

INTRODUCTION

"Communications" means many things to many people. In this text on information systems security and control, communications means "electronic communications." That is, signals sent on a wire, or over microwave, or by satellite, or by optical fiber or however, but electronic in nature. Further, voice communication among people is not significant for this purpose; various forms of computer-readable communications are the subject.

This leaves a very wide range of possibilities, from 110 baud ("baud" is a measure of the speed of communications; 1200 baud is roughly 1200 words per minute, or 120 characters per second) teletype to megabits-per-second direct computer linkages. This text does not go into the various communications possibilities such as 300/1200 baud modem links, or whatever; from a security standpoint the specific details do not matter very much, although of course technical details do matter for solutions. The concentration in this chapter is on the kinds of exposures which occur in data communications links involving computers. Where a specific problem is very common, details may be given, but usually it is enough to consider the origination, transmission, and reception of communications for security attention.

Every successful communication has an originator, a transmission medium, and a receiver. In addition, there is the message content. For human beings, the message content in one person's mind is "encoded" into a spoken language, transmitted by means of vibrations in the air, received by another person's ears, and "decoded" into meanings understood by the listener. Computers are no different in principle. A computer has a "message" internally; this is "encoded" into a form which will go onto a telephone line (by a modem), it is transmitted via electrical signals along the telephone system, it is received and decoded into a signal the receiving computer can "understand," and finally action occurs.

If the human originator does not speak the same language as the receiver (say, German at origination and Russian at reception), communication will fail. Similarly, if the originating computer "speaks" ASCII and the receiving machine "speaks" EBCDIC, communication will fail. If the room is noisy, people may not hear each other, or may miss part of the signal; this is "noise." Noise can occur on data communication lines as well, and must be handled or, again, the communication will fail. Two people having a conversation may be overheard; this is "interception." A tap on a telephone line is one way to intercept computer communications. People in a noisy environment may shout at each other and not be understood; this is "distortion." Electrical and electronic signals are subject to various forms of distortion as well.

Technical means for minimizing various data communications problems exist; they require specialized training which is outside the scope of this text. The emphasis here is on security; security is satisfied if the signal is noise-free and undistorted, and not intercepted, regardless of how this is accomplished.

Readers of this chapter will benefit from studying one of the many references on data communications.

10.1 ELECTRONIC

Computers are electronic machines. They generate electromagnetic fields during operation, and they can be affected by fields around them. In Japan, so-called "killer robots" have been traced to outside interference in the computers which control industrial robots. Until shielding standards were improved, personal computers often interfered with television and radio reception. (There is a modem in the author's home which causes diagonal interference on some television channels' video signals.) Static electricity -- which is generated by people moving around, among other ways -- can destroy unshielded chips totally.

This section discusses some of the more common problems involved in this topic area, and the easiest solution.

10.1.1 Incoming: Interruptions, Static

The computer operation can be affected by "electronic pollution" from outside the machine. "Electronic pollution" can be defined as any electronic signal not wanted in the vicinity; interference on radio or television is a familiar example. Other common examples include radar near an airport (or from a speed trap outside a house), strong signals near a radio or television transmitting station, CB radios, and mobile telephones. Static electricity is generated by weather (at the extreme, it causes lightning) and by almost anything which moves. A static electricity field generated by a person walking on a wool carpet in a low humidity area easily can be 50,000 volts or more; probably everyone has had the experience of getting shocked by touching a doorknob. None of these forms of electronic pollution do a computer any good if they reach the chips.

10.1.2 Outgoing: Leakage

Computers also generate electronic signals. There is a "clock" oscillator in every digital computer, that generates a signal at the "clock frequency" as it works (this controls internal timing). The movement of signals within a chip, or along buses among components, generates electromagnetic fields which can affect things outside the computer. Modems can generate signals which will interfere with television and radio reception. In past days, one diversion sometimes practiced was to put a radio receiver on top of the CPU; the signals generated when a program ran could be picked up at the right frequency. It is possible to control the frequency of the audio signal received by doing such things as varying the number of times a loop executes. People have written "music compilers" which cause radios placed on CPU's to pick up a "tune." Peripheral equipment (such as printers) also generates signals; it is possible to determine what is being printed, or typed on an electric or electronic typewriter or computer keyboard, by analyzing these leaked signals. It has been demonstrated that unshielded computers emit strongly enough that sensitive equipment outside the building can detect the signals and determine what the computer is doing (it takes about one van full, though such spy equipment also is getting smaller).

There have been reports in the press that satellites can detect such leakage, although these reports are not confirmed.

10.1.3 Solutions: Shielding

The generic solution to the problems described is shielding. If a grounded metal "cage" surrounds the equipment, most electronic signals will not pass outside the cage. An application of this principle is shielding of computer rooms: grounded wire mesh is placed in each wall, floor, and ceiling during construction, and the computer then will be unaffected by interference from outside the room, and will not emit detectable signals past the shielded boundary. (Expert advice is needed when installing such shielding; for example, sometimes things like metal water pipes for the air conditioning can act as antennas and defeat what looks like good shielding.) Similar shielding is now standard for microcomputers; the power supplies, chips, and other parts which may emit signals or be affected by incoming signals are surrounded by grounded metal. (The author once decided to demonstrate leakage in a classroom, and found during testing that the computer used was too well shielded; no signal could be picked up by the radio.)

There is a United States Department of Defense standard named "Tempest" which describes very complete shielding so that signals cannot be detected outside the computer itself, even by very sensitive equipment. Usually, this requires a complete metal case rather than simply shielding around some parts of the machine. (For military purposes, it would be embarrassing at best if an enemy could detect and read what is being typed into, or displayed on the screen of, a computer on a battlefield.) Tempest equipment is also very well protected against outside interference. Because of the all-metal construction and for other reasons, Tempest equipment can be rather expensive and relatively heavy.

The shielding problem may ease in the future. Optical fibers do not leak electronic signals and are immune to electronic interference or to interception. Future optical computers can be expected to be similarly immune. Some computers already use fibers to transmit internal signals (because they have a wide bandwidth and are very fast, not because of leakage), and optical computers have been built as laboratory test beds.

10.2 COMMUNICATIONS

When computers communicate with one another, simple shielding is not a solution: for communications, signals need to go out and to be accepted; keeping them from doing so means no communication is occurring. The shielding must have intentional "doors" or "gates" to allow desired signals to leave and enter.

10.2.1 Value-Added Communications

"Value added communications" is a term which means that the fact of having a linkage adds value to what is being done. For example, working on a spreadsheet may give great satisfaction and may be valuable; however, it is likely to be much more valuable if someone other than the originator sees the results. This involves communication. The value may be increased further if others can see the results *quickly*, or perhaps even can interact with the originator while the work is performed. In cases like this, the communication link has *added value* to the work. A computer time-sharing network has value for a number of reasons; one reason is that electronic mail systems are possible: "value added" to the timesharing network by the communication happening.

It is impossible to express the complexity and value of the data communication happening continuously today. Electronic mail, funds transfer, access to more "written" information in seconds than existed fifty years ago through data bases, control of traffic lights coordinated with conditions all over a city, similar control of rail equipment over a continent, power networks responding to an outage in one place without affecting others. The list could go on and on. Computers plus communications permit things like telecommuting (Chapter 4). This list has not even touched on Local Area Networks (LAN's); from a security view, there is little difference whether the wire between computers goes to a telephone line or to another computer in a LAN. (In practice, the LAN is *more* secure because it does not extend outside the area; it often is *less* secure because the wires commonly are not shielded as well as public carriers' lines.) Communication *will* happen, and adds enormously to the value of information systems.

Communicating adds value but involves added risk as well.

10.2.2 Communication Exposures Incoming: Noise and Interference

Noise and interference are significant problems on incoming (and also on outgoing) data communication lines. The first attempt at a solution should be to try to ensure that the lines themselves are physically good (no breaks in insulation, "conditioned lines" from the telephone company, and so on). This is not always enough, or the physical condition of the lines may be outside the organization's control; the generic solution for this problem in computers is "error detecting and correcting codes." The parity bit in an ASCII code is a simple error-detecting method; if the parity bit is wrong it is clear that one, three, or five of the other bits are wrong and the byte should be rejected. (A single parity bit will not catch an even number of errors since parity would not be affected.) Much more sophisticated error-detecting and also error-correcting codes exist. They are used as standards in data communications, with the precise encoding depending on the type of communication link involved. Encryption schemes normally include extra error-detecting and correcting codes.

Noise problems are minimized to some extent by the nature of a digital signal: the noise is random, and unless it happens to match the waveform representing a bit, and at the right time, it will be ignored. A familiar example of this is the lack of noise on a compact audio disk: the music is digitally encoded; any noise would be analog and is ignored by the processor, so no "record hiss" or "tape hiss" comes through. Unfortunately, the function of a modem is to modulate or demodulate a digital signal to match the telephone line: the modulated signal is not digital; thus noise is a greater problem when telephone communication using modems is involved.

"Packet switching" involves using telephone lines to transmit *digital* information; higher speeds are possible because the analog noise is ignored for much the same reasons that CDs are noise-free. (Not all telephone lines will accept this digital material, because telephone systems originally were set up to handle voice, an *analog* signal. Newer systems translate the analog voice signal to digital forms and are structured to handle this information format. Anything going through a satellite is digital as well.)

Interference can include noise, or other signals which distort the incoming signal or drown it out. Some common sources of interference include electric motors of all kinds, other unshielded computer equipment and peripherals, weather, static electricity, airport and police radar, CB and aircraft radios, and passing automotive traffic. The exposure to interference depends on such variables as site location, shielding of the equipment and of the room in which it is located, and similar considerations.

One risk related to communications has nothing to do with noise or interference. "Freeware," or public-domain programs, is available (in several variants) on many bulletin boards which can be accessed using a computer and a modem. It is known that at least some of this freeware contains "viruses" or "worms," program constructions which can degrade an operating system, destroy data files, and do much damage to the information a computer works with. (There are three *Scientific American* articles in the "Computer Recreations" columns which describe viruses and worms in some detail, for those who want more information on the topic.) No one knows exactly which programs are thus booby-trapped. A perfectly communicated program which proceeds to wipe out your data files and file allocation tables is a risk of "downloading" and running freeware from public bulletin boards. The only solution seems to be either to avoid the exposure -- do not download or run *any* freeware -- or to take extreme precautions in doing so (back up all files, test the program as if you are convinced it is trying to harm you, then *perhaps* run it, if you are willing to risk that subtle damage is being done without obvious signs).

10.2.3 Exposures Outgoing: Interception, Replacement

In sending a signal outside your premises, at least two new risks have been added: someone may *intercept* the signal and read it, and someone may intercept your signal and *replace* it or parts of it with his or her own. If the data are sensitive, unauthorized reading is a problem. A penetration method for computer systems has been to intercept one signal, then replace it with another (the replacement might contain a command to change or print the password, for example, and would be accepted because the legitimate user is already signed on). If a signal is a transmission of financial data, it could be of great benefit to someone to have certain numbers be larger or smaller than intended by the originator.

10.2.4 Solutions: Physical Measures

Physical measures to deal with noise and interference include selection of the type of transmission line, and control of access to the line. Coaxial cable is not nearly so subject to interference, or to tapping, as is a simple telephone line. Optical fiber is totally unaffected by electronic interference and cannot be tapped without leaving obvious physical signs. If an unauthorized person can reach a twisted pair line, a simple induction loop around the line will pick up enough signal to allow analysis.

Selecting the type of line may be the best solution, if it is a possible one. Within a single installation, it is entirely possible, although expensive, to use optical fiber protected by being buried in concrete to link computers. This is an extremely secure link, assuming the endpoints are also secured. Shielded or coaxial cables are reasonably secure as well. Standard insulated twisted pair wiring is not secure at all. This kind of choice may not be available, and certainly is not available for any transmission using public carriers.

One way to obtain security is to keep potential perpetrators away from the lines. Consider, however, what may be involved in doing so. A communications link involves many nodes and channels, not all of which may be within the scope of a security officer's authority. For example, the elements of a data link involving public carriers may include:

1.   Originating equipment
2.   Modem
3.   Telephone connection inside the room
4.   Organization's switchboard or Private Branch Exchange (PBX)
5.   Telephone master connections for the floor and for the building
6.   Telephone lines from the building to the pole
7.   Telephone lines to a substation

8.   Whatever equipment is in the substation
9.   Lines from the substation to a "long line"
10.   Microwave transmission towers or satellite uplinks
11.   Satellite downlinks
12.   The inverse of longline-substation-lines-building-room-equipment at the other end

Any point in this link can be a place where noise or interference may intrude, and where an unauthorized person may be able to intercept the signal and read it, or (at some points) replace it with one of his or her own. In particular, a satellite downlink is a radio frequency transmission from a satellite which can be received by anyone with a proper antenna and sensitive equipment within many kilometers of the legitimate satellite receiving dish, and can be analyzed and read. Most of the elements of the path described are outside the practical control of a security officer or individual organization.

The linkage described is common and occurs billions of times a day (millions in the case of satellites, which would be long-distance). Much more complex linkages can occur.

Many simple physical measures can be taken which are within the domain of the organization's security personnel. Access control to the room minimizes the chance that someone will tap the phone or the lines inside. Shielding minimizes other radiation which could be detected, and also helps with telephone lines. Locks on the rooms containing the floors' telephone boards, and again on the building's nexus, are essential. (If someone can access these rooms easily, they have access to all the telephone lines for a floor or building. These rooms tend to be small, in accessible public areas such as beside elevators, and seldom visited. Who pays attention to someone in coveralls with a tool box, working on something or other in a small room full of unidentifiable equipment?)

Even if physical measures minimize this sort of exposure, other exposures outside the domain of control exist. Once the signal leaves the premises the security officer has almost no further control over its security. The only feasible solution is to send a signal which can't be used by unauthorized people who may receive it: encryption of some form.

10.2.5 Solutions: Encryption

Perhaps the best (indeed, perhaps the *only* effective) solution to problems relating to communications is to "encrypt" the signal at each end. Then, if someone intercepts the signal, possession of a key would be needed to make use of it. Similarly, only with the encryption key could someone insert a correctly encoded message into a communications link. In addition, the algorithms which currently are used to encrypt signals contain enhanced error-detection coding, and the chance of an undetected error caused by noise is much lessened, as is the possibility of recreating a distorted signal using error-correcting features.

The RCMP have reported in their July 1987 *EDP Security Bulletin* that a communications link which has user identification and password authentication, encryption, and which has a dial-back capability, can be considered as secure as a hard-wired situation. (The dial-back capability means that after the system identifies the user, the system disconnects and calls the number associated with that user to initiate the session. It is often combined with terminals which contain hardware to identify themselves.)

Chapter 11 describes some basic principles and usages regarding encryption.

10.2.6 ISO OSI Communications Standard

The International Standards Organization (ISO) was founded in 1946 with 25 charter member countries. Today, it is headquartered in Geneva, Switzerland and is comprised of the national standards bodies of 89 countries. The ISO has had working groups looking at the area of communications standards for many years.

One of the results of these efforts has been the "Open System Interconnection" standards (OSI). (An open system is distinguished from a closed network which cannot be entered from outside the network. Many LANs are closed; when *any* link to outside, even a single telephone link, is added, the network becomes "open.") Over time, the ISO/OSI standards and the standards promoted by certain prominent manufacturers, have converged; it seems likely that in the near future the ISO/OSI standards will be accepted fairly universally.

The ISO OSI standards consist of seven layers, which include not only communications standards but also definitions of security at each level. While the security varies by level, one comment summarizes the ISO work for purposes of this text [ISO 1984]:

Within the OSI framework, the only known method of protection must be the encryption of data on the physical links. (Techniques such as physically securing a line, or the use of fiber optic links, are not within the OSI framework.)

This, along with the authors' experiences and other researchers' conclusions, forms the basis for the comment in the first paragraph of this subsection, that encryption may be the *only* effective security measure in any open communications situation.

To discuss the security specified for the ISO/OSI framework, the seven levels are listed first. Little detail is given since this framework is widely known and published.

The layers are:

1.   Application
2.   Presentation
3.   Session
4.   Transport
5.   Network
6.   Data Link
7.   Physical

The *application layer* is where the system interacts with the end-user application.

The *presentation layer* prepares the information for the application (such as reformatting for transfer between devices or programs).

The *session layer* establishes the communication link between network nodes.

The *transport layer* translates requirements from higher layers into a protocol that can be used by the network, thus providing a common interface to the communication network.

The *network layer* establishes the logical transmission path through a switched network (assuming alternate paths exist).

The *data link layer* performs functions necessary to move data through an electrical connection.

The *physical layer* describes the physical and electrical connections in the network.

The report [ISO 1984] suggests that there are three primary categories of security features that relate to the basic OSI reference model just briefly described. These can be paraphrased:

Basic features (those feasible now)

Desirable features (may or may not be feasible now)

Important features that are outside the OSI model, or not feasible with to-day's technology

Basic Features

...The basic features are the protection of connection-oriented data transfer with regard to:

Confidentiality;

Integrity;

Authentication;

Protection against traffic analysis;

Protection against deliberate denial of service;

Security audit;

Compartmentalization.

Desirable Features

Signature service -- protection against repudiation or forgery [i. e., denial of transaction or a counterfeit one];

Network security access control;

Protection of connectionless data transfer;

Selective field protection [protection of only parts of a message];

Protection against covert or unauthorized overt information channels;

Protection against traffic analysis (e. g., deriving information relative to the number and duration of connections, message format characteristics, origin-destination identities and traffic patterns).

Features Outside Present Scope

Physical security;

User authentication [i. e., advanced technologies];

Security within end systems [i.e., operating systems];

Audit record review for security purposes;

Electronic radiation emanation protection;

Trojan horse protection.

Many of the items noted in the preceding quote are covered in various places in this text. The critical point remains as noted already: encryption may be the *only* way to ensure security in an open network.

A great deal more information is available about the ISO/OSI framework for those interested in communication issues in detail. For purposes of this text, the security issue in essence is that only encryption can provide adequate protection. Note that this is essentially the conclusion which forms the basis of the RCMP report in their July 1987 bulletin reported above.

10.3 NEW TERMS

New terms introduced or defined in this chapter include:

Baud
Dial-back system
Distortion
Electronic communications
Electronic pollution
Encoding
Error detecting and correcting codes
Freeware
Interception
Noise
Originator
Private Branch Exchange (PBX); also, PABX -- Private *Automatic* Branch Exchange
Receiver
Replacement
Satellite downlink
Shielding
Tempest
Transmission medium
Value added communications
Viruses and worms

10.4 QUESTIONS

10.1 Describe the communication process. For your own organization, identify the elements in this process which you invoke when you use a computer.

10.2 Noise and distortion are both problems in communications. Use examples to describe clearly the difference between noise and distortion. Explain why a solution which overcomes a noise problem may increase a distortion problem.

10.3 Find two computers with similar capabilities available for retail sale, one shielded to the "Tempest" standard and one not. Compare the prices and availability of each.

10.4 Why is interception likely to become less of a problem in the future?

10.5 What element of the ASCII code helps with error detecting? How does it help? What is one limit to the help?

10.6 You are an industrial spy trying to intercept communications between computer terminals and the computer in an office building where sensitive work is being done. Write out a strategy which you think might allow you to do this.

At the beginning of your report, identify any assumptions you have to make about the nature of the building, network, or other communications links.

For each action in your plan, indicate:

    what your target is
    why you think it may be vulnerable
    what you hope to gain.

10.7 After you have created the penetration strategy for Question 10.6, take the part of the information security officer for the company in the building. Using the same assumptions as you did for your previous answer, describe how you would stop the industrial spy from succeeding by the methods proposed.

10.8 Using the answers to Questions 10.6 and 10.7, identify each strategy or counter as to its place in the ISO/OSI framework and associated security considerations.

10.9 Is a "computer virus" contagious? Explain how it can be caught, or explain why it is not contagious.

Chapter 11

ENCRYPTION AND HARDWARE

INTRODUCTION

This chapter represents a difficult compromise: the treatment of encryption has been kept to what amounts to an outline of the factors involved. Many texts on computer security present considerable detail about encryption and other cryptography topics, and of course there are numerous complete texts in the area. Because the literature is so extensive, the choice has been made for this text to concentrate on those factors of immediate relevance to security personnel.

Thus, for instance, there are many methods of encryption; however, a security practitioner in the commercial world normally will use some available package, probably DES in some variation. The details of the encryption are givens which can be accepted or rejected, but not changed; only operating considerations are within the security practitioner's domain of control. This text tries to concentrate on that domain of control.

Cryptography has been around for thousands of years, and the reader is referred to a book such as *Cryptography and Data Security* (Denning, Dorothy Elizabeth Robling, Addison-Wesley, 1983) for a much more detailed treatment than in this chapter. The concern in this text is with the use of encryption for purposes of information systems security, and for that purpose it is sufficient to know of the existence of encryption and the main standard, the impacts on a system, and a few terms which will be encountered.

11.1 ENCRYPTION

11.1.1 Definition

Encryption is the process of using an "encryption unit" and an *encryption key* to change *plaintext*, or the normally-understandable information, into *ciphertext*, which (hopefully) is not readable without the encryption device's inverse and a key. *Decryption* is the process of changing the ciphertext into plaintext. The encryption unit can be anything from pencil and paper, to computer software and/or chips, to special-purpose devices (one of the most famous is the "enigma" device used by the Germans in World War II and captured by the Allies).

Historically, any information which people have had to send to someone else along channels which are not secure, has been encrypted in some fashion before transmission. This could be anything from credit or financial data, to personal private information, to military communications. Because of the inherent vulnerability of data communication channels on public carriers, particularly microwave and satellite transmissions, and because of technological advances, encryption has become a cost-effective way to ensure secure data transmission. The costs have dropped so far that encryption using the most common method ("DES," Section 11.1.3) is quite inexpensive, and is widely used (but see Section 11.1.4 for some comments).

11.1.2 Public Key and Private Key

Two basic encryption systems are common today: *public key* and *private key*. In a private key system, encryption and decryption are done using the same key. The key must be kept secret. Anyone with the key can both encrypt and decrypt data. In a public key system, two keys are used, one to encrypt and one to decrypt. The two keys are related mathematically in a way which cannot be determined using "reasonable" computational methods. (Mathematicians consider that very great effort, perhaps thousands of years of supercomputer time, would be needed to crack the coding. This sort of analysis is risky, as new developments in mathematics can offer new ways to crack codes and invalidate such analyses.)

Thus, the encryption key may be published; anyone can encrypt and send messages to whomever owns the decrypting key but only the owner of the decrypting key can read any such encrypted data. This has the advantage that only one copy, or a small number of copies, of the private key needs to be kept secure. As well, anyone can *send* encrypted data using the public key but only a receiver possessing the private key can read the message.

As at November 1986, there were no internationally defined standards for modes of operation for public key systems (RCMP *EDP Security Bulletin*).

11.1.3 DES

It is probably true to say that there are presently two major encryption methods applicable in informatics: DES and "all others." Many security packages (IBM's Resource Access Control Facility [RACF] for example) have their own proprietary encryption algorithms; these must be accepted by a security officer on a "take it or leave it" basis, and thus are not covered in this text. "DES" is the *D*ata *E*ncryption *S*tandard which has been adopted by the United States Government (Federal Information Processing Standards Publication 46, January 15, 1977 [FIPS 1977]). It is a private key encryption method developed by the IBM corporation, which agreed to grant nonexclusive, royalty-free licenses under its patent, to other organizations wishing to make, use, and sell apparatus which complies with the standard.

DES has mathematical flaws which need not be addressed in this text; it is considered sufficiently secure for most commercial, nonmilitary systems. (The U. S. National Security Agency may not endorse DES past 1988 for more sensitive situations due to these flaws and to developments in mathematics [factoring large numbers] useful for cracking DES-type encryption schemes.)

"DES chips" (computer chips containing the DES algorithm) are easily available in North America for a low price, and many software packages include DES as an option. Normally, a chip is far preferable because the software implementations significantly degrade system performance. Variations are available for communication lines, and for encrypting data into files in many computers, including personal computers.

Readers with an interest in DES are referred to the FIPS standard [FIPS 1977] for mathematical details.

As with any other non-public-key system, the key used to encrypt must be held by both originator and receiver, and the key itself must be kept secure, as must the transmission channel for the key.

11.1.4 Advantages and Disadvantages

The obvious advantage of any good encryption scheme is that the coded material cannot be used without the key. This means that, for example, one need not worry about someone tapping the telephone line, or intercepting the microwave signal -- the intercepted transmission is useless without the key. Similarly, encrypted data on diskettes is not at risk of disclosure unless the key is obtained along with the diskette. In essence, encrypted data in any form and on any medium, assuming DES or an equivalent or better coding scheme is used, reasonably may be considered not to be subject to disclosure or to use by unauthorized people, in nonmilitary situations.

Encryption does have disadvantages. Lose the key, and the data or whatever will not be available to you, the authorized user. The penetration effort shifts emphasis to the key: people must remember to keep that key confidential. (Personal Identification Numbers [P. I. N.] are issued by banks along with cards which will access automated teller equipment; an amazing percentage of people write their P. I. N. *on the card* -- thus destroying any security offered by use of P. I. N.s.)

The biggest disadvantage of encryption probably is performance degradation. To use any data or program which is encrypted, information first must be encoded, then stored or transmitted, then, later, decoded; in principle, this can slow a system down by as much as a factor of three. If the system has reasonable performance in the first place, this may not be too much of a problem, but it certainly *can* be a problem. Encrypted data may take more storage than plain text; this can be a problem if storage is at a premium. (Eventually, storage *always* is at a premium; that is why people buy so many "hard disks." Throughout the history of informatics, memory size, storage capacity, and operating speed have been, or very rapidly have become, "insufficient." Encryption [or a database management system] causes storage to become a limitation a lot faster than it might without such "storage-eaters.")

Somehow, the key needed to read encrypted data must be given to the intended user. The method of communicating such keys must be extremely secure, or encryption using the keys is useless. However, this is the reverse of the microcomputer problem mentioned in Section 11.2.2; far fewer keys need to be transmitted, and far less often, than encrypted data. Protection which would not be cost-effective in bulk can be cost-effective for infrequent short messages such as keys.

The best advice on encryption would be to be sure that extremely sensitive material (for example, tables of passwords and authorization codes, or encryption keys during transmission) is encrypted. Most material is not that sensitive and probably should not be encrypted. The risk analysis outlined in the first two chapters of this text should have identified the really sensitive material. This advice will change as costs change and the cost-effectiveness of encryption changes. Costs are dropping, and in the near future it may be cost-effective to encrypt basically everything.

In some cases, there may be no option: for example, United States law requires banks with automated teller devices to utilize DES or better encryption by 1989. Sometimes the no-option works the other way: it may be unlawful to take any computer containing a DES chip into a Soviet-bloc country, for example.

11.1.5 Future Developments

The International Standards Organization (ISO) was referred to in the previous chapter. The ISO has working groups examining the area of cryptography and encryption, particularly "SC20" committees.

With the lack of public key modes of operation, and the anticipation that the United States National Security Agency may not endorse DES past 1988, activity in SC20 and changes in the near future seem assured. Developments in Japan are becoming significant as well.

11.2 HARDWARE

11.2.1 Computer Room Considerations

Security considerations for large computer installations generally amount to providing a proper environment for the equipment and controlling access. Since there usually is only one large installation per company, a special room is a normal solution. The room can be designed with access control and special equipment needs in mind.

Computer rooms need careful design consideration, and it is wise to engage professional advice. It usually is necessary to remodel normal office environments substantially to create a good computer room.

First, the room for a large minicomputer or a mainframe probably needs to be an environmentally controlled area. The equipment generates heat and has special cooling needs. Numerous cables connect the various pieces of hardware, and they have to be located somewhere that people won't trip over them. Cables carrying significant power are a fire hazard as well, and special monitoring systems may be needed (and are available). A common solution to this need has been a raised floor, with cables (and often chilled air) running underneath. False ceilings can represent an exposure; fire and access control partitions should extend all the way to the real ceiling, not leave a gap above a false ceiling. Acoustic materials are needed in the construction, since many of the peripherals generate considerable noise.

Be certain that the floor of the proposed room can withstand the weight of all equipment, people, and supplies which might be in the room at once.

The computer room should be located away from an outside wall, if possible. Vehicles do crash through walls and do the contents no good. Also, any attempts to eavesdrop are more difficult if several walls intervene.

In the past, the computer was a "showpiece" for many companies; the computer room was on display behind glass windows. The firebombing incident in Montreal, and other incidents, have changed this. The computer needs physical protection. There should be good locks on doors, and there should be a supplies storage area which can be accessed without also accessing the computer itself (so personnel without security authorization can replenish supplies).

Combustible supplies such as large amounts of paper should not be in the computer room itself. Ideally, the supply room should be isolated from the computer room by fire protection barriers.

The environment in the computer room should be isolated from the building. In particular, ventilation and air conditioning systems are common avenues for the spread of fires; the computer should have its own system. Environment control for the computer itself will vary depending on the specific equipment.

Do not overlook the location of air intakes and exhausts for the computer room. Any environment system would have a problem if the intake is near a loading dock and sucks in Diesel exhaust, for example.

Although they are cost-effective in reducing noise, carpets, even the anti-static variety, generate dust and do not belong near computers.

If there is a media library for tapes and disk packs, it should have its own fire control, separate from the computer. Many computer media are fairly serious fire hazards; it's not easy to ignite a reel of magnetic tape, but if one succeeds, the resulting fire is very difficult to extinguish.

The best fire control for a computer room may be a Halon system as mentioned in Chapter 8. Opinions vary on this: fire departments believe water is the best extinguisher, and that clean water does less damage even to computers than other consequences of a fire. Most computer centers use Halon.

Smoking should not be permitted in the computer room, nor in the supplies or media storage areas.

Even if sensitive data and eavesdropping are not issues, a computer room should be shielded from radio frequency interference (RFI). Examples have been given previously of some consequences of unwanted signals coming into a computer such as an industrial robot controller. Modern cities are places of substantial electronic pollution. Grounded wire mesh on all sides of the computer room works well. Do not forget that any metal going through the mesh may act as an antenna: this includes power supply wiring, ventilation ducts, water pipes, window frames, possible hangers for false ceilings, telephone lines, and other items often overlooked.

It may be cost-effective to include an uninterruptible power supply (UPS) (see also Chapter 6) for the computer, depending on the consequences of an interruption. Details of power requirements for the equipment and the consequences of various lengths of downtime will determine what sort of UPS is needed.

11.2.2 Special Microcomputer Problems

Microcomputers have become a dominant force in informatics, and in offices in general. Microcomputers pose a number of security exposures which are not present, or not present to the same extent, in mainframes or minicomputers.

Perhaps the primary difference between personal computers and mainframes is that there are *many* microcomputers. There are at least millions in use, and over four million new units are sold each year. The sort of control which can be enforced with mainframes or other systems located in a small number of locations would be prohibitively expensive applied to all locations where there are micros. Yet, the value of the data stored in a microcomputer may be no less than that of data stored on a mainframe. Offsetting this somewhat is that microcomputers are relatively cheap; the loss of a stolen microcomputer is in the low thousands of dollars rather than a million or more dollars if a mainframe were stolen. Security specialists do not have any universal solutions for these exposures, particularly data exposure (for example, there is so far no practical method of stopping "piracy," or unauthorized copying of diskettes, in any environment at all extended).

One solution which has merit in many cases is to identify which data and programs are truly sensitive, and then apply more stringent control measures, such as locked doors and file storage areas, to the micros which work with those data. Data encryption can be a help as well.

By their nature, microcomputers are small, and they normally are used for individuals (indeed, "personal computers" may be a more accurate name than microcomputers). This means two things: first, micros are installed in normal office areas rather than in well-secured central operations areas. Offices are not as secure, and the environment (temperature, humidity, static, etc.) is not as controlled. Second, micros can be picked up and carried away, which is not a common problem with mainframes.

The normal office is not a very secure place, even when there is only one person per office and there is a door to lock. Most office doors have no locks, and most of the locks which are installed can be opened faster with a credit card than with a key. Obviously, better locks can help minimize unauthorized entry. Applying the "rings of protection" concept, one would try for reasonable building security, perhaps guards and alarm systems. Then there should be reasonably good locks on the doors of offices containing microcomputers (and barriers to prevent people coming past doors and over walls through the false ceilings in most buildings; these barriers may also help prevent the spread of fires). As a final ring of protection, the microcomputer itself can be attached to the desk. Even if the attachment does not lock, it takes time to detach, and time is a valuable commodity for a thief.

In environments where microcomputers must be accessible to the public, such as educational institutions, another alternative is available for physical protection. Faced with the problem of equipment disappearing from labs, staff at the University of Victoria developed an inexpensive cabling system, which includes (optional) monitors of various sorts to report on disturbance of the equipment protected. A number of universities in the United States and Canada have adopted this system.

It is a good idea to install anti-static carpeting in offices containing microcomputers. In climates with harsh winters, inside conditions may be very dry in winter, and static can be a real problem. Many solutions of various types (and effectiveness) are available for controlling static problems.

Otherwise, as a rule microcomputers have been designed by their manufacturers to withstand normal "people" environments. While this has not always been true, today any good-quality micro will be "comfortable" in any environment people find comfortable. Even things like spilled coffee are not likely to be a disaster any longer; product improvement and competition has led to things like rubber shields under keys on entry boards. (It still isn't a good idea to eat or drink or smoke near *any* computer, however; diskettes are *very* vulnerable, and things like peripherals [such as some printers] may contain sensitive exposed machinery.)

Microcomputer systems using the standard Microsoft Corporation operating systems are single-user systems. There is no way to prevent access to the system if someone has access to the computer itself. Locking up data and program diskettes can help, but "hard disks" are becoming more popular as the prices drop, and they contain the operating system. As noted in previous chapters, the DELETE function often does not actually erase data; it remains available for possible browsing (see Chapter 12) until overwritten. Encryption can help to solve this access problem: there are software and hardware products available which will allow the micro user to encrypt data and program files. A penetrator would have to have the key diskette, or magnetic card, or whatever is used in an individual system. (As with other encryption, the user must not forget or lose the key, or the system will be unavailable to him or her as well.) Some computers come with keys; they must be unlocked before they can be used. This may be as useful as encryption, and more likely to be used (and does not degrade system performance).

The newer, 386 chip-based computers, combined with announced operating systems being developed by Microsoft and IBM, will support more than one user simultaneously. Increased exposure, and a need to apply the same sort of controls as now common on mainframes, can be expected as a consequence.

11.3 NEW TERMS

New terms introduced or defined in this chapter include:

Ciphertext
Cryptography
Data Encryption Standard (DES)
Decryption
Encryption
Encryption key
Plaintext
Private key system
Public key system

11.4 QUESTIONS

11.1   Define: encryption, decryption, encryption key

11.2   What are the major advantages and disadvantages of using encryption?

11.3   You are an industrial spy who wants to get the encryption key that will allow you to read sensitive material you can record easily from the signal spilling over the dish in a satellite downlink. What would your best strategy be?

11.4   Why should you not have large glass display windows to show off the company's latest $30 million supercomputer?

11.5   Your company doesn't have any really sensitive data on the computer, and there are no communication links to the outside. Why bother to shield the computer room from RFI?

11.6   What is the most common loss experience involving microcomputers? Why is this the case?

Chapter 12

SOFTWARE AND OPERATING SYSTEM CONTROLS

INTRODUCTION

This chapter contains three major sections: operating system security, system and program development controls, and some consideration of controls in the maintenance process (that is, keeping the system going properly).

The chapter does not delve deeply into the details of operating system security; that is an extremely technical subject involving sophisticated mathematics. The purpose of this chapter is to present an outline of the history of the development of the "secure operating system" concept, particularly as it relates to the "kernel" concept. (This is not the same "kernel" which refers to the memory-resident part of an operating system; see below for more). Over time, guidelines and standards for secure operating systems have been developed; the most important of these is mentioned. (While detailed technical material is avoided, the reader will benefit from a familiarity with operating systems and how they are designed and function.)

A few of the more common methods of penetrating operating systems security which have been observed are reviewed, with comments on the simplest methods of foiling these common penetration attempts. One of the easiest and most common methods of helping improve security involves password control systems. Some discussion of this topic, including some of the ways the method is implemented poorly and why, is presented.

There are many excellent texts in the area of system and program development. Most of them concentrate on using development methodologies to control the work involved, with perhaps a comment on security. It has been pointed out already that "bugs" are by far the worst security problem; system and program development methodologies as ways to improve security, partly by avoiding bugs, are presented here. Management of a development effort is not treated in much detail since the purpose in this text is to review security and control implications. (It is assumed that readers are familiar with at least one development methodology, and with structured programming and systems concepts.)

As with development, there are excellent references which go into detail about maintenance of existing systems; this text assumes the reader has some familiarity with the area. The coverage of maintenance here is from a security and control viewpoint, not from a perspective of "how to manage maintenance."

Since maintenance involves many of the same things as development (when maintenance is done properly, that is), issues common to both are covered in whichever section is convenient, and may not be repeated in the other section. This text espouses the principle that maintenance is a "mini-development," and that a maintenance effort should follow much the same problem definition, justification, analysis, design, testing, and implementation steps as a development would (in the case of maintenance, many things legitimately can be shortened, however).

12.1 SECURE OPERATING SYSTEMS

12.1.1 History

The history of concern for the security of operating systems follows closely the history of increasing accessibility of computer systems. As time-sharing became common, it became clear that security of some sort was needed to protect users from each others' activities, whether intentional or accidental. Paging systems with protection keys, and virtual storage mechanisms, partially addressed the security need. As charging systems for the use of computer resources became more common, increased security began to be seen as a real need. The explosion of millions of people with training in computer programming, plus the enormous increase in accessibility provided by more and more sophisticated communications, plus the easy availability of significant computer power in the form of microcomputers, has led to several major efforts to address the problem of security in operating systems, and in systems in general.

In the early operating systems, it was all too easy to penetrate the system. The growth of more capable systems usually involved more complexity; the problem of security got worse, as it turned out that very complex systems are not more secure than simpler ones (rather the reverse, usually). Adding communications capability to complex systems allowed many more people the opportunity to try to penetrate already shaky security, and the problem continued to worsen.

It is reasonably well established by now that complex operating systems, which did not have security as a major design factor, are inherently insecure. Security packages installed with already-developed operating systems, such as IBM's Resource Access Control Facility (RACF), are "add-ons" and help a lot. Unfortunately, the problem is not soluble in general; the add-ons make access from outside and sometimes access inside (legitimate users of the system accessing other users' files, for example) more difficult, but they do not make an originally non-secure system into a secure one.

More than one investigator has concluded that any operating system which allows programming is not secure and cannot be secured; a group in the Netherlands has made a name by publishing successful penetration methods for each new "fix" as it came out. Penetration methods such as those outlined in Section 12.1.4 worked on all systems, and still work on all too many systems.

The picture is not totally bleak, however. While operating systems which were not designed for secure operation cannot be made completely secure, the problem has been known for some time. New operating systems designed since about the mid-1970's have had consideration of security as a significant design parameter, and mainframe operating systems which are in common use on today's fourth and fifth generation computers are fairly good. Some minicomputer operating systems are reasonably secure as well. (This is not true now for most personal computer operating systems or for all minicomputer systems, however. With the latest machines introduced, and current developments in operating system software for microcomputers, the situation may improve for personal computers as well.)

Results of investigations into the problems of operating system security, along with a number of well-publicized problems, have led interested parties such as accountants and others to examine security in other aspects of organizations. If the operating system is inherently not secure, then "compensating controls" in other parts of the information system to a large extent can make up for the lack. A major thrust of this book is that the security problem is not primarily a technical one, and that good organizational measures, such as recommended previously, can be much more important than technical details.

The investigations into operating system security have been fruitful as well. The concepts of "security kernel" designs and of "trusted computer" systems have led to design of systems which are provably secure, and which have not been penetrated. These are covered in the next section.

Absolute security probably is impossible. Reasonable security combined with reasonably "user-friendly" and usable computer-based information systems is achievable and has been achieved. Most modern computers can be penetrated, but it is much more difficult than it was, and the penetration is likely to be detected by other controls in the information system. Future systems designed for security in the first place will be quite secure indeed. The largest risk today is posed by the 41% of organizations with no security at all, and by general lack of appreciation of the importance of security in the profession and by senior management. Education and reasonable professional standards can help solve this kind of problem.

12.1.2 Concepts: Capabilities, Reference Validations, Kernels

12.1.2.1 Secure Kernels

The word "kernel" has been used for some time to denote the part of the operating system which is memory resident at all times (as contrasted to less-used parts that are paged in and out as needed). The word has a different meaning in the context of secure operating system design.

In a secure system, the **kernel** is a small module which is a portion of the operating system. *All* references to information and *all* changes to authorizations must pass through the kernel. The kernel needs to meet three basic conditions:

1.   Completeness

All accesses to information must go through the kernel.

2.   Isolation

The kernel itself must be totally protected from any form of unauthorized access or alteration.

3.   Verifiability

The kernel must be small and simple enough that it can be proven that the kernel meets design specifications.

Development and verification of the security kernel uses mathematical concepts and techniques which are beyond the scope of this text. The development normally includes four important factors:

1.   A *mathematical model* defines the rules for demonstrating that system security is preserved.

2.   *Formal specifications* bridge the gap between the mathematical model and actual implementation of the kernel. The formal specifications also must be proven mathematically.

3.   The kernel is implemented in a *high-order language* which can be verified for correctness mathematically. (This does not mean a "high-level language" such as COBOL or ADA; see below.)

4.   *Implementation* of the kernel, using the three elements above, is verified mathematically.

If the three basic conditions are met, and all four elements listed above are present, then the kernel may be considered secure. Since the kernel has been verified, and cannot be changed without authorization, and all references must pass through the kernel, the operating system is secure.

There are two points which need to be mentioned here:

First, there are reasons in mathematics to question the applicability of this sort of proof.

Second, whether the mathematics is valid or not, using a kernel involves greatly increased system overhead.

In theory, the mathematical verification is itself subject to at least some question. The Gödel work on mathematical consistency indicates some theoretical reasons for this concern. (*Gödel's Proof*, by Ernest Nagel and James Newman, New York University Press, 1967, is a readable treatment of Gödel's work for interested readers with a mathematical background.) It is doubtful whether this theoretical possibility has real existence, but it cannot be determined mathematically, and some question must remain.

The high-order language mentioned must be one of a class of mathematically-provable languages which has been developed as part of research into provability of program correctness. These languages are developed by creating canonical forms which are small enough to be proven, then combining the canonical forms into more complex language components, using mathematically provable methods such as logical operators. No commonly used computer language meets the provability criterion. ALGOL 68 may have come closest, but it failed to win commercial acceptance at least in North America.

Even neglecting this rather esoteric consideration, there remains the problem of the correctness of the mathematical model itself. Using any computer language, provable or not, to write a program amounts to creating a mathematical model of the process being programmed. There is an extensive history of mathematical models which have proven incorrect or incomplete even after extensive use; Newton's theory of gravitation or Euclidian geometry are examples. The history of incorrect or incomplete computer programs probably includes every program of significant size ever written.

More pragmatically, there is considerable overhead in having all references to any information go through the kernel. Security is gained at the expense of system performance. Given the trend of cheaper hardware, it may be more cost-effective to ensure security by providing non-communicating, separate systems for such things as development, than to have the production machine slowed by a kernel approach.

12.1.2.2 *Reference Validations and Capabilities*

For the purposes of this text, *reference validation* and *capabilities* can be understood sufficiently by considering them as part of a system with a security kernel. (The kernel includes reference validation and may use capabilities and thus is "stronger" than reference validation or capabilities alone -- and also involves more overhead.)

One form of reference validation is the storage protection key normally implemented in any paging system. Simplifying, if a process trying to make a reference does not have the proper protect key, the reference is denied (in this case, by the kernel). More complex kinds of reference validation exist.

Capabilities are "tokens" that may be compared to storage protect keys or perhaps to a ticket to enter various areas in a major sporting event. Capabilities are more encompassing than protection keys: they include not only the right to access something, but also what kinds of access are permitted. *Every* physically or logically possible action inside the computer is associated with a capability (under control of the security kernel, capabilities are created, modified, and sometimes revoked, as the computer functions). A capability in computer terms might include information as to whether what is referenced can be *read, written, executed,* or *erased.* For example, a process might have execute capability only for an object module: the process is not allowed to read the object code, erase it, or change it; it can only be run. Another process, presumably with more restricted access itself, may be able to change the module but not to erase it. (As an analogy, a sporting event ticket may include access to public viewing areas but not to locker rooms. The ticket would not grant the holder a capability to do other than watch the game. A reporter, on the other hand, would have greater access privileges and the capability to interview athletes, perhaps only in the locker room or perhaps on the field's sidelines.)

The security kernel is responsible to examine the capability presented by a process attempting to access information. The kernel ensures that only actions permitted to processes with that capability (reference, changing, deletion, running a process, and so on) can occur, and that the capability is permitted by the characteristics of the information referenced. (The information may not have the characteristic of permitting execution even if the process's capability includes execution, for example.) This is *reference validation*.

12.1.3 Present Guidelines and Standards

"Trusted computer systems" are

> operating systems (including the underlying hardware base) capable of preventing users from accessing more information than that to which they are authorized (Nibaldi, G. H., *Proposed Technical Evaluation Criteria for Trusted Computer Systems*, M79-225, Contract No. AF 19268-80-C-0001, Mitre Corporation, Bedford, Massachusetts, Oct. 25, 1979).

The task of certifying computer systems as "trusted," under the published Department of Defense (DOD) criteria, has proven to be difficult. The problem seems to be that commercial operating systems simply are too complex to be tested exhaustively, and since they were not designed using security kernel or other mathematical concepts, they cannot be proven mathematically with tools now available. Research continues.

The DOD criteria referred to in the previous paragraph are specified in a publication produced in 1983 [DOD 1983]. They define evaluation classes ranging from Division D "minimal protection" to C "Discretionary protection (need-to-know)," then B "Mandatory protection," to Division A "Verified protection -- Utilizes formal verification procedures to assure protection of mandatory and discretionary controls." Each level includes all protection features found in every lower level. As noted above, Division A verification has proven a difficult problem.

Other classification schemes exist; for purposes of this text this example is sufficient. Security professionals need to know about the existence of such standards and probably will encounter the DOD standard if they encounter any.

12.1.4 Common Penetration Methods

Over time, a number of methods have been used to penetrate operating systems. Many operating systems share common flaws which make penetration easier than it should be. Some of these flaws are:

1.   Encryption: Lists of sensitive data such as the table of account and password identifications should be encrypted, so that anyone who manages to access the files cannot read them. This is not always done.

2.   Implementation: There may be a well-designed security system provided in the operating system but not used by the organization, or not implemented properly.

3.   Implied sharing: The system may place sensitive operating system control information in the user's workspace; under some conditions, the user may be able to read this. (For example, a program error, perhaps deliberately induced, that causes a memory dump may cause a printout of everything in the workspace, including anything the operating system may have stored there.)

4.   Legality checking: the system may not check on the parameters a user supplies it.

5.   Line disconnect: The user in a time sharing or other remote system mode may hang up without disconnecting; another user may be able to get in without proper validation. Not all systems "hang up" properly when a line is disconnected.

6.   Operator carelessness: Operators may inadvertently mount the wrong disk packs or tapes; some cases have been reported where penetrators telephoned the operator and were able to trick the operator into giving out sensitive information.

7.   Passwords: Passwords may not be used, they may be simple to guess, or the system may allow repeated attempts. (A microcomputer easily can be programmed to try to log on by repeatedly selecting passwords from a list.) The next section looks at passwords in more detail.

8.   Repetition: Systems may allow users an indefinite number of attempts to sign on, thus allowing use of a microcomputer and repeated guesses. The system should disconnect or hang up after some small number of unsuccessful attempts, and the event should be reported to the operator or security officer.

9.   Shielding: As noted in Chapter 10, wires emit signals which can be detected and analyzed. Unshielded lines with non-encrypted data are a significant exposure in many systems.

10.   Waste: sensitive printouts may be discarded; more than one system has been penetrated by people who found lists of user identification and passwords in a waste container.

Several penetration methods have been used many times to cause successful system penetration. Many of the common methods make use of the flaws noted above. Unfortunately, it still is very common to find that systems are vulnerable to these methods, even though the methods are well-known and often easy to defeat. A security specialist should work with information systems personnel to ensure that at least these common "holes" are plugged.

1.   Between lines: a special terminal is used to tap into the communication line used by a legitimate user while the user is not active. Terminals should never be left signed on and unattended, and lines should be shielded.

2.   Browsing: The user searches through the computer system, or through files, attempting to locate sensitive information. Such action is controllable through file and other access controls. Commonly, a table listing what the user may access is created, and the user is restricted to only those accesses. Files may be given individual passwords in some systems.

3.   Denial of use: the user is able to "crash" the system, or hang it up by putting a program into an endless loop. At least one commercial time-sharing system allowed jobs to submit other jobs; it was possible on that system (by submitting a job that submits itself) to fill up the job queue with jobs waiting to be processed so that the computer became unavailable to anyone else.

4.   Hidden code: programs may contain undocumented code which does things other than what is described in the manuals. Poorly controlled maintenance often allows an opportunity for a programmer to insert a routine which should not be in the program. A program library and controls over maintenance will make this difficult or impossible.

5.   Interrupts: a penetrator may cause program or system interrupts; some operating systems allow such a user to enter a privileged mode with more access than usual, while processing an interrupt.

6.   Line disconnect: the user signs off, or the line "goes down," but the system has not yet acknowledged and terminated the user's session. Until this termination occurs, another user may be able to use the session.

7.   Masquerade: the penetrator obtains identification and passwords and signs on with someone else's account. A user pretending to be someone else by grabbing a line as noted above, is a form of masquerade.

8.   Operator deception: a penetrator may, for example, convince an operator to divulge a password (perhaps by claiming to have just changed the password and miskeyed the new one).

9.   Piggyback: the penetrator intercepts a communication line and substitutes his or her own messages to the legitimate user and/or to the system. (For example, simulates the signon program and thus gets the user to give out identification and password information.)

10.   Salami technique (not strictly an operating system penetration, but a common fraud): the classic example is a program which accumulates all roundoff figures for a bank's loan calculations into one account. Each "slice" is less than 1/2 cent and is not noticeable; over thousands of accounts the cumulative effect can be large.

11.   Trojan horse: this is a generic name for the "hidden code" penetration method. Something is in a program that is not supposed to be there, which causes sensitive data to be available. Or, the program does not do what it is supposed to; the name is misleading. It is possible to put a Trojan horse into a system which would, for example, simulate the logon messages; after collecting user data the Trojan horse would put the data somewhere accessible to the perpetrator and then remove itself from the system.

This is not an exhaustive list; it only is some of the more common penetration methods. The cures generally are rather obvious and often do not cost much money or degrade performance.

12.1.5 Password Control Mechanisms

One of the easiest and most effective access control methods is passwords. The user is assigned an identification and then is assigned or creates a password; the system will not allow logon, or file access, or generally access to password-protected resources, without the correct identification and password. Most multi-user systems have this capability. Often, it is not used, or is used improperly.

Some general rules about passwords should be obvious but are often violated:

1.   Do not allow repeated attempts. Disconnect after some small number of unsuccessful tries.

2.   Log unsuccessful signon attempts and system disconnections.

3.   Make sure someone reviews the log and follows up on patterns.

4.   Never write down a password and account together, never tape a password to a terminal or to the phone list on a desk "pull-out shelf," or in a file folder labelled "passwords," or in any other obvious place.

5.   Select unusual passwords which are several characters long; preferably at least eight characters. Use mixed alphabetic and numeric data for passwords to make them harder to guess. (*Any* actual word may be in a spelling dictionary, and a microcomputer can be programmed to try using words from such a dictionary as password guesses.) Do not use the user identification account number or personal names.

6.   Change passwords frequently.

7.   Passwords should be easy to remember but hard to guess correctly.

8.   Never tell anyone else your password; change it immediately after the other's use if there is a legitimate need to tell someone else.

9.   Do not allow others to watch while you key in a password.

10.   The system should not display the password; the screen should display nothing at all, or overstrike characters, or some other means to be sure the identification is not visible.

11.   Job streams which are not stored in a secure manner should not contain signon information. This applies particularly to personal computers, where it is common to store such data in "macros" so the user presses only one key for commonly accessed services. (It once was common to see card decks containing a sign-on card, with identification and password information, stored in a publicly accessible area along with the output from the run; signon information in macros is a more modern equivalent.)

12.   Passwords assigned to users must be sent via secure transmission methods.

13.   Password tables should be encrypted.

Passwords are convenient, relatively cheap ways to improve on system access security, when used properly. In practice, their use helps, but people defeat the system by carelessness or improper use in all too many instances. The organizational climate should stress proper use of passwords, and reminders need to be frequent.

Passwords may be chosen in any of a number of ways. Today, most systems allow users to choose their own. If the user chooses the password, it should be chosen to be unusual. Lists with titles like "The One Hundred Most Common Passwords" are published in many places; reproducing such a list and posting it may discourage users from trying their own "unique" ideas. One method which yields reasonably good passwords which are hard to guess, is:

Choose two words or numbers which are easy to remember.

Using some rule, combine them. One possible rule is to use alternate letters.

Using this method, one might select, say "1066" and "ABCD." The resulting password would be A1B0C6D6, which is much less obvious than either of the easily remembered sequences. Other sequences -- for instance, height and maternal grandmothers' maiden initials -- may serve the need to be easily remembered but create a good password when combined.

In principle, passwords created by the system using a random number generator are more secure; in practice, people are less likely to remember nonsense, and thus more likely to write down the password. The same applies to long passwords: the longer, the more secure and the more difficult to remember. The method described in the previous paragraph has the virtue that the resulting password looks like nonsense and is hard to guess, but the components and combining rule are easy for the user to remember; thus the user is less likely to write it down.

If the system generates a password, it must be communicated to the user somehow. The transmission channel is subject to compromise, from human error (lost mail) to eavesdropping through communication taps. Whether using system generated passwords is a good idea depends on the circumstances.

A system which has good communications security, which uses encryption when appropriate, and which has users making proper use of password controls, is very difficult to access without authority.

12.2 SOFTWARE CONTROLS: DEVELOPMENT

12.2.1 The Real Problem: Bugs

"Bugs" are things which go wrong with information and other systems. The term "computer bug" has been attributed to a technician finding a dead moth crushed between the relay contacts of a very early digital computer, which had caused the computer to malfunction. "Debugging" is the process of removing bugs.

Repeatedly in this text, it has been stressed that by far the largest security exposures are errors and lack of training, not actual deliberate attempts to compromise information systems. When a systems analyst makes an error in describing the proposed system, or when a user forgets that seemingly insignificant but critical item, an error has occurred. This may lead to a system "bug." When a programmer writes the wrong code by error, this is a program bug. If all systems analysts were perfect, and all programmers always wrote perfect code, and all users really knew exactly what they needed, then there might be no bugs. In the real world, no one is perfect, and errors occur.

As much as 85% of the total effort in a large data processing shop may be dedicated to "maintenance." Maintenance includes changing programs to reflect new requirements and changed circumstances (and this kind of maintenance will be covered later in this chapter). Most maintenance, unfortunately, consists of fixing problems which should not have been allowed to occur in the first place.

From a security and control standpoint, the best idea is to avoid having errors in the systems or programs at all. The best time to effect this is as early as possible in the development process; fixing a system design error may cost easily 1000 times as much during the "maintenance" period as it would during the design effort and before any code is written.

A tool which has been developed to help with avoiding errors initially, is structured methodologies: so-called "structured programming" and "structured analysis."

12.2.2 Structured Methods

Structured analysis and structured programming were developed in the 1970's by Constantine and Yourdon, among others. They used "data flow diagrams," and consideration of certain mathematical characteristics of the graphs formed by data flow diagrams, to derive principles which, if followed, minimize the chances of inserting bugs into systems and programs in the first place, and minimize the problems in removing them when discovered. Recently, graphics capabilities of reasonably affordable computers have reached the point that data flow diagrams, linked with data element definitions or data dictionaries, can be handled with a microcomputer in much the same way as numeric data works with a spreadsheet, or a word processor handles text.

In essence, structured analysis involves identifying activities performed by an organization and the data flows which drive those "processes" (this process is not the same as the technical term used above in discussing secure operating systems). The data flows contain data elements, and when the data flows and data elements are defined, a "data dictionary" results. Programs are written using modular code corresponding to processes (at a very detailed level, of course), and using the data dictionary developed. Modules, in systems or in programs, should not affect each other ("low coupling") and should be reasonably self-contained and do one single logical thing ("high cohesion").

When systems are designed, and programs written, using these structured concepts, certain mathematical developments apply (coupling and cohesionare English expressions of some of these mathematical concepts from set and graph theory), and programs and systems can be treated to proofs of correctness, mathematical simplifications, and other methods which avoid some of the human problems that make correct systems and programs so difficult to create.

Perhaps most importantly of all, any *defined* means of creating systems, particularly one with a mathematical basis such as structured analysis, allows one to set standards, measure performance against those standards, and correct problems. In principle, an organization should have a business plan, which breaks down into systems and subsystems, which have systems definitions, which are implemented using structured programming techniques. The logical linkage is maintained; senior and user management function within defined responsibilities; users are ensured to be involved in system design and testing; and excellent systems with minimal future problems will be created. (This ideal is not likely ever to be achieved in practice.)

The security personnel's main involvement in this sort of process, which really is the domain of information system management, would be to help ensure that methodologies are followed, approvals requested, procedures in place, and so on. EDP auditors will be allies of security personnel in this area; they are trained to look at such methodologies, or lack of them, during an audit. Involvement of auditors and security personnel during the design of system controls may lead to much better controlled and more secure systems.

12.2.3 Program Library/Librarian

A control which helps keep intruders and unauthorized changes away from systems under development as well as existing systems, is the use of a program library, usually computer-maintained, and a program librarian whose responsibility it is to ensure that the program library is maintained.

All copies of data dictionaries, programs, load modules, and documentation would be under the control of the program librarian (in principle; in practice people will retain working copies of some documentation). The program librarian has the responsibility to ensure that programs are not added to the production library until they are properly tested and authorized. Programmers should not be allowed access to production programs; only the program librarian should be able to alter any production program. Thus unauthorized alterations are much less likely.

Whether done by computer or manually, a program library needs to hold *current* versions of programs and documentation. It needs to hold a record of changes made, by whom, when, authorized by whom, and what the changes are. Test data used to verify that changes are done correctly, and user signoffs indicating correct testing, should be in this library. Much of this can be done nearly automatically when the library is automated, and such an automated program library is highly recommended for any installation of significant size.

12.2.4 Data Dictionary as a Control

When developing programs, programmers may wish, or be forced, to invent names for data elements which are common among several programs. The data dictionary, whether as part of a database management system or as part of a program library, is simply a listing of every data element used in any program, with the data element characteristics, a cross-reference of what programs use the data element and what files it is in, and similar data.

The data dictionary serves as a control, particularly in conjunction with a program library, when programmers are required to use variable names from the program library. This ensures that all programmers use the same name (allowing changes to an element to be made easily, perhaps even automatically, in many programs written by different people), and that there is control over creation of new names (the program librarian).

If the program library is automated, a data dictionary normally will allow copying of definitions into new programs, which saves time and minimizes errors. The same holds true for standard modules in a program library.

12.2.5 Conversion and Implementation

Every new system must be implemented. Most new systems require conversion of data, sometimes a great deal of data, from the format used in a previous system to a new format for the new system. *After thorough testing*, and *user sign-off* that the test system works as it should, conversion can begin.

Controls which applied to the data before the conversion process must be reviewed and the equivalent controls maintained during the conversion. Data entered into the new system must be as complete and as accurate as previously, and converted or new data must retain the integrity of the previous system (at least; ideally, the new system will have higher standards).

During testing and implementation, parallel runs are common. In parallel running, the same data are presented to both systems; hopefully, the same results will be produced, unless different results were part of the design. In practice, results will vary. Do not assume that the new system is in error. As noted in the previous sections, a carefully constructed new system will contain few errors; it is more probable (as much as 90% more) that the discrepancy is caused by an error in the old system which was never discovered. User resistance to acknowledging this is common, and testers need to be prepared to prove their case.

12.3 SOFTWARE CONTROLS: MAINTENANCE

12.3.1 Separation of Duties

Maintenance programming involves changing production programs to fix errors, and modifying programs to produce different results for many reasons (government regulations or withholding tax changes, for example). To retain control over system security, some separations of duties are needed.

Operators should not be programmers, and should not be able to change programs. Programmers should not be able to change production programs directly. Systems analysts normally need not have any access at all to programs, particularly production programs. Users should not have any access to the computer room or to programs. Program librarians are strongly indicated as a control over this area.

The *Computer Control Guidelines, Second Edition* [CICA 1986] indicates that the following roles are incompatible and should be performed by different people or groups:

1.   Users
2.   Information system development
3.   Information systems processing
4.   Information systems support

Rules such as those given in this section may be difficult or impossible for smaller organizations, where there are fewer staff. In a case where segregation is not possible or is prohibitively costly, compensating controls should exist elsewhere. An example could be a "one person shop," where the information systems manager is also the analyst, programmer, and operator. There is no control other than such things as professional certificates in this case; however, if this person has no access to financial assets and cannot cause inventory to be diverted, a compensating control exists which lessens the exposure. A security specialist or at least an accountant should review such situations, to ensure that reasonable control is maintained.

12.3.2 Testing Controls

All changes to any production system need to be tested. The user management has the responsibility for the user organization's data, and user management should be required to sign off the results of tests. The program librarian should retain the test data used during implementation of the system, which was the basis for user acceptance signoff; this test data bank can be used to test modifications to be sure the system still works as intended after the changes.

Testing never should be done with production data or files. In a parallel run, a separate copy of production data should be used, with copies of master files rather than production versions. Some organizations go so far as to have a separate computer for testing, or to rent time on someone else's machine. (This can be combined with a test of contingency backup arrangements, thus doing two good things with one action.)

12.3.3 Change Control

One of the common methods to compromise systems has been to insert code into production programs that does something other than what the program is supposed to do (decrease one person's loan account balance, or increase the checking account balance, for example). A change control mechanism needs to be in place which ensures that all changes are:

1.   Authorized
2.   Tested to ensure correctness
3.   Recorded

As noted in 12.3.1, programmers never should have access to production programs, nor should they be allowed to make changes without proper recording and authorization. The best way to ensure this is to use a program library and librarian, plus proper logs and approval forms. The change needs to be *requested*; the change must be *done*; the change must be *documented* in program comments, manuals, operating instructions, and wherever else necessary; the change must be *tested*; the production program must be *modified*. All these events need *recording* and *authorization*.

In some organizations, programmers are not allowed to initiate change requests; the request must come from the user. This can be cumbersome, but it provides an excellent level of control.

There always will be need from time to time for emergency changes. The times will be few if the system is well-designed and tested, but no perfect computer systems have been reported yet. Controls are subject to being relaxed during such events. The Security Officer should work with user and information systems management to ensure that control is maintained as far as possible during emergency modifications, and that emergencies are logged for later review by senior management. Contingency plans (Chapter 8) need to consider maintenance of as much control as realistically possible.

Ideally, the change process should be a "mini development" process. The development process includes a project proposal, a feasibility study, alternative analysis, system design, program design and construction, testing, approval, implementation, and follow-up. A change to an existing system needs to be considered just as carefully, although some elements of the full system design process may be abbreviated.

A need should be established (the change request), a cost study should consider alternatives, the changes must be planned and program alterations made, the system needs to be tested again using the original test data, etc., and similar sign-off rules apply.

12.4 NEW TERMS

New terms introduced or defined in this chapter include:

Capability
Change control mechanism
Cohesion

Compensating controls
Completeness
Coupling
Data dictionary
Data flow diagrams
IBM's RACF
Incompatible roles
Isolation
Kernel
Operating system flaws:
    Encryption
    Implementation
    Implied sharing
    Legality checking
    Line disconnect
    Operator carelessness
    Passwords
    Repetition
    Shielding
    Waste
Penetration methods:
    Between lines
    Browsing
    Denial of use
    Hidden code
    Interrupts
    Line disconnect
    Masquerade
    Operator deception
    Piggyback
    Salami technique
    Trojan horse
Program library
Reference validation
Structured analysis and structured programming
Trusted computer systems

Verifiability

12.5 QUESTIONS

12.1 List the actions you must take to access your organization's computer. For each action, indicate what, if any, security consideration is involved.

(*Hint*: the actions probably include dialing a phone number -- is it published?; you probably have a user identification and a password -- are they protected? how is the password chosen?)

12.2 A secure system kernel must meet three basic conditions.

(a)   List them.

(b)   For each, give an example of what could happen if the basic condition were *not* met.

12.3 Give an example of a mathematically correct model which does not succeed in the real world.

12.4 Secure operating systems cost more to run due to overhead in things like reference checking. Using concepts from this text, write out, in one page or less, what factors would cause your organization to choose a more secure system, or to accept less security. (That is, what are the common tradeoffs?)

12.5 Why might a data dictionary save an organization money as well as improve security?

12.6 Compare a "Trojan horse" with a "computer virus" (Chapter 10). Does the ISO/OSI framework relate to Trojan horses? to viruses? How?

12.7. (case) Systems Development and Maintenance Audit

Using the case material in Chapter 7, Question 7.5, comment on the client's situation from the standpoint of systems development and maintenance.

Required:

Prepare your initial outline of the report requested by ABC Inc.

Organize your answer under the following headings:

I. Systems Development and Maintenance Control Review

A. Strengths

B. Weaknesses

C. Exposures and Recommended Improvements

Remember that you should concentrate on *systems development* and *maintenance*; other weaknesses/strengths are for other chapters.

SECTION IV: LEGAL ENVIRONMENT AND PROFESSIONALISM

Chapter 13

THE INFORMATION SECURITY
SPECIALIST AND THE LAW

INTRODUCTION

This chapter addresses some of the specifics in a very complex profession, the law, which relate to computer security and controls. Because of the nature of the legal field, and because it is changing rapidly, the style of this chapter is somewhat different from that of the rest of the text. This change is partly to emphasize that legal matters and their relationship to computers comprise a different field, and that any professional working in security areas who comes into significant contact with the law is strongly advised to obtain knowledgeable legal advice.

The material in this chapter was contributed by Martin P. J. Kratz, who manages the Advanced Technology Law Department at Ogilvie and Company, a law firm in Edmonton, Canada.

The purpose of this chapter is to provide a basic framework for the understanding of the role of law in planning, implementing and sustaining information security systems. The information security attorney is one of the partners in the information security strategy for any organization seriously attempting to protect its proprietary assets.

It is important for the information security specialist to understand some basic concepts about a number of diverse areas of law in order to more fully appreciate the design, implementation and execution of a truly comprehensive information security program. This chapter does not purport to provide specific legal advice pertaining to any specific fact situation. Rather, it is intended to introduce the reader to global concepts and establish a framework for the future working relationship between the information security specialist and the information security attorney. To that end, a number of critical legal topics are addressed here. It should be apparent that in an introductory text the devotion of one chapter to this topic cannot hope to address all areas of law which might be relevant to the information security manager. In particular, local variations of general principles and application of general law relating to possession and control of real property, the torts of false arrests, malicious prosecution, the tort libel, slander, conspiracy to injure, interference with advantageous business relationships, conversion, detenue, and such other general areas cannot be adequately dealt with in a space of this size. To that end, the reader is recommended to review current introductory texts in the appropriate areas of law. The topics addressed in this chapter will, rather, be the specialized legal subjects which have and continue to evolve to deal with more difficult problems of protection of intangible assets such as confidential information, data, computer programs or the like.

Most legal systems distinguish between civil laws (that is law governing disputes between individuals) and criminal law (that is law governing disputes between the individual and the State). The purpose of this section is to examine the elements of both systems and thereby highlight some significant differences and approaches in systems of protection of data and information.

The intention is to provide a background for the intelligent assessment of legal options in the design of security systems and also to provide a background to the policy issues which may motivate legislative reform. With this understanding, it is anticipated that the security professional may play an active role in the law reform process and ensure that the development of law in this fast changing industry will be consistent with the needs of that industry.

Related to issues of data and information protection are issues of transborder data flows or transborder information flows. Some of the policy arguments behind the need for free and uninhibited flows of data are reviewed.[1]

As a result, this paper is intended to provide a background to the continuing evolution of legal solutions to information and data protection legislation. If those solutions are to have any meaningful effect on the significant problems of data and information protection, then the security professions must be an informed and fully participating part of the development of those solutions.

The law enforcement official requires access to a wide range of data and materials in conducting an information abuse investigation. Often, privacy legislation is seen as a barrier to access of information which may be useful in the investigation of such criminal conduct. However, such legislation may also serve as a very useful tool in the protection of data and information. In particular, such legislation provides options for enforcement of rights which may better reflect commercial reality. It is important for the security professional to be involved in the development of these remedies so that they can be a real balance between all of the interests involved.

13.1 PLANNING FOR LEGAL ENFORCEMENT ALTERNATIVES

Legal systems provide for rights and obligations and methods of enforcing those rights or obligations. As a result, the legal solutions often play an active role generally only *after* a breach of security has occurred. Competent security planning provides for these legal options *before* a possible breach and therefore minimizes some sources of risk.

13.1.1 Law as a Security Tool

Criminal law generally provides for sanctions, investigated and prosecuted by the State, in relation to certain conduct which the appropriate State's legislative body deems sufficiently reprehensible so as to bring the might of the State's law enforcement machinery against such conduct. Criminal law provides sanctions in the form of monetary fines or deprivation of liberty. The monetary fines are usually paid to the State but, in some circumstances and in some jurisdictions, may be paid to the injured party. The deprivation of liberty can take the form of incarceration or of mandated conduct (such as carrying out certain public service work or the like).

Civil law generally governs a relationship between private individuals, whether persons, bodies corporate, or otherwise. The civil law provides remedies in the form of money compensation for injuries done or court orders to require certain conduct from a particular individual. The civil action is brought by the aggrieved or injured individual against the wrongdoer. The injured party must carry the cost and burden of bringing legal action to redress the wrong done. The individual injured, if successful, also reaps all of the benefits of the award and, from the perspective of the information security specialist, most importantly, the injured party also has absolute control over the law suit. It may be that the information security specialist would rather settle a law suit with a particular wrongdoer so as to achieve broader corporate goals such as the protection of confidential information, reputation of the corporation for security, or other purposes. The criminal action is investigated and prosecuted by the State and generally the victim has little influence over the direction or outcome of that criminal prosecution.

A further factor must be identified as a preliminary matter. Except in very unique cases of threatened wrong doing, the law generally provides remedies to redress an injury which has *already* occurred. That is to say, the law provides compensation for injuries and, hopefully, deters wrongdoers by the smooth and efficient operation of the legal machinery. The law does not generally provide a remedy if no injury has occurred. The law then acts as a shield through its deterrent effect and not in a proactive manner. Where it is vital that the injury does not occur, then the physical and environmental controls described elsewhere in this text must be utilized as additional barriers against the wrongdoer. On the other hand, after a wrongdoer has compromised the physical or environmental security arrangements, the law is generally the only tool available to the information security specialist to minimize the injury already done and to deter, so far as is possible, future wrong doing.

By way of example, signing non-disclosure agreements with one's employees *prior* to giving sensitive or secret data or information to such employees serves as an advance warning or reminder to the employees. Since the relationship has been clearly defined, then there will be less potential risk of abuse of the confidential materials. Secondly, having clearly established these legal relationships, enforcement action is less costly and more certain of a successful outcome.

The information security specialist must not rely on legal mechanisms of security (such as creation of rights or obligations) in lieu of the technical and organizational security measures implemented in the environment. There also must be a sense of practicality and sensitivity introduced which will assist in ensuring that employees respect and understand the obligations under which they work. It may be far easier to deter security risks if employees understand their obligations, respect the information security specialist, and understand the consequences of breach of their obligations.

As noted above, the creation of legal relationships in advance of potential problems is an important and vital role in protecting against breaches of security. Much of the remainder of this chapter will focus on some of the issues raised in establishing those relationships. Risks are reduced by effective advance planning of these relationships, and new options may be established for enforcement. In this way advance planning provides for new arrows in the legal quiver. However, a fundamental problem with many legal solutions is that they become active only *after* the breach. Of course, there are also several actions that can be taken in cases of *anticipated* risk which can be most effective. Interim injunctive relief, for example, may be granted in such cases. Similarly, tracing remedies permit the courts in some jurisdictions to follow confidential information or data into the hands of an innocent third party.

The planning of security systems must take into account all of the legal options available and blend those most applicable to the particular situation into the overall security plan.

13.2 SURVEY OF LEGAL OPTIONS

In the following pages, the critical elements in a number of the most common legal remedies used in enforcing security systems are surveyed. The problems of information system security are not exclusive to any jurisdiction but constitute, rather, a world-wide phenomenon. Illustrations will reflect the international scope of these problems. Many of the same rules apply in the United States and in other jurisdictions. The purpose of the following materials is to provide a short checklist to facilitate decision making and provide a base point for further study.

13.2.1 Copyright Law

Copyright law provides a very significant legal tool for use, both before a security breach and certainly after a security breach dealing with possible misappropriation of data, computer programs, blueprints, plans, laboratory notes, or similar material. It is for that reason that the information security specialist will want to be familiar with some basic concepts related to copyright law.

The United States, United Kingdom, Australia, and many other countries have now amended or revised their copyright legislation to explicitly provide that computer programs are protected by copyright law.[2] In other countries, such as Canada, the courts have held that the unrevised *Copyright Act* is broad enough to protect computer programs.[3] In many of these other countries, the reform of copyright law is actively underway.[4] The piracy of software is a serious security issue in many environments. Yet the significance of this development is perhaps more important in relation to the protection of unique data.

The traditional view was that copyright, actually a bundle of related rights, was intended to protect forms of creativity. The problem then arose of how to deal with determination of the relative merits of creative works. In a landmark case, <u>Leiber Code</u>,[5] the Court held that the law would not rule on the relative merits of a creative work but would protect any work that was an original creation: the product of an author's labor, skill and judgment and fixed in a tangible form. Under this rule a wide variety of creative works were protected by copyright law. Examples of such works are:

(a)   Codes consisting of otherwise unintelligible numbers[6]

(b)   Grids of computer generated sequences of letters[7]

(c)   Telegraph Code[8]

(d)   A fixed odds football pool form[9]

(e)   A timetable index[10]

(f)   A street directory[11]

As a result, it is clear that any data that is an original work of authorship may be protected by copyright law. The implication of this development is that all of the tools available under copyright law may be used in cases where data or software is copied illegally. Similarly, courts have held that selling of pirate materials is fraud[12] and the unauthorized interception of copyright protected materials may be a basis for criminal prosecution or private civil action.[13]

Another requirement of copyright law is that the subject matter be fixed in some tangible form. This may mean that details stored on some magnetic or other media are protected. However, it also means that transitory data, such as may be developed in random memory and which is not yet fixed, may not be protected.

Generally, worldwide copyright law has continued to expand in scope and in the types of works protected. This expansion has been met by a reactionary argument that would see copyright law restricted to its traditional place of protecting artistic forms of creativity.[14] Basically the argument is that some other form of protection, or no protection at all, should be used for utilitarian forms of creativity. This is basically what the author has previously called the "aesthetic purpose test."[15]

This argument runs counter to the principle, discussed above, in the Leiber Code decision. Basically the Court is placed in a situation where it must determine whether or not a work has aesthetic merit. This was the impossible situation that the decision in Leiber Code avoided.

Given that copyright law may have application to data as well as to software, the next step is to briefly examine the general elements in copyright law.

Copyright law exists under the appropriate *Copyright Act*[16] and provides a right, in the first creator, to prevent another person from making copies or translations of that creative work without the creator's permission.[17] Note that in some jurisdictions it may be necessary to register or comply with other formalities in order to create these rights.

A copyright is a right which is distinct from the object or work the right relates to. For example, one might purchase a book from a bookstore and have a complete right to possess that book. One may wish to read the book, not to read it, destroy it, throw it away, or give it to another person. Yet, the purchaser of the book does not have all the rights in the book. The copyright holder still retains the copyright. The copyright prevents the purchaser of the book from being able legally to make copies of the book or substantial parts of the book without the copyright holder's permission. Other rights are paternity rights and moral rights. A paternity right is the right of the author of a work to claim authorship of that work. A moral right relates to the alteration or display of a work in a manner which might harm the reputation of the author.

The *Copyright Act* does recognize that certain situations may exist where there should be a limit to a copyright holder's monopoly on copying. As a result there are a number of exemptions under the Act under which copying is permissible. Briefly, some of these are:

(a)   Any fair dealing with any work for the purpose of private study, research, criticism, review or newspaper summary.

(b)   For educational use, short passages suitably acknowledged may be reproduced so long as "not more than two such passages from works by the same author are published ... within five years."

(c)   Recitation in public of any reasonable extract of a work.

The United States has a broader fair use exemption than the "Fair Dealing" exemption seen in many Commonwealth countries. Under 17 USC, Section 107 states:

Notwithstanding the provisions of Section 106, the fair use of a copyrighted work, including copying of such work by reproduction copies or phono records or by any other means specified by that Section, for purposes such as criticism, comment, news reporting, teaching (including multiple copies for classroom use), scholarship, or research, is not an infringement of copyright. In determining whether the use made of a work in any particular case is a fair use, the factors to be considered shall include:

(1) the purpose and character of the use, including whether such use is of a commercial nature or for non profit educational purposes;

(2) the nature of the copyrighted work;

(3) the amount and substantiality of the portion used in relation to the copyrighted work as a whole; and

(4) the effect of the use upon the potential market for or value of the copyrighted work.[18]

In all cases it should be remembered that a copyright protects only the form of the author's creative expression. The ideas or underlying concepts are not protected by copyright law. Thus, copyright law is generally effective in dealing with software, or data piracy, or direct copying of a computer program or data without permission. However, copyright law is not effective in preventing a competitor from examining the program or data and using the concepts or ideas or other information therein. The competitor cannot make a copy but he or she may be able to use those ideas, concepts, or information in another product.

If copies are made without the permission of the copyright holder, or without the aid of an exemption, then an action may be brought for damages, an accounting for profits, or for an injunction (a court order) ordering the wrongdoer to refrain from continuing to infringe the copyright and also ordering that all copies made without permission be delivered up by the wrongdoer. The copyright holder may also seek to have the summary procedure in the act invoked, in which case the wrongdoer may become liable to pay a fine.

Copyright law becomes a valuable consideration for the information security specialist because many cases of breach of security involving loss of information or data will involve copyright issues. Of particular relevance is the ability to bring both civil or criminal action under many copyright statutes. This makes copyright a very flexible and adaptable tool for the information security specialist.

In summary, copyright law may be effective where identical or substantially similar copies are made of a protected work. The process may be expedited through use of interim injunctions in serious cases and the rights, under the copyright law, apply against all persons in the jurisdiction.

13.2.2 License Agreements

Another area of law used to protect computer programs or data is contract law. By contract, the program developer may often grant the user a license which is a right to use the computer program. A *license* must be distinguished from a sale. They are very different relationships. As noted above, a purchaser of a book can do very many things with that book in addition to reading (ie. using) the book. Under a license agreement, the user has a right only to use the work, say in the case of a book the right to read that book. The book still belongs to the vendor.

Under the license agreement, the right to use a computer program, data, or other confidential information may be limited and defined by a number of conditions. Often, failure to carry out the terms set out in the license agreement will result in the termination of the right to use the program or data. The user will be under a legal obligation, in most cases, to return the program, data, and materials to the vendor. Therefore, it is important to remember that one does not own the computer program under a license arrangement. Rather, the user must continue to comply with the terms of the license agreement in order to continue the right to use the program and data.

The law of trade secrets is based, in common law countries, upon the broad principles of Equity. This branch of law will, in appropriate circumstances, enforce obligations of confidentiality or secrecy in relation to ideas, know-how, data, or other information. As it is the one legal avenue that provides some protection for ideas, the law of trade secrets is often used when dealing with confidential or sensitive information.

The law of trade secrets will be discussed in more detail below. However, it is important to note that these obligations of secrecy are very often imposed through license agreement.

As a result of its flexibility of application, a license agreement can, in the right situation, be a very powerful tool in the security plan. The license agreement has the ability to provide a custom-designed relationship between the rights holder and the user of data or programs. The agreement has the advantage of informing the user of the restrictions on use in advance and so eliminating misunderstandings and some security risks. It also has the advantage of tying other, chiefly financial, interests in to the user's compliance. As a result, it may be very disadvantageous to breach the terms of the license.

In summary, the license agreement may serve as a flexible way in which the respective rights of different parties may be determined. In the employment situation, properly drafted employment agreements may have the same desirable effect. It may clarify the obligations on a potential security risk and at the same time provide a mechanism for enforcement of those obligations.

Many criminal laws rely on a concept of authorized use or permitted use. As a result, it is very important for the information security specialist to know precisely what is permitted and what is not permitted under the licensee's contract or that of the licensee's employees.

13.2.3 Trade Secret Law

Very often a breach of security involves a misuse of secret or confidential information. There may be elements of other law involved, such as copyright law in relation to reproduction of data. However, the obligations and responsibilities in relation to the secret or confidential information come under the general head of trade secret law.

The law of trade secrets is based on a relationship between two or more parties in which there is an express or implied obligation of confidentiality as pertains to certain information. The roots of this branch of law go back to the industrial revolution.[19] Unlike the law of patent or copyright, the law of trade secret acts *in personam*, that is, between the parties and not against all the world.

Since this branch of law can be of some importance to the security professional, it will be covered in somewhat greater detail.[20]

There are many definitions of a trade secret corresponding to the very extensive protection this branch of law provides. Basically, trade secret law protects ideas, unlike copyright or patent law. This very much broader protection has resulted in making trade secret protection, in conjunction with contractual provisions, the widest form of legal protection used to protect confidential or technical information.[21] A widely used definition is that of the United States *Restatement of Torts*, which indicates a trade secret may consist of:

> any formula, pattern, device or compilation of information which is used in one's business, and which gives him an opportunity to obtain an advantage over competitors who do not know or use it. The subject matter of a trade secret must be secret ... so that, except by use of improper means, there would be difficulty in acquiring the information. An exact definition

of a trade secret is not possible. Some factors to be considered in determining whether given information is one's trade secret are: (1) the extent to which the information is known outside of his business; (2) the extent to which it is known by employees and others involved in his business; (3) the extent of measures taken by him to guard the secrecy of the information; (4) the value of the information to him in developing the information; ...; (6) the ease or difficulty with which the information could be properly acquired and duplicated by others.[22]

The law of trade secrets has not seen such an attempt at codification in England, Australia, or Canada and so appears to be somewhat more flexible though courts generally take into account the same considerations.

The underlying theme of trade secret protection was summed up by Lord Denning in Seager v. Copydex, Ltd.[23] where he quotes Roskill J in Cranleigh Precision Engineering Co. Ltd. v. Bryant:[24]

> the essence of this branch of law, whatever the origin of it might be, is that a person who has obtained information in confidence is not allowed to use it as a springboard for activities detrimental to the person who made the confidential communication, and springboard it remains even when all the features have been published or can be ascertained by actual inspection by any member of the public.

Lord Denning then sums it up:

> The law on this subject does not depend on any implied contract. It depends on the broad principle of equity that he who has received information in confidence shall not take unfair advantage of it. He must not make use of it to the prejudice of him who gave it without obtaining his consent. The principle is clear enough when the whole of the information is private. The difficulty arises when the information is in part public and in part private ... When the information is mixed ... then the recipient must take special care to use only the material which is in the public domain.

Information to qualify for trade secret protection need not be novel or original. It is sufficient that the information provides a competitive edge.[25]

The elements of the action for breach of confidence were stated by Justice Megary in Coco v. A.N. Clark (Engineers) Ltd.:[26]

> First, the information itself, in the words of Lord Greene M.R. in the Saltman case on page 215, 'must have the necessary quality of confidence about it.' Secondly, that information must have been imparted in circumstances importing an obligation of confidence. Thirdly, there must be an unauthorized use of that information to the detriment of the party communicating it.

(a)   Quality of Confidence

This requirement means that the material is not in the public domain. The information or data, to qualify for trade secret protection, must contain concepts that, when considered as a whole, have qualities that are outside the area of public knowledge[27].

(b)   Obligation of Confidence

There must be a relationship between the parties which, expressly or implied, creates an obligation of confidence. This duty of confidence may be created under a contractual relationship and this is, in fact, the most common method used to expressly state the limits of the confidence. As mentioned above it is common to create these obligations in license agreements but this could also be done in employment agreements or consultancy agreements. Of course, there need not be any agreement, say as during negotiations, and yet the obligations of confidence may still exist.

These obligations may also arise by operation of law. It has long been an implied term in the employment agreement that the employee has a duty of fidelity to the employer.[28] This contractual obligation of fidelity may prevent a skilled employee from giving his assistance to a competitor despite the fact that the assistance is provided on the employee's own time and despite the fact no confidential information might have been disclosed to the employee under an obligation of confidence. (There are two issues here: is it confidential; is there an obligation of confidence?) Basically, the employee cannot put himself into a position where he can injure the employer,[29] such as by competing with the employer or by assisting a competitor.

(c)   Disclosure Resulting in Detriment

It is rarely difficult to show some detriment through the unauthorized release of confidential data. If nothing else, control over the data has been lost and this can have a very serious impact on an enterprise or individual.

The security professional should be aware that the obligations under trade secret law may be, in the proper circumstances, an effective tool to control abuse of data. This is a complex area of law and one where the definition of obligations in writing has significant importance.

Trade secret law, unlike copyright law, gives only rights against those persons who are under obligations of confidence. It may be a powerful tool to protect ideas and know-how but this limitation must always be kept in mind.

13.2.4 Non-Disclosure Considerations

A number of specific factors should be considered by the information security specialist in conjunction with the information security attorney. In particular, the establishment of employee agreements and consultant agreements can provide the legal basis for subsequent prosecution in the event of breach of the security guidelines. Some of the significant elements in such agreements are set out below.

1. Acknowledgement of the value of trade secrets. There may be a distinction between valuable trade secrets and confidential information without commercial value for the purposes of criminal law and particularly for the purposes of civil remedies available. As a result, the agreement may indicate clearly that valuable trade secrets are involved.

2. Non-disclosure requirement. This requirement will provide the essential obligation of confidence and secrecy in relation to the trade secrets or other confidential information.

3. Non-use requirement. This provision is also often included to as to preclude use of the trade secrets or confidential information by the party restrained. When obligations of confidence are discussed herein, it is assumed a non-use restriction is also included.

4. Detail of the scope or definition of the trade secrets. Agreements are more effective when they are certain. As a result, it is of advantage to define with as much precision as possible the confidential information subject to the obligations of confidence. An example might be definition, in a detailed form, of a particular semiconductor design project. The security manager may wish to ensure that the types of activities or the access to certain processes, products or resources which may constitute confidential information are clearly defined.

5. Obligations continuing beyond termination. It is clear that obligations of confidence must continue past the termination of the assignment by the consultant or the employment by the employee. Otherwise, of course, there would be no remedy to deal with the employee who absconded with valuable trade secrets of the former employer. One should also note the necessity of continuing obligations when dealing with general releases of individuals who are fiduciaries (that is, have relationships with high trust such as senior officers or directors of corporations).

6. Restraints on duplication of materials. In some circumstances, it may be necessary to provide a clear restraint on an individual's ability to take copies of materials, particularly data and computer programs. These obligations may be important in triggering civil and potentially criminal liability in relation to such unauthorized reproduction of certain materials. These restraints should be clearly integrated into the company's policy in relation to access and use of the firm's computer systems.

7. Exit review. At the termination of access or of employment, it is very practical and advisable to conduct a review of the confidential information that the employee or consultant has had access to, and to review the continuing obligations of confidence in relation to that valuable confidential information. Such an exit review performs an educational function and provides some certainty for the employee and employer in ascertaining the information restrained. It should, of course, be in writing and it may be placed in the form of an agreement between the parties.

8. Delivery of documents on termination. There should be a clear obligation on the employee or consultant to return all documents upon termination of the employment or engagement. This avoids the prospect of confidential information disclosed in such documents being outside the control of the employer.

There are numerous other terms which may exist in such employment or consultant agreements and, in particular, related to the assignment and ownership of inventions, discoveries, improvements, or works of authorship developed or created by the employee or consultant. It is not within the scope of this text to deal with such additional terms. However, the information security specialist should examine all of these issues in detail with the information security attorney.

13.2.5 Computer and Information Crime

The legal protections provided by copyright law and under license agreements often are not sufficient to curb widespread abuse of computer systems. Software piracy is epidemic in scope. Estimates range from 10 to 30 illegal copies for each legitimate copy in circulation.[30] Such widespread piracy acts as a serious disincentive to the development of high quality software as it becomes more difficult to recover one's investment in time and money. Similarly, the loss of valuable confidential data can destroy commercial opportunities or in some cases destroy entire enterprises. Given a problem on such a wide scale, numerous jurisdictions have taken strong measures through the enactment of tough new computer crime laws.[31]

In 1987 there were 35 bills introduced into fifteen state legislatures concerning computer crime. Out of that 35, 13 were made public law, 10 are pending until 1988, 2 were replaced by others, and 10 died in committee.[32]

For ease of discussion, since criminal jurisdiction in the United States rests with each state and therefore has led to a plethora of different approaches, we will use the example of Canada in which the legislative authority for criminal law rests with the federal government.

The major categories of computer crime identified by most legislators are listed below. Also included are examples of each type of conduct.

1. Unauthorized use of computer systems or services:
   An employee may use the computer system or service for personal use, such as moonlighting. A stranger may, through devious means, gain access to use of your computing system or services and use that system or service without authorization or compensation to the system or service operator.

2. Theft of computer hardware or computer programs:
   An individual may steal a personal computer or components thereof. An individual may steal a third party's programs or internally generated computer programs or data.

3. Destruction, alteration, or abuse of data:
   A student may alter grades in an educational institution's data base of the student's academic record. An employee may alter remuneration calculations in the employer's payroll system. A third party might gain access to a computer system and destroy data necessary for decision making, such as patient treatment records used by a hospital.

4. Destruction or theft of tangible assets through use of the computer as a tool:
   False invoice records or shipping documents could be used to acquire possession of tangible assets or property. Abuse of electronic fund transfer systems or automatic teller machines may occur for the purposes of embezzlement or fraud.

There are many reasons why legislators have felt a need to enact specific computer crime laws. There are many factors which make computer crimes much more difficult to detect than traditional criminal conduct. Some examples of such reasons are:

1. Informal sources indicate that average computer crimes (such as embezzlement or fraud) are able to succeed in obtaining larger sums than traditional crimes. For example, once the criminal has breached a financial institution's security system, it may be just as easy to take a large amount as a small amount.

2. Many computer crimes are not detected. Since no paper trail is left in respect of many computer transactions, it may be very difficult to detect a specific incident.

3. Computer crime occurs on a different time scale than traditional crime. Many traditional crimes occur on a time scale of minutes, hours, or even days. A computer fraud may be executed in less than a second.

4. There is a broader geographical scale involved in computer crime than traditional crime. For example, an individual using a lap-top terminal in Atlanta may commit a fraud on a computer in Los Angeles through use of dial-up access. To make it even more difficult to detect, the computer criminal could initiate the call from a public telephone booth.

These and other characteristics provide significant challenges for the law enforcement official as well as the information security specialist.

The information security manager must be very familiar with the appropriate criminal law in his or her jurisdiction. The criminal law provides the greatest deterrent sanctions for would-be wrongdoers. Other advantages of criminal prosecution are the public nature of many prosecutions, the fact that the State usually pays the costs of the prosecution, and the severe penalties, including fines and loss of liberty. An example of a specific computer or data crime law exists in Canada under Bill C-18.[33]   The computer crime provisions in this legislation became law in December 1985.

There are two basic provisions. Firstly, (in Section 301.2) it states:

S. 301.2   (1) Everyone who, fraudulently and without colour of right,

(a) obtains, directly or indirectly, any computer service

(b) by means of an electromagnetic, acoustic, mechanical or other device, intercepts or causes to be intercepted, directly or indirectly, any function of a computer system, or

(c) uses or causes to be used, directly or indirectly, a computer system with intent to commit an offence under paragraph (a) or (b) or an offence under Section 387 in relation to data or a computer system

is guilty of an indictable offence and is liable to imprisonment for ten years or is guilty of an offence punishable on summary conviction.

Subsection (2) goes on to provide definitions of "computer program," "computer service," "computer system", "data," "electronic, acoustic, mechanical or other device," "function," and "intercept." These definitions use other specialized concepts or words from data processing practice. These additional concepts or words are not defined. The result will likely require experts from the data processing industry to provide expert evidence about the meaning of these concepts and words (ie. such things as "logic" or "storage and retrieval").34

As one can see, these new computer crime laws can be quite broad and have criminalized areas of human behavior which were not formerly criminal conduct. At this early stage one can only speculate on the effect of these new computer crime laws.

This section should provide a criminal sanction in cases where a person wrongfully gains access to a computer system and so it could deal with the problem of "system cracking" (breaking into computer systems through use of telecommunications). However, the section also provides a sanction where an employee wrongfully uses a computer system.

These provisions are similar in concept to those found in many other jurisdictions. As a result, information security specialists must carefully review their internal operating procedures to familiarize themselves with the permitted uses of the company's computer and information systems. It will be very difficult for a company to sustain a successful criminal prosecuting or even civil action where the scope or ambit of authorized activity is not clearly defined.

On the other hand, it is also important that the information security specialist exercise a certain amount of common sense in relation to the definition of what is authorized and what is not. As seen above, the definition of authorized use of a computer system or service can have a significant effect on users. For example, if word processing for personal use is prohibited, then an employee printing Christmas card labels may have committed a criminal offence. As a result, while the computer use guidelines should be clear and precise, they also should be meaningful and likely not to be violated by routine or normal practices.

Another example occurs in the case of databases. Many companies specifically prohibit their employees from using the company databases for personal use. If this is the case and if an employee, knowing of this prohibition, acts in violation of it, then that employee risks criminal liability. Similar examples occur in relation to personal computing projects. Some companies encourage programmers to experiment with new ideas or personal computing projects on the company system. If that is the case then no liability will attach under Section 301.2.

It is very important for the information security specialist and the data processing manager to define the scope of permitted uses of the computer and information systems. These permitted uses should then be communicated, in writing, to all employees or persons having access to the computer system. This section provides that it is an offence to gain access to, use or attempt either to gain access to or use a computer system without authorization.

This is a hybrid offence, meaning that the Crown prosecutor has the choice of proceeding by Indictment (for serious situations) or by a Summary procedure (for less serious situations). The maximum penalty for conviction under Indictment is ten years imprisonment.

The second provision is found in Section 387 (1.1) which states:

(1.1) Every one commits mischief who willfully
   (a) destroys or alters data;
   (b) renders data meaningless, useless or ineffective;
   (c) obstructs, interrupts or interferes with the lawful use of data; or
   (d) obstructs, interrupts or interferes with any person in the lawful use
   of data or denies access to data to any person who is entitled access
   thereto

Alteration or destruction of data or programs may be an offense under this section. As with Section 301.2, the offence is hybrid and the maximum penalty for conviction by indictment is ten years imprisonment.

These new computer crime laws are added to the existing body of criminal law. One should not assume that because Sections 301.2 and 387(1.1) are specific computer related offenses, there are no other offenses which might arise out of misuse of computing resources. Courts in all jurisdictions have not been slow to find that the Criminal Code governed many types of abuse involving computers.

In R v. Kirkwood the Ontario Court of Appeal held that the selling of pirate copies of a copyright protected work constituted the criminal offence of fraud on the copyright holder. If you make illegal copies of a diskette you are violating the *Copyright Act*. If you then sell those copies, you have also committed a criminal offence.

Unauthorized interception of private communications is another area in which criminal law has evolved in response to growing abuse.[35] In Canada the *Criminal Code* provides that such interception is a criminal offence under Section 178.11(1), which states:

Everyone who, by means of an electromagnetic, acoustic, mechanical or other device, willfully intercepts a private communication is guilty of an indictable offence and liable to imprisonment for five years.

Section 178.1 defines "private communication" as follows:

"private communication" means any oral communication or any telecommunication made under circumstances in which it is reasonable for the originator thereof to expect that it will not be intercepted by any person other than the person intended by the originator thereof to receive it.

Special provisions exempt telephone operators and similar persons from the operation of this section.

In the United States Title III of the *Omnibus Crime Control and Safe Streets Act of 1986*[36] provides criminal sanctions where wire communications are intercepted without authorization. Similarly, Section 605 of the *Communications Act*[37] also prohibits the interception of certain signals.[38] The new technologies were not in existence when the U.S. Bill of Rights was enacted but there are some who feel that the Fourth Amendment, which protects against unreasonable search and seizure, will also protect the privacy of individuals using such devices as cellular telephones and electronic mail.[39]

The *Interception of Communications Act 1985*[40] is the applicable legislation in the United Kingdom and it attempts to deal with the unauthorized interception of private communications. Section 1(1) provides that:

> ... a person who intentionally intercepts a communication in the course of its transmission by post or by means of a public telecommunications system shall be guilty of an offence.

The maximum penalty for commission of this offence is two years of imprisonment. Note that a key element of the offence is the interception of a private transmission through a public media (ie. post or telecommunications). Therefore, the provision differs from the Canadian section in that internal communications, such as in a network, and unauthorized access via a public telephone line would not be covered.[41] The legislation in Canada, the United States, and elsewhere provides for specific exemptions for certain law enforcement purposes. In most cases, the legislation provides for an obligation to appear before a judge and request a warrant or order permitting the intercept. The case law surrounding the validity of such orders is quite complex and should be examined in detail whenever it is it is desired to obtain permission to intercept private communications.

Software, know-how, and data may be protected under a license agreement that provides an obligation to keep the program contents secret. This protection is an attempt to use trade secret law to provide additional protection. In Canada, as in many countries, the legal basis for "theft" of such confidential information is very controversial. The Ontario Court of Appeal has found, in a split decision in the case of R v. Stewart,[42] that confidential information could be property for the purposes of the *Criminal Code* and so it could be stolen. The Alberta Court of Appeal unanimously held the opposite in R. v. Offley,[43] relying on the English Court of Appeal decision in Oxford v. Moss.[44]

It is important to distinguish between the object holding the information and the information itself. It is clear that a diskette, being a physical object, can be stolen. However, the law has difficulty with the misappropriation of confidential information. If you take my idea I still have full possession of the idea. I have, however, lost control over the dissemination of the information. If you took my diskette, I no longer have the diskette.

The Stewart case found that misappropriation of confidential information could be theft. Justice Houlden J.A. (Justice of Appeals) stated the policy behind his decision at page 597:

> The last half of the twentieth century has seen an exponential growth in the development and improvement of methods of storing and distributing information. I believe that S.283(1)[45] of the Code is wide enough to protect the interests of those who compile and store such information and to restrain the activities of those who wrongfully seek to misappropriate it.

And at page 599 Justice Cory J.A. stated:

> Information and its collection, collation and interpretation are vital to most modern commercial enterprises. Compilations of information are often of such importance to the business community that they are securely kept to ensure their confidentiality. The collated, confidential information may be found in many forms covering a wide variety of topics. It may include painstakingly prepared computer programs pertaining to all aspects of the firm's business; meticulously indexed lists of suppliers with comments as to their efficiency, reliability and time required for delivery; laboriously compiled lists of customers and their needs; instructions as to manufacturing processes learned from months of experimentation and trial; lists of employees, including reference to their physical well-being and disciplinary history that may be required to be kept confidential in compliance with the terms of a collective bargaining agreement. For many businessmen their confidential lists may well be the most valuable asset of their company. Their security will be of utmost importance to the firm.
>
> If questioned, a businessman would unhesitatingly state that the confidential lists were the "property" of his firm. If they were surreptitiously copied by a competitor or outsider, he would consider his confidential information to have been stolen. The importance of confidential information will increase with the growth of high-technology industry. Its protection will be of paramount concern to members of industry and the public as a whole.

This logic was followed in Alberta in R v. Tannis,[46] a case involving a charge of theft against a computer programmer. However, in the later case of R

v. Offley, the Alberta Court of Appeal took the opposite approach. The policy reasoning of the Court appears to be stated by Justice Belzil at page 7:

> What constitutes anything "animate or inanimate" in s.283 must, in my view, be determined by the intrinsic nature of the "thing" and not by its quality. If information *per se* is intrinsically incapable of being an "inanimate thing," the qualifying of it as being "confidential" will not make it so. The concept of "returning" (ie. bringing back that which had been previously taken away) something to the owner when he has never been deprived of it is difficult to grasp. How can something which has never been taken away be returned to the person from whom it was never taken? Is the person who reveals a personal secret entrusted to him by a friend to be guilty of theft? Or the person who reads a confidential memo inadvertently left on his desk?

And at page 9, quoting from Glanville Williams' *Criminal Law*:[47]

> ... the definition of theft does not well fit cases of industrial espionage. There is a very strong case for extending the criminal law to the protection of trade secrets and other valuable confidential information (such as the scenario of a play) deliberately obtained by industrial espionage or knowingly in breach of confidence, but the way to achieve this is some- how to goad Parliament into action on the subject.

Between Stewart and Offley we see two different approaches. In Stewart, the Court was willing to apply a flexible definition so that the obvious wrong could find a remedy. In Offley, the Court recognized that finding a property right in information required a major policy decision that should properly be made by elected representatives. Yet, the problem remains.

Legal systems around the world still struggle with this problem. However, as information and know-how becomes increasingly important as we move to in- creasing dependence on knowledge and idea based industries, legal systems will have to choose between the alternatives and find a solution.

In summary, criminal law has several advantages. Firstly, the state, and not the complainant, pays for the investigation and prosecution. Secondly, the penalties imposed may be very strong, often involving a term of imprisonment, which may have a deterrent effect. However, there are also disadvantages to criminal prosecution. Most importantly, the complainant loses control over the dispute and becomes merely a witness in the prosecution. Police or the state may not always treat the confidential information, data, or know-how as confi- dentially as would the owner of the information. Finally, once the criminal op- tion is pursued then it becomes difficult to try to settle the dispute with the wrongdoer as one might do in a civil law case.

A study of the development of computer and information crime laws will serve the security manager in making cogent arguments to his or her government and in ensuring that the law that develops is appropriate for the needs of the security profession.

13.2.6 Issues Arising From Transborder Data Flows

As you read these words electrons speed from country to country along the silver threads of telecommunications networks. Those electrons, by their characteristics, carry information. That information may be temperatures from a weather reporting service, stock quotations from an exchange, a salesman making a sale and recording the transaction, or the personal comments of a traveller to his loved one separated by so many miles.

Each of these communications, and so many others, pass through various nodes or links in those telecommunications networks. The information may come from a database in a computer in another country.

The complexity of these transborder data flows, the international nature of the flows, and the ease with which a private individual can gain access to foreign information without passing through any censors or customs bureau raises a number of problems.

The number of people who have potential or actual access to such information can be large and so there is a need to provide protection from abuse. Actions by one country may be quite ineffective as the information can easily pass through several national telecommunication systems. As a result, some form of international cooperation is required to set standards for the protection of private communications. The Organization of Economic Cooperation and Development (OECD) has begun that process.

The OECD: has prepared a set of Guidelines[48] for the handling of private non-data and data communications. These guidelines serve to identify the relative responsibilities of the database operator, the telecommunication system operator, the person assembling the data in the first instance, and also the end user. These are new rules that will eventually provide us all with greater personal privacy in an age when computerization and telecommunications have laid much of our private lives open to view.

Another example of such cooperation is the Canada-United States Free Trade Agreement. In this historic agreement, both countries agree to eliminate certain trade barriers and that future legislation and practice will not increase such barriers, in respect of a wide range of services including computer services.

Computer crime has also entered an age when international cooperation is needed to deal with crimes which may be committed in Texas by a person sitting at a terminal halfway around the world. This problem is complex. In such a case, where did the crime occur? In Texas where the injury was done -- or at the terminal in Sweden where the criminal controlled the process? This question becomes important as the law of the place where the crime was committed may be very different.

Pornography and hate literature may be imported through the use of data telecommunications and avoid any border screening by customs officials. At the present time there is no feasible way to intercept all transborder data flows and subject them to scrutiny. In fact the effort to do so would cost so much and create a bureaucracy so large that more serious problems would be created by the solution than by the problem.

The new information based industries must react and act more rapidly today than at any previous time in human history. This is only accomplished when information from the farthest corners of the globe is available to the user without delay and at least cost. This is the age of information industries. To cut the flow of information would be as harmful as it would have been to cut the flow of water to a water mill centuries ago.

The end result is that the citizens of advanced industrialized societies must learn to deal with the added strength and the new problems which arise from transborder data flows. The world continues to become more and more complex. There is no alternative but to adapt to these changes but in a way which serves to strengthen our traditional values and beliefs.

The information security professional must play a role in helping the society interpret and understand the competing needs of personal privacy and the needs of secure free flows of data.

13.3 THE INFORMATION SECURITY SPECIALIST'S ROLE

The information security attorney, as discussed earlier, is an important member of the information security specialist's crisis team. It is important for the information security specialist to establish a team who can immediately investigate a situation of possible wrong doing, preserve evidence both for the purposes of the investigation and for the purposes of subsequent criminal or civil legal action, and also to protect the company, its assets, and the members of the information security team.

In order to avoid claims of slander, libel, or defamation, the information security specialist must be very careful about making allegations of wrongdoing against any individual or corporation. It will be very important for the information security specialist to fully assess all of the facts and to make accusations only after receiving appropriate legal advice.

It is very important that evidence of wrongdoing be properly preserved so as to avoid exclusion of such evidence because of inappropriate handling, or for several important legal reasons. Again, it is important that the information security specialist obtains appropriate legal advice to preserve the best evidence to maintain the option of criminal or civil action.

The foregoing comments are very important. Imagine you are the information security specialist at an important defence establishment. At 4:00 a.m. you observe one of the employees at the outside gate passing a large box over the fence to another person who quickly drives away. You telephone ahead but the description of the car is common and it is only some ten miles later that the highway patrol pulls over a car of that description containing a box, as you described, with important data from the company. The information security specialist may make the accusation against the employee and feel satisfied that the situation has been encapsulated and resolved so quickly.

However, unfortunately, the information security specialist may also find himself faced, the next morning, with a law suit for defamation, wrongful dismissal, malicious prosecution, or any number of other legal actions. In many cases these actions may merely be a smoke screen in an effort to intimidate or threaten the information security specialist or the company into dropping any action against the rogue employee. It is to prevent, or at least minimize, the likelihood of such action that it is important that the information security specialist obtain early and effective legal advice to help ensure that after a breach of all of the physical and environmental security precautions, the perpetrator is not able to escape upon a legal technicality or a failure to properly preserve evidence for subsequent prosecution.

The information security specialist must also be prepared to act as a witness in criminal or civil actions. Your information security attorney or District Attorney (or Crown Prosecutor) will assist you for your presentation of evidence. There are many basic rules or principles which you must always keep in mind. Remember that the courtroom is also a battlefield and that you must follow very carefully the instructions and directions of your attorney.

1. Answer only and precisely the question which you have been asked. If you attempt to elaborate or discuss in broader terms, you may disclose information which would be useful to the defence or upon which they could build an attack on your attentiveness or credibility.

2. Do not become emotionally involved. A tactic used by many defence attorneys is to attempt to upset you, get into an argument with you, or otherwise put you off balance. It is important that you maintain a cool, detached, and professional attitude throughout the presentation of your evidence so that you can avoid being pushed into making foolish and damaging statements.

3. Tell the facts as you witnessed them with your own senses. The hearsay rule may preclude admissibility of certain evidence which you obtained from a third party. It is important that you do not make assumptions about your observations.

4. If you do not understand a question or if the question is too complicated or contains too many elements, then do not hesitate to ask that the question be repeated or phrased in a manner which does not lead to improper inferences from the way in which the question is asked. For example, the question "Are you still beating your wife?" leaves no satisfactory answer because of the way the question is phrased. If you answer "no," the implication is that you formerly *did* beat your wife. If you suspect that a question has been unfairly stated in an effort to create unfair inferences, then it is most likely that your attorney will object to the question in the form it is phrased. If your attorney does not do so, and you think the question is unfairly phrased, then you should object to it on that basis and request that the question be more fairly phrased.

5. Describe your observations in a clear, chronological, and logical sequence. Do not jump ahead or raise tangential or irrelevant matters that will only make it more difficult for a judge or jury to understand your evidence.

In some circumstances, depending upon your experience and training, you may be called upon as an expert witness. An expert witness is entitled to give opinion evidence to a court. Typically, an expert witness will be given a hypothetical fact situation and be asked to provide an opinion based on that hypothetical fact situation.

Normally, an expert witness will have to be qualified before the court (unless having been previously so qualified). This is usually done by submission of the expert witness' resume, textbooks, or articles to the court, and a brief examination of the witness's expertise. In some cases, defence attorneys will attempt to minimize or limit the area in which the expert is qualified to give opinion evidence. They will do this by focusing upon those areas in which the expert witness is truly expert and attempting to limit or minimize those areas. A rough example would be the introduction of a purported expert witness on computer program and system designs. It may be, after examination of the expert witness's qualification, that the expert's qualifications are restricted to experience in a particular environment (such as mainframe or minicomputer and, perhaps, only in relation to specific languages, such as, for example, Pascal and Cobol). However, the dispute before the court may relate to alleged unauthorized use of a computer program, written in C, in a microcomputer environment. In this way, a defence attorney will attempt to minimize or limit the strength or effectiveness of any opinion evidence which might be given by an expert witness.

The information security specialist, in helping to select such expert witnesses, should be aware of the possibility of such limitation, and should ensure that the appropriate expert has been retained for the nature of the specific case.

Furthermore, information security specialists who do become expert witnesses themselves must ensure that they are absolutely candid and frank with the court about their qualifications and their opinions. Any attempt to appear one-sided or to attempt to shift the analysis to favor the client (who after all has paid for the evidence the expert witness is providing), not only will damage the case but also can completely destroy the reputation of the expert witness and end any future likelihood of a career as an expert witness.

The defense attorney may prepare for your testimony by reading your publications or even by obtaining copies of your previous testimony in court in other cases. Any discrepancy between your present evidence and your publications or prior testimony likely will be used by the defense attorney to cast doubt on your present evidence.

The foregoing material has attempted to provide a very basic introduction to a number of legal issues which may be of significant relevance to the information security specialist dealing with advanced technology security concerns, data, computer programs, and the like. It is important that the information security specialist consult with a qualified information security attorney to help in the planning, implementation, and conduct of an appropriate information security plan. This cooperation will result not only in greater likelihood of success for the information security plan, but also greater protection from personal liability for the information security specialist.

13.4 CONTROL OF STRATEGIC MATERIALS

Certain materials, know-how, information, devices, plans, blueprints, computer programs, assemblies or parts thereof, in a wide range of areas of advanced technology dealing from composite materials through micro electronics, semiconductor design, radar, guidance, communications, laser or similar fields, are of strategic importance to the security of your country. As a result, most jurisdictions have legislation controlling the import and export of strategic goods and materials. It is important for the information securities specialist to make him or herself aware of the provisions of these laws and establish relationships with local customs or special officers enforcing them.

In the event of breach of security at an installation involving strategic goods, information, or other materials whose export may be controlled or restricted, it is important that you notify the appropriate officers so that they may increase their vigilance for attempts to export that strategic technology.

It is very important that the information security specialist be aware that approaches may be made to his company from another friendly country. However, that friendly country may, in some cases, be an inadvertent host for operation of those who wish to divert strategic technology in breach of legislation controlling or prohibiting export of such technology.

If the company is in the business of supplying products or services dealing with such strategic technologies, then a number of indicators may lead to suspicion in relation to a proposed transfer export of such strategic technologies. Some of these indicators or factors are:

1. Major new customers who ask to pay in cash.

2. Customers who do not want after-service or maintenance contracts.

3. Customers who ask for voltage differences from their own country's.

4. Customers with unusual shipping instructions, such as requesting crates that do not identify the contents.

The information security specialist may save his company embarrassment and significant liability (both in fines and criminal prosecution) under applicable strategic technology control legislation by being aware of these potential threats and incorporating them into the overall information security plan.

FOOTNOTES

1   In respect of personal data, the *Guidelines on the Protection of Privacy and Transborder Flows of Personal Data*, Organization for Economic Co-operation and Development, Paris 1981 and other policy viewpoints should be examined.

2   In the United States: *Computer Software Copyright Act* Publ. L. No. 96-517, s.10; 94 Stat. 3028 (codified in 17 U.S.C. s.101, 117; In England: The *Copyright (Computer Software) Amendment Act 1985*, c.41; In Australia: *Copyright Amendment Act 1984*, enacted June 7, 1984.

3   See, for example, <u>Nintendo of America, Inc. v. Coinex Video Games Inc. (1985) 69 C.P.R. (2d) 122 (Fed. C.A.); Bally Midway Manufacturing Co. v. Coinex Video Games Inc. (1983) 71 C.P.R. (2d) 105 (F.C.T.D.); Midway Manufacturing Co. v. Bernstein (1982) 67 C.P.R. (2d) 112 (F.C.T.D.); Spacefile Ltd. v. Smart Computing Systems Ltd. (1983) 75 C.P.R. (2d) 281 (Ont. H.C.); Apple Computer, Inc. v. Computermat Inc. (1983) 75 C.P.R. (2d) 26 (Ont. H.C.); Bally Midway Manufacturing Co. v. Fountainhead Amusement Corp. Ltd. (1984) 79 C.P.R. (2d) 241 (F.C.T.D.); I.B.M. v. Spirale (1984) 80 C.P.R. (2d) 187 (F.C.T.D.); F & I Retail Systems Ltd. v. Thermo-Guard Automotive Products Canada Ltd. (1984); 1 C.P.R. (3d) 297 (Ont. H.C.); La Societe D'Informatique R.D.G. Inc. v. Dynabec Ltee Unreported August 14, 1984 (Que. S.C.); Canavest House Ltd. v. Lett Unreported November 29, 1984 (Ont. H.C.); and also Apple Computer Inc. v. Macintosh Computers Ltd. (1986) 28 D. L. R. (4th) 178 (F.C.T.D.)</u>

4   See Bill C-60, 2nd Session, 33rd Parliament, 35-36 Elizabeth II 1986-84

5   <u>D.P. Andreson & Co.</u> v. <u>The Leiber Code Co.</u> [1917] 2 K.B. 469 (K.B. Div.)

6   <u>D.P. Andreson & Co.</u> v. <u>The Leiber Code Co.</u> [1917] 2 K.B. 469 (K.B. Div.)

7   Express Newspapers PLC v. Liverpool Daily Post & Echo PLC [1985] Fleet Street Reports 306 (Ch. D.)

8   Pitman v. Hine (1884) 1 T.L.R. 39 (Q.B.) followed in Canavest House Ltd. v. Lett Unreported November 29, 1984 (Ont. H.C.)

9   Football League v. Littlewoods [1959] Ch. 637; Ladbroke v. William Hill [1964] 1 W.L.R. 273 (H.L.)

10   Blacklock v. Pearson [1915] 2 Ch. 376

11   Kelly v. Morris (1966) L.R. 1 Eq. 697

12   R v. Kirkwood (1983) 148 D.L.R. (3d) 323 (Ontario Court of Appeal) A case involving the sale of pirate video tapes.

13   Chartwell Communications Group v. Westbrook 637 F. 2d 459 (6th Cir. 1980); National Subscription Television v. SALT TV 644 F. 2D 820 (9TH Cir. 1981)

14   See for example comments in Case No. 7-0-143/80 (Mannheim District Court); and the defendant's argument in Apple Computer Inc. and Apple Computer Australia Pty. Ltd. v. Computer Edge Pty. Ltd. and Michael Suss Trial decision, not recognizing copyrightability, reported at [1984] 10 F.S.R. 246 *Reversed on Appeal* [1984] 11 F.S.R. 481 (Federal Court of Australia).

15   M. Kratz, "The Creator and the Benefits of Creation: The Protection of Computer Programs in The Information Revolution" (1985) 9:3 Dalhousie Law Journal 555

16   R.S.C. 1970, c.C-30; The Canadian example is used. There are similarities in these basic elements in most advanced legal systems.

17   A form of copyright notice which is not required by Canadian law or that of other Berne Convention countries but may be required in the United States or under the Universal Copyright Convention.

18   The leading cases in relation to the interpretation of this section include Sony Corp. of America v. Universal City Studios, 222 USPQ 665(USSC); Folsom v. Marsh, 9 FCAS 342 (C CD MASS. 1981); Grey v. Russell, 10 FCAS 1035 (C CD MASS. 1839).

19   For example, see Prince Albert v. Strange 18 L.J. Ch. 120 (1849); Morison v. Moat 20 L.J. Ch. 513 (1851)

20   For a more complete discussion of this area of law see: M. Kratz, "Trade Secret Law" (1985) 1 Canadian Computer Law Reporter 219 (Part 1) dealing with the law; and 1 C.C.L.R. 231 (Part II) examining several agreements in detail.

21   Palmer & Resendes, *supra*, at 92 discussing Miller's 1974 and 1977 surveys (1978) "The CONTU Software Protection Survey" 18 Jurimetrics J 35

22   Restatement of Torts s.757, comment b (1939)

23   [1967] 2 All E.R. 415 (C.A.) at 417

24   [1956] 3 All E.R. at 301, 302

25   Telex v. I.B.M. 367 F. Supp 258 at 323 (N.D. Okla. 1973 *affirmed on the trade secret issue* 510 F. 2d 894 (10th Circuit) *certiorari* dismissed 423 U.D. 802 (1975) (U.S.S.C.)

26   [1969] R.P.C. 41 at 47

27   Talbot v. General Television Corporation Pty. Ltd. [1980] V.R. 224 (Australia); For example, where a competing product was developed using information available to the public: Half Court Tennis Pty. Ltd. v. Seymour (1980) 513 F.L.R. 240 (Queensland S.C.); O'Brien v. Komesaroff (1982) 56 A.L.J.R. (Australian H.C.) and Molnar Lithographic Supplies Ltd. v. Sikatory (1974) 12 C.P.R. (2d) 197 (Ont. C.A.)

28   See Lord Greene M.R. in Robb v. Green [1985] 2 Q.B. 315 at 320

29   Wessex Dairies, Ltd. v. Smith [1935] 2 K.B. 80

30   Kratz, "The Creator and the Benefits of Creation: Protection of Computer Programs in the Information Revolution" (1985) 9:3 Dalhousie Law Journal 555 at page 563

31   Canada, like the U.S., Australia and West Germany, is a federal country in which the sovereign powers are divided according to a written constitution. In Canada the Federal level of government has the ultimate responsibility for Criminal Law and so Canadian Criminal Law, unlike that in the U.S. where the similar responsibility is at the State level, is uniform throughout the Country.

32   Arkansas Senate Bill 671, David Malone (D-6) public law; California Assembly Bill 426, Norman Waters (D-7) public law, Assembly Bill 1241, Norman Waters (D-7), pending in Public Safety, Assembly Bill 1246, Norman Waters (D-7), pending in Public Safety, Assembly Bill 1480, Dominique Cortese (D-24), discharged by Ways and Means Committee, Senate Bill 255, Ed Davis (R-19), public law 87-139; Florida House Bill 945, Fred Lipman (D-97), public law, Senate Bill 833, Robert Crawford (D-13), replaced by House Bill 945; Idaho Senate Bill 1046, public law; Illinois Senate Bill 1132, public law, Senate Bill 1250, David Barkhausen (R-30), Public Health Committee, Senate Bill 1259, David Barkhausen (R-30), Judiciary Committee, Senate Bill 1335, Arthur Burman (D-2), passed over Veto; Massachusets House Bill 1644, Kevin Blanchit (D-16), replaced by House Bill 2276, House Bill2276, Salvatore Dimasi (D-3), died in Justice Committee, House Bill 3738, Lucille Hicks (R-13), died in Committee; Minnesota House Bill 1685, Randy Kelly (DFL-36A), House Judiciary Committee, Senate Bill 1553, Darril Wegtscheid (DFL-37A), Senate Judiciary Committee; Mississippi Senate Bill 2354, Smith, House Bill 426 , Ralph Doxey (D-5), passed Senate and reported favorably to House Judiciary; Missouri House Bill 208, Judy O'Connor (D-7), public law; New Mexico House Bill 44, Thomas Foy (D-39), public law, house Bill 585, Cheney, died in Judiciary Committee; North Dakota House Bill 1038, public law; Pennsylvania House Bill 132, Edwin Johnson (R-80), pending until 1988 in House Judiciary Committee; Texas House Bill 1401, Albert Luna (D-143), public law, House Bill 1402, Albert Luna (D-143), public law, House Bill 1763, John Culbertson (R-125), Barry Connelly (R-126), died in science and Technology Committee, Senate Bill 777, Chet Edwards (D-9) died in House science and Technology Committee, Senate Bill 778, Chet Edwards (D-9), died in House Science and Technology Committee; Utah Senate Bill 145, Fred Findlayson (R-8), public law. See also the model Computer Crime Bill of the Data Processing Management Association, attention Governmental Affairs Manager, Joseph E. Collins, Park Ridge, Illinois.

33   *Criminal Law Amendment Act*, 1985, 33-34 Eliz. II

34   The Law Science and Technology Committee of the Canadian Bar Association expressed concern about the Computer Crime laws in general and specifically about the complex definitions used.

35   See, for example, "On-Line User Says Privacy Invaded" Infoworld June 9, 1986 p. 13; "Computer Wiretaps" Infoworld May 19, 1986 p.1; "Dangers of a National Data Centre" Computerworld May 12, 1986 p. 16; "Computer Blacklists" Time May 19, 1986 p. 104; A more detailed overview of the situation may be found in *Electronic Surveillance and Civil Liberties* (1985) Office of Technology Assessment or in the Reports of the Canadian Privacy and Computer Task Force.

36   18 u.s.c. 2510-2520

37   47 u.s.c. 605

38   These enactments should be read in light of the passing of the *Electronic Privacy Bill 1986* HR 3378 by the House of Representatives in June 1986. See also a similar Senate Bill, S1667.

39   See **Congressional Quarterly Weekly Report** May 31, 1986 Volume 44 No. 22 Pg. 1233

40   This act owes its existence to a decision of the European Court of Human Rights which held that the previous procedures regarding interception of postal and telecommunications were contrary to Art. 8 European Convention on Human Rights. See Malone v. United Kingdom (1985) 7 E.H.H.R. 14.

41   For a more detailed review of this law, see B. Mitchell, The Interception of Communications Act 1985 (1986) 48 Computer and Law 28

42   (1983) 149 D.L.R. (3d) 583 (Ontario Court of Appeal)

43   Unreported May 29, 1986 (Alberta Court of Appeal)

44   (1978) Cr. App. R. 183 (Div. C.); See also the decision of the House of Lords in Boardman v. Phipps [1967] A.C. 46 (H.L.); In Malone v. Commissioner of Police of the Metropolis (No. 2) [1979] 2 All E.R. 620 the court held that there was no property in words transmitted by electric impulses.

45   The general theft provision.

46   Unreported December 1984 Alberta Court of Queen's Bench

47   Second Edition at page 717

48   These Guidelines are the result of studies by a group of experts led by Justice M.D. Kirby, Chairman of the Australian Law Reform Commission, and were adopted by the Council of the OECD on September 23, 1980. The text of the Guidelines should be reviewed for any detailed study.

13.5 QUESTIONS

13.1. How does civil law differ from criminal law?

13.2. What are advantages and disadvantages of civil action?

13.3. What are advantages and disadvantages of criminal prosecution?

13.4. What are the advantages of copyright law?

13.5. How is a license different from a sale transaction?

13.6. What is a major advantage of trade secret law over both copyright and patent law?

13.7. What are the elements of an action for breach of confidence?

13.8. What are some considerations in establishing a non-disclosure relationship?

13.9. Should theft of confidential information be a criminal offense? Why or why not?

13.10. What are some problems for the security specialist arising from transborder data flow or communications?

13.11. Why is it important to properly preserve evidence of wrongdoing?

13.12. What are some materials which might be strategic goods and whose export might be controlled or restricted?

13.13 (Discussion Example) The Disgruntled Employee

You are the information security manager of XYZ Computer Systems Development Inc. ("XYZ"). XYZ is in the business of developing, manufacturing, and selling two kinds of software. Firstly, they have a software product which provides control and co-ordination over electrical and electronic components used in large power stations (the "Process Control Software"). Secondly, XYZ does custom programming work for the Department of Defense on specialized control systems used by the Department of Defense in certain missile guidance systems (the "defence" work).

Joe has been one of the senior programmers and systems analysts of XYZ. However, in recent years, Joe has felt passed over for promotions he feels he deserves and has generally become disgruntled with his position and the amount of recognition he gets at XYZ.

Joe has recently, while still employed by XYZ, seen a new market opportunity for the general Process Control Software developed, manufactured, and sold by XYZ. Joe feels that with small changes to the software, he will be able to sell or license the software to a new market which XYZ is not presently active in. Joe has signed a non-disclosure agreement with XYZ and is aware that the source code of the Process Control Software is kept confidential by XYZ and considered valuable property of XYZ. However, Joe feels that making minor changes to the software will mean he is no longer using the software of XYZ but rather something he has developed himself. Besides, Joe feels that since he de-veloped much of the Process Control Software, he has a right to have greater recognition and to profit from sales of that software.

It is a common practice in XYZ for programmers working on design projects or in correction of programming bugs to work at home on company supplied microcomputers or on the microcomputers available in the XYZ premises. There is no system requiring employees of XYZ to specifically sign out software they take home. However, there is a system requiring employees of XYZ to sign out hardware (the microcomputers) which they take home for such development work.

Joe's dissatisfaction has been encouraged over the last year by Jane, who operates a small company, ABC Inc., which is a competitor of XYZ. Jane has proposed to Joe that they become active partners in this new enter-prise.

Not presently known to you as security manager is the fact that Jane believes that Joe will be able to develop a completely new system based only on general principles which he has learned in the industry. She is not aware that Joe is planning to merely keep a copy of the source code, make minor revisions to it and market the revised software. However, Jane has suggested to Joe that it might be of advantage to have a list of XYZ's present and past clients and in particular any clients for whom numerous service calls were necessary. Jane thinks these would be a good start for increasing the client base of her company, "ABC Inc."

Two and a half weeks ago, Joe handed in his resignation giving two weeks notice. XYZ has no special exit review procedure requiring an employee to review the matters involving secret or confidential information which the employee had access to during the term of his employment. As a result, at the end of last week, Joe picked up his final check, cleared out his desk, and went home.

This morning you, as security manager of XYZ, read in the paper a large announcement by ABC Inc. that Joe has come to join ABC Inc. Furthermore, the announcement also indicates release of a new process control software by ABC Inc. The performance specifications of this new software are suspiciously close to that of the Process Control Software developed by XYZ.

The President of XYZ has just now come into your office holding a copy of the announcement by ABC Inc. He wants to know what he can do.

Consider the following questions in your discussion:

1. Has Joe done anything wrong:
    (a)   Ethically wrong?
    (b)   Civilly wrong?
    (c)   Criminally wrong?

2. What recourse might XYZ have against Joe, if any:
    (a)   Under the terms of a non-disclosure agreement?
    (b)   Under copyright law?
    (c)   Under applicable criminal law?

3. What recourse might XYZ have against Jane, if any:
    (a)   Under trade secret law?
    (b)   Under copyright law?
    (c)   Under applicable criminal law?

4. What recourse might XYZ have against ABC Inc., if any:
    (a)   Under trade secret law?
    (b)   Under copyright law?
    (c)   Under applicable criminal law?

5. What evidence do you think you will need to help support of any criminal or civil prosecution, if any?

6. What defenses might be available to Joe?

7. What defenses might be available to Jane?

8. What defenses might be available to ABC Inc.?

9. Is there any risk to you or XYZ if you, as information security manager of XYZ, see Joe and "ream him out" for "stealing our software," particularly if this happens in front of other people who know both of you?

10. What recommendations might you make to improve the position of XYZ in the future if such a situation should arise again?

Chapter 14

PROFESSIONALISM EFFORTS

INTRODUCTION

A primary way to meet the human motivational characteristics necessary to have dedicated and secure personnel is the development of a sense of "professionalism." As with doctors, lawyers, accountants, and engineers, computer professionals should share a common background and expectation of behavior.

People with professional designations have a valuable asset (the certification) which they are very careful to protect. They normally are much less likely to take a chance at crime since the consequences of being caught can be severe. If convicted of a crime or of professionally inappropriate conduct, they can be debarred from their professional society and lose the designation which they have worked hard to obtain. (Some designations require seven years of education and job experience, in addition to examinations. All of those listed above require at least five years of education and job experience, in addition to success in demanding professional examinations.) As well, people working towards a professional certificate (such as articling students in an accounting program) are aware that being convicted of committing a crime may wipe out their chance of being admitted to the professional institute.

Webster defines a *profession* as a calling requiring specialized knowledge and often long and intensive preparation. In reality, however, the general recognition and acceptance of a particular occupation as being a profession is the determining thing.

First, let us review the notion of professionalism. Aspects of a profession include:

1. Image in the public mind
2. Codified body of knowledge
3. Accredited education program
4. Uniform examinations and certification of knowledge
5. Apprenticeship or internship
6. Code of ethics
7. Code of Conduct and good Practice
8. Oversight by society (Governments)

There are many combinations of letters which indicate a profession when written after a person's name. Here are a few of these.

Ph.D. and M.D.

These designations, which result in the person being titled "Doctor," are attained after extensive schooling.

CPA

The Chartered Public Accountant (CPA), or the Canadian equivalent Chartered Accountant (**CA**), is a widely recognized designation which is significant in this discussion because, like the CDP and others presented later, the CA or CPA (or CGA etc.) is not a required license but rather a *voluntary* certification attained by some people who practice accounting.

PE

The PE, or in Canada, P. Eng., is a professional engineer. This designation is conferred by the appropriate state or provincial licensing society (often incorporated under a law defining the profession, or an act such as the Professions and Occupations Registration Act in Alberta and Ontario). It represents a *license* to practice certain aspects of the field of engineering. To achieve the P.Eng. or its variations, an engineer must pass difficult comprehensive examinations and meet other experience and ethical requirements.

CDP

CSP

The CDP (Certificate in Data Processing) and CSP (Certified Systems Professional) are *not* licenses but rather certifications which can be attained by a person who has experience in computer based information systems. There is much discussion about licensing of those who are responsible for computer based information systems: practitioners currently have a choice as to attainment of these designations.

The four groups of greatest interest in the area of information systems *professionalism* in North America are:

ICCP (Institute for Certification of Computer Professionals, Chicago, USA);
CIPS and DPMA (Canadian Information Processing Society and Data Processing Management Association, and DPMA Canada ACFOR);
BCS (British Computer Society).

The ICCP operates the oldest certification program, including now the CDP, CSP, ACP (Associate Computer Professional), and CCP (Certified Computer Programmer). The BCS operates in the UK and in a number of Commonwealth countries such as Hong Kong & Singapore and administers various degrees of Fellow of the BCS (FBCS). CIPS and DPMA are members of ICCP and in addition, in Canada, are examining the issues involved in creating a *Canadian* professional designation.

The EDP Auditors' Foundation, Inc. (EDPAF) operates similar programs for the Certified Information Systems Auditor (CISA) certification, another certificate of significance both to accounting and informatics professionals.

A rather important part of the discussion about these professional certifications and efforts is: how are the CDP and similar certifications recognized by individuals and corporations employing Data Processing personnel?

An individual may attain the CDP for purely personal reasons. Many do just that; over 5000 people in Canada and over 35,000 in the United States have demonstrated their commitment to the profession by attaining the CSP or CDP.

Many companies, in the United States and in Canada, support the CDP programs in various ways. This can range from recognition to actual company support; some companies even present review courses and pay employees to take the programs and the exams (and promote employees or give them raises on successful completion).

In the United States, the federal government explicitly recognizes the CDP. Companies and individuals thus have a significant motivation: it improves people's employability and the value to the company of the candidate or employee. In Canada, advertisements sometimes mention the CDP, but the level of awareness is not as high. In a number of countries, particularly in Southeast Asia, the BCS and ICCP certificates are recognized and valued highly.

The ICCP certifications are recognized by the American Council for Accreditation (ACE), and may qualify for college-level credits at colleges and universities which subscribe to the ACE programs.

Another important reason for the development of professional bodies and their certification standards in new fields such as informatics is the market effect of these standards. In a fast growing set of disciplines such as the information processing industry, the ability to show the consumers of information processing services that one has satisfied certain minimum standards is often a commercial advantage. At an advanced level, professionalism may result in the formation of organized, self-governing societies who police their own members in an effort to maintain minimum standards for the protection of the public.

The environment is changing, both in Canada and in the United States. The ICCP added the Associate Computer Professional (ACP) program in 1985. Also in 1985, the Association for Systems Management gave the CSP program to ICCP to administer. In Canada, both DPMA and CIPS continue to support the ICCP programs strongly. DPMA Canada ACFOR and CIPS also are exploring whether there is a need for a unique Canadian certification program, and, if so, what form it should take.

There are no firm answers yet. Entering computer people will see the results over the first years of their professional lives. They may join in the efforts underway as part of their own personal commitment to the information processing profession. Their interest and help will be welcomed.

14.1 BRITISH COMPUTER SOCIETY

The British Computer Society (BCS) was founded in 1957. It has grown so that it now contains over 30,000 members in over 40 local groupings in the United Kingdom and other Commonwealth countries. In July of 1984, the Society was incorporated under a Royal Charter. The BCS is comparable in size to DPMA in the United States, but operates more internationally.

The BCS program is a focus of intense interest in Canada and this interest may well lead to creation of a Canadian professional computer designation.

The British Computer Society publishes examination regulations and an examination syllabus, much as ICCP does for North America. They are similar in that each contains the rules under which examinations will be held and marked, and each syllabus (or "Official Study Guide") has a detailed outline of the contents of every examination section, and lists of references for study and review.

The BCS examinations are in two parts, aptly named "Part I" and "Part II." Part I has a general examination section (a several-hour examination given under controlled circumstances, testing knowledge similar to that described in more detail for the CDP in Section 14.2); a "Part I Paper" which must demonstrate the candidate's understanding of informatics; and a "Report of Project," which must demonstrate the successful achievement of a significant project proving that the candidate has the skills and experience to be considered a professional. The BCS considers that the level of ability and learning demonstrated by successful completion of the Part I examination is roughly equivalent to a four-year college degree in North America. Part II of the BCS examinations is examination in depth in one or another specialization. The BCS considers that the candidate should demonstrate a depth of knowledge in the specialization equivalent to a Master of Science in the area.

As with the ICCP, the BCS has developed review courses and other educational materials, and accredits courses for their examinations and recertification.

The BCS has all of the trappings of professionalism noted in the Introduction to Chapter 14, including a Code of Ethics and Codes of Practice, formal examinations, prescribed curricula of study, and rather greater visibility through the Royal Charter than DPMA and CIPS have yet achieved in North America.

The BCS material is not immediately relevant in Canada or the United States, but as it derives from the British legal system it may well be adopted by CIPS or DPMA Canada as the pattern to follow in the future in Canadian professional certification. Other Commonwealth countries that share the British legal heritage can be expected to consider both the ICCP and BCS patterns, as Canada is doing now.

14.2 NORTH AMERICA: DPMA AND ICCP

The Data Processing Management Association (DPMA) was founded in 1950 in the United States (as the National Machine Accountants' Society). Today, there are some 40,000 members, in Canada and the United States, and in a few in other countries such as Brazil.

DPMA is an ICCP member, and in fact developed the CDP program and started ICCP. An important component of DPMA's contribution to professionalism in informatics is the Special Interest Group for Certified Professionals (SIG-CP). Through SIG-CP, a network of "Region Certification Ambassadors" has been established in each DPMA Region and in Canada. These people aid local chapters in matters related to the CDP and other ICCP examinations, and in interaction with ICCP.

The Institute for Certification of Computer Professionals (ICCP) was founded in 1973 by DPMA (US) and was given the CDP program and the responsibility to administer it. The ICCP programs are the most long-lived in the information processing industry.

The members of ICCP are:

ACM	Association for Computing Machinery
ADAPSO	The Computer Software and Services Industry Association
AICCP	Association of the Institute for Certification of Computer Professionals
AIM	Association for Information Management
AISP	Association of Information Systems Professionals
ASM	Association for Systems Management

AWC	Association for Women in Computing
CIPS	Canadian Information Processing Society
COMMON	An IBM Computer Users Group
DPMA	Data Processing Management Association
HKCS	Hong Kong Computer Society
IACE	International Association for Computing in Education
ICCA	Independent Computer Consultants Association
IEEE-CS	Computer Society of the Institute of Electrical and Electronics Engineers

These groups collectively represent over 200,000 computer professionals in North America. CIPS was involved, as the Canadian representative, in the creation (in 1975) of ICCP as it now exists. New members join ICCP regularly, and the membership list changes frequently.

14.3 CANADA: CIPS AND DPMA

14.3.1 CIPS

CIPS is the Canadian Information Processing Society. It was founded in 1958 and grew from interest mainly in Canadian universities to become the largest single information processing group in Canada. CIPS now has over 5000 members in Canada. CIPS is the official Canadian representative to ICCP and the International Federation for Information Processing (IFIP).

CIPS has begun investigating the issues of professionalism in Canada. There is a national-level professionalism committee, which is looking at issues such as Canadian certification, and licensing under provincial jurisdictions. There is no formal conclusion or majority agreement yet.

This investigation is of interest especially in Canada. In December, 1985, Bill C21 *The Professions and Occupations Registration Act* was passed in Alberta; this law allows professional societies who can prove they represent 25% of the members of a profession, and can meet other criteria, to be established as provincial licensing bodies. There is a similar law in Ontario. CIPS potentially could follow the BCS path in Alberta, as it has done in Ontario. The present situation is that CIPS have decided to wait until a *national* agreement can be evolved.

14.3.2 DPMA Canada

DPMA Canada was founded as a DPMA-US Region, and incorporated in Canada in 1976 as DPMA Canada ACFOR (the "ACFOR" part of the name represents a French language equivalent of Data Processing Management Association, *Association des Cadres de l'Informatique du Canada*). It has since become Region 16 but remains incorporated in Canada. DPMA has about 1100 members in Canada. DPMA Canada has representation in all major Canadian cities, including some representation in Quebec and Montreal. Unlike DPMA, DPMA Canada ACFOR is bilingual in concept.

DPMA Canada has, through the Vancouver Chapter, accreditation capabilities for a two-year Computer Information Systems curriculum, as developed and maintained by the DPMA Education Foundation (DPMAEF). The Vancouver Chapter also has headed the creation of a committee at the National level to explore the need for a Canadian certification program.

14.4 Certificate in Data Processing (CDP)

To give a picture of professional examinations in the information processing industries, the CDP will be examined in somewhat more detail. Other professional examinations in informatics have similar characteristics, although there are detail differences. For example, the BCS Part I contains essay sections, and the CISA examination has different skill sets than the CDP or BCS examinations.

The Certificate in Data Processing (CDP) is a recognized professional standard in the computer information systems industry worldwide. It is awarded by the ICCP to those who have 60 months' professional experience, and who pass the CDP examination and agree to subscribe to the ICCP Codes of Ethics and Practice.

Some facts about the CDP are:

The first exam was administered in 1962 by DPMA

In 1975, the exam was administered by the new ICCP organization

More than 30,000 persons now hold CDP's

There are about 160 testing centers in countries all over the world

In 1985, the CSP program developed by ASM was given to ICCP; there are now over 7000 CSP holders as well.

The CDP examination consists of 5 sections, each containing 60 questions for a total of 300 questions. Fifty minutes are allowed for each section, so a total of 250 minutes (4 hours and 10 minutes) is allowed for taking all five sections. By comparison, the *complete* BCS test set would require over 12 hours, and is essay rather than multiple-choice; the multiple-choice examination for the

Certified Information Systems Auditor (CISA) certificate contains 350 questions and requires 8 hours. The CDP sections are as follows:

1   Computer Hardware

Computers and peripherals that are used to effect Data Processing Solutions

2   Computer Programming and Software

Logical flow of programs and how they interact with operating systems/ advanced programming concepts and tools / ANSI COBOL programming language

3   Principles of Management

Management techniques and application to Data Processing planning, development and operations

4   Methods and Applications

Vocabulary, basic analytical methods and tools employed by major users of Data Processing services; includes accounting, mathematics, statistics, and management science

5   Systems

Project definition, systems analysis and design of automated information systems

Passing these examinations is not the only qualification for attaining the CDP or CSP. Each society requires passing its examination, and also work experience, and adherence to a code of ethics. The exact amount of experience varies, and in many cases formal education will be accepted in place of most of the experience. Typical is a five-year requirement, up to two years of which may be waived for possessors of University degrees in appropriate disciplines.

14.5 QUESTIONS

14.1 What is "licensing?" How does it differ from simple certification? Give at least two examples of professions in your area which require licenses to perform at least some activities.

14.2 Which professional associations are active in your area? What are their main activities? Do they support student chapters?

(*Hint*: Look at the list of ICCP members and contact senior managers or your instructors to find out who may be a member of one of the associations. Once you locate the local chapters' executives you almost certainly will receive eager cooperation.)

14.3 One criticism of the ICCP programs has been that, with the CDP, then the CCP, and now the CSP and ACP as well (and with pressure for a so-called "capstone" in addition), the profession risks losing the value of the certifications in "alphabet soup." Write out your opinion on this question, including your justifications.

(*Hint*: Check out other professions, such as accounting, medicine and engineering. Do they also have many designations? Do they suffer from the alphabet soup problem?)

SECTION V: CICA COMPUTER CONTROL GUIDELINES

Chapter 15

CROSS-REFERENCE TO CICA COMPUTER CONTROL GUIDELINES

INTRODUCTION

One of the most recent efforts of the accounting profession to offer guidance to people who are working with information systems is the Canadian Institute of Chartered Accountants (CICA) *Computer Control Guidelines, Second Edition*, published in 1986. The first edition of this book was accepted widely by accountants and was translated into French, German, Spanish, and Japanese. The Control Objectives and Minimum Control Standards shown in the summary of the CICA *Guidelines* (pages 176-197) are reproduced here, with the permission of the copyright holder, the Canadian Institute of Chartered Accountants, Toronto, Canada. Each objective and standard is cross-referenced to one or more parts of this text. Within the *Computer Control Guidelines*, these are also cross-referenced to the body of that reference. Those who are interested in the accounting aspects of information system security, as well as those whose interest is primarily informatics, should find this double cross-reference a valuable guide to further study.

This text concentrates on *information systems* security. Accounting concentrates on effective use of an organization's *financial resources*, and controls to prevent fraud and errors. While there is much overlap, there are differences in emphasis. Many of the CICA guidelines are not directly related to information systems security and have few or no references in this text. Many others have numerous cross-references. The cross-references to this text are usually the first, or the most important one, plus a few others which are significant. There is no attempt to be exhaustive.

For readers from a computer background, "control point" is the same for either accounting or computer usage. A "control" in this chapter is a specific accounting term corresponding to what computer people would mean by using "safeguard."

It should be noted here that these guidelines are those proposed by a research study group of the Canadian Institute of Chartered Accountants. Guidelines from other sources may not agree completely. The field is in a state of constant and rapid change, and any security professional will have to become familiar with the latest and best material available, and then exercise *judgment*.

The format of this cross-reference looks like:

Control objectives are   indented;

Minimum control standards are indented one further level;

Cross-references are indented one more level, and are *italicized*.

15.1. RESPONSIBILITY FOR CONTROL

Control Objective:

A.   To establish control over information and information systems.

Chapter 3; Chapter 4; Chapter 7; Chapter 9; Chapter 10.

Minimum Control Standards:

A1. Senior management should establish policies governing the information systems of the entity.

Chapter 4, especially Section 4.2; Chapter 9.

A2. Senior management should assign responsibilities for information, its processing and its use.

Chapter 4, Section 4.2.

A3. User management should be responsible for providing information that supports the entity's objectives and policies.

Chapter 4, Section 4.2, 4.3.

A4. User management should be responsible for the completeness, accuracy, authorization, security and timeliness of information.

Chapter 4, Section 4.3.

A5. Information systems management should be responsible for providing the information systems capabilities necessary for achievement of the defined information systems objectives and policies of the entity.

Chapter 7; Chapter 4, Section 4.3.

A6. Senior management should approve plans for development and acquisition of information systems.

Chapter 4, Chapter 9.

A7. Senior management should monitor the extent to which development, operation and control of information systems complies with established policies and plans.

Chapter 4.

15.2. INFORMATION SYSTEMS DEVELOPMENT AND ACQUISITION

Control Objective:

B. To ensure that the information systems selected meet the needs of the entity.

Chapter 4; Chapter 8; Chapter 12.

Minimum Control Standards:

B1. The decision to develop or acquire an information system should be made in accordance with the objectives and policies of the entity.

This relates to overall organizational planning, which is not emphasized in this text. Some references occur in the body in comments on planning, especially Chapter 8 on Contingency Planning and in the portion of Chapter 12 dealing with system development methodologies.

B2. There should be procedures to determine costs, savings and benefits before a decision is made to develop or acquire an information system.

Chapter 12, Sections 12.2, 12.3.

B3. Procedures should be established to ensure that the information system being developed or acquired meets user requirements.

Chapter 4; Chapter 12, Section 12.2.

B4. Information systems and programs should be adequately tested prior to implementation.

Chapter 12.3; comments in several places about program "bugs".

Control Objective:

C. To ensure the efficient and effective implementation of information systems.

In effect, this objective recommends creating a defined planning process, and defined documentation standards. Chapters 3 and 4 relate; Chapter 12, Sections 12.2 and 12.3 discuss signoffs; Chapter 8 considers contingency planning.

Minimum Control Standards:

C1. Responsibility should be assigned for implementation of information systems.

Chapters 3 and 4; Chapter 12, Section 12.2.

C2. Standards should be established and enforced to ensure the efficiency and effectiveness of the implementation of information systems.

Chapter 8; Chapter 12, Section 12.3.

C3. There should be procedures to ensure that information systems are implemented in accordance with the established standards.

Chapter 3.

C4. An approved implementation plan should be used to measure progress.

Chapter 12, Sections 12.2, 12.3.

C5. Effective control should be maintained over the conversion of information and the initial operation of the information system.

Chapter 12, Section 12.3.

C6. User management should participate in the conversion of data from the existing system to the new system.

Chapter 12, Section 12.3.

C7. Final approval should be obtained from user management prior to operation of the new information system.

Chapter 3; Chapter 12, Sections 12.2, 12.3.

Control Objective:

D. To ensure the efficient and effective maintenance of information systems.

Chapter 3; Chapter 4; Chapter 12, Sections 12.2, 12.3; Chapter 7, Chapter 8.

Minimum Control Standards:

D1. There should be procedures to document and schedule all planned changes to information systems.

Chapter 12, Section 12.3.

D2. There should be procedures to ensure that only change authorization authorized changes are initiated.

Chapter 12, Section 12.3; Chapter 7.

D3. Only authorized, tested and documented changes to information systems should be accepted into production.

Chapter 12, Section 12.3.

D4.   There should be procedures to report planned information systems changes to information systems management and to the users affected.

Chapter 3; Chapter 4; Chapter 12, Section 12.3; Chapter 7.

D5.   There should be procedures to allow for and to control emergency changes.

Chapter 8.

D6.   There should be procedures to ensure that controls are in place to prevent unauthorized changes to information systems.

Chapter 7; Chapter 12, Section 12.3.

Control Objective:

E.   To ensure that the development and acquisition of information systems are carried out in an efficient and effective manner.

Chapter 3; Chapter 4; Chapter 7; Parts of Chapter 5, Chapter 12.

Minimum Control Standards:

E1.   Standards should be established and enforced to ensure the efficiency and effectiveness of the systems development and acquisition processes.

Chapter 12, Section 12.2 in particular.

E2.   There should be procedures to ensure that all systems are developed and acquired in accordance with the established standards.

Chapter 12, Section 12.2.

E3.   An approved development and acquisition plan (project plan) should be used to measure progress.

The topic of project control is not addressed directly in this text.

E4.   All personnel involved in systems development and acquisition activities should receive adequate training and supervision.

Chapter 5 on personnel selection and training.

15.3. INFORMATION SYSTEMS PROCESSING

Control Objective:

F.   To ensure that present and future requirements of users of information systems processing can be met.

Some of the material on the System Security Officer in Chapter 4 relates to this. Standards F4 and F5 have peripheral references in Chapter 7 on Operations management. The security function normally is not very involved in this area. It is a normal management responsibility to ensure proper reporting and control, and an information systems management responsibility to monitor changing technology as part of planning.

Minimum Control Standards:

F1. There should be written agreements between users and information systems processing, defining the nature and level of services to be provided.

F2. There should be appropriate management reporting within information systems processing.

F3. Information systems processing management should keep senior and user management appraised of technical developments which could support the achievement of the objectives and policies of the entity.

F4. There should be procedures to examine the adequacy of information systems processing resources to meet entity objectives in the future.

F5. There should be procedures for the approval, monitoring and control of the acquisition and upgrade of hardware and systems software.

Control Objective:

G. To ensure the efficient and effective use of resources within information systems processing.

Chapter 7; otherwise, this is another management topic which usually does not involve the security function directly.

Minimum Control Standards:

G1. A budget for information systems processing should be prepared on a regular basis.

G2. Standards should be established and enforced to ensure efficient and effective use of information systems processing resources.

G3. There should be procedures to ensure that information processing problems are detected and corrected on a timely basis.

The control techniques recommended involve recording problems and resolutions, and making sure that historical records are reviewed and reported to senior management. Chapter 7 touches on this.

G4. Users of information systems processing facilities should be accountable for the resources used by them.

Control Objective:

H. To ensure complete, accurate and timely processing of authorized information systems.

Chapter 7, especially Sections 7.3, 7.4, and 7.6; some of Chapter 3, notably Section 3.4.4; some of Chapter 12, Section 12.3; parts of Chapter 8, Section 8.1.

Minimum Control Standards:

H1. Standards should be established and enforced to ensure complete, accurate and timely processing of authorized information systems.

H2. There should be operating procedures for all functions of information systems processing.

Written procedures are mentioned in a number of places, including Chapter 7 on operations, Chapter 8 on contingency planning, and in the systems development and implementation part of Chapter 12.

H3. Information systems processing activities should be recorded and reviewed for compliance with established operating standards and procedures.

This refers mainly to system logs, which are mentioned in several places. Chapter 3, Section 3.4.4; and Chapter 7, Sections 7.2 through 7.5 are the most relevant.

H4. There should be written agreements between users and information systems processing, defining the nature and level of services to be provided.

H5. Information systems processing activities should be scheduled to ensure that the established user requirements can be met.

Agreements and scheduling are management responsibilities and are mentioned in Chapter 7.

H6. Appropriate maintenance should be applied to hardware, systems software and storage media.

Mentioned in Chapter 8; Chapter 7; Section IV.

H7. Only authorized, tested and documented new and changed information systems should be accepted into production.

Chapter 12, Section 12.3.

15.4. SEGREGATION OF INCOMPATIBLE FUNCTIONS AND SECURITY CONTROLS

Control Objective:

I. To ensure that there is an appropriate segregation of incompatible functions within the entity.

> *Separation of duties is mentioned frequently. Chapter 7, Sections 7.1, 7.2, 7.6; and Chapter 12, Section 12.2 delve into the topic area in some detail.*

Minimum Control Standards:

I1.   The organization structure established by senior management should provide for an appropriate segregation of incompatible functions.

> *See especially the "typical organization" examples in Chapter 7, Section 7.1.*

Control Objective:

J.   To ensure that all access to information and information systems is authorized.

> *Chapter 12; Chapter 9, especially Section 9.2; Chapter 7; Chapter 3, Section 3.4.*

Minimum Control Standards:

J1.   There should be procedures to ensure that information and information systems are accessed in accordance with established policies and procedures.

> *The control techniques recommended here include eighteen specific methods involving security classification of data, communications security, control of access to system utilities, passwords, and so on. Much of Chapters 7 and 12 is devoted to this area. It is referred to in Chapter 9 as well.*

Control Objective:

K.   To ensure that hardware facilities within information systems processing are physically protected from unauthorized access and from accidental or deliberate loss or damage.

> *This objective relates to physical security, environmental control, access control. Chapter 6; some of Chapter 7; Chapter 8, Section 8.1.3; and Chapter 3, Sections 3.4 and 3.5 all touch on this area.*

Minimum Control Standards:

K1.   Hardware facilities within information systems processing should be physically separated from other departments in the entity.

> *Chapter 6, Section 6.1.*

K2.   Physical access to hardware facilities within the information systems processing should be restricted to authorized personnel.

> *Chapter 6, Section 6.2; Chapter 7, Section 7.1.*

K3. There should be procedures to ensure that environmental conditions (such as temperature and humidity) for hardware facilities are adequately controlled.

Chapter 3, Section 3.4; Chapter 6, especially Sections 6.3 and 6.4; Section 7.5; and Chapter 8, Section 8.1.3.

Control Objective:

L. To ensure that information systems processing can be recovered and resumed after operations have been interrupted.

In essence, Chapter 8 is devoted to this objective. The training aspects are mentioned there and in Chapter 4, Section 4.4 and Chapter 5, Section 5.4.3. Part of the control techniques (L1-3 for example) refer to exposure identification, which is the topic of Chapters 1 and 2.

Minimum Control Standards:

L1. There should be procedures to allow information systems processing to resume operations in the event of an interruption.

Chapter 8.

L2. Emergency, backup and recovery plans should be documented and tested on a regular basis to ensure that they remain current and operational.

Chapter 8.

L3. Personnel should receive adequate training and supervision in emergency backup and recovery procedures.

Chapter 4, Section 4.4; Chapter 5, Section 5.4.3

Control Objective:

M. To ensure that critical user activities can be maintained and recovered following interruptions to normal operations.

This is the user side of the considerations mentioned in the chapters referred to under objective L. The references are the same.

Minimum Control Standards:

M1. There should be backup and recovery plans to allow users of information systems to resume operations in the event of an interruption.

Chapter 8.

M2. All information and resources required by users to resume processing should be backed up appropriately.

Chapter 6, Section 6.7; Chapter 7, Section 7.5; Chapter 8, Sections 8.1.1, 8.2.2.

M3.   User personnel should receive adequate training and supervision in the conduct of the recovery procedures.
Chapter 4, Section 4.4; Chapter 5, Section 5.4.3.

15.5. APPLICATION CONTROLS

Control Objective:

N.   To ensure that application controls are designed with due regard to the controls relating to segregation of incompatible functions, security, development and processing of information systems.
> *This refers to the design of controls which are all-encompassing; that is, if there is a weakness in one area such as operations, then there should be a corresponding compensating control elsewhere.*

Minimum Control Standards:

N1.   Application controls should be designed with regard to any weaknesses in segregation, security, development and processing controls which may affect the information system.
> *This is a specific instance of the principle of compensating controls. There may be unavoidable weaknesses in one area, such as operating systems; if so, a corresponding application control should ensure that control is maintained elsewhere.*

Control Objective:

O.   To ensure that information provided by the information systems is complete, authorized and accurate.
> *This whole topic area is addressed in Chapter 7, Sections 7.2 through 7.6 and in a number of other locations in the text. Such things as automatic editing, reasonableness tests, limit tests, suspense account analysis, various reports documenting activities in files, exception reporting, control totals, and generally the sort of system audit trail found in good system design are found in Objective O. Parts of this are referred to many places in the text.*

Minimum Control Standards:

O1.   There should be procedures to ensure that all transactions (including those used to change semi-permanent data and to correct errors) are initially recorded.

O2.   There should be procedures to ensure that all accepted transactions are authorized.

O3.   There should be procedures to ensure that all authorized transactions are recorded accurately.

O4. There should be procedures to ensure that all authorized transactions are processed.

O5. There should be procedures to ensure that all authorized transactions are processed accurately.

O6. There should be procedures to ensure that output is reviewed by users for completeness, accuracy and consistency.

O7. There should be some method of ensuring that control procedures relating to completeness, accuracy and authorization are enforced.

Control Objective:

P. To ensure the existence of adequate management trails.

See the previous objective.

Minimum Control Standards:

P1. Policies and procedures for record retention should be established.

This topic is covered in passing in parts of the text which discuss backups. The specific sub-topic of record retention is a specialized area of "Records Management" outside the scope of this text; legal requirements for records retention are involved as well as computer backup principles.

P2. There should be some method of identifying and locating the component records involved in the processing of a transaction and in the production of information.

Time stamps and other means of identifying transactions to permit recovery and audit are mentioned in several places.

REFERENCES

The references used directly in the body of the text are listed where they are used. This section collects the major references used, and also adds some further references of interest. This section is adapted from *A Computer Security Bibliography*, an annotated bibliography maintained by the author (Fites). The bibliography is kept up-to-date; the material herein is from the March 1988 version.

This is not at all a complete list; the primary source contains nearly 800 entries and grows weekly.

1.   AFIPS, Security: "Checklist for Computer Center Self-Audits," AFIPS Press, Washington, DC, 1979.

2.   *AFIPS Systems Review Manual on Security*, AFIPS Press, Montvale, NJ, 1974.

3.   "Backup Supplies Power for Orderly PC Shutdown," *Canadian Datasystems*, March 1987, p. 20. Product announcement regarding microcomputer UPS.

4.   Bell, D. E., and L. J. La Padula, "Secure Computer Systems: Unified Exposition and MULTICS Interpretation," MTR-2997, rev. 1, Mitre Corporation, Bedford, Mass., November 1973-June 1974, Vols. I-III.

5.   Beker, Henry and Fred Piper, *Cipher Systems*, John Wiley & Sons, New York, 1982.

6.   Beker, Henry and Fred Piper, "Cryptography for Beginners," *New Scientist*, July, 1983.

7.   Bill C-60, "An Act to Amend the Copyright Act and to Amend Other Acts in Consequence Thereof," THE HOUSE OF COMMONS OF CANADA, 2nd Session 32nd Parliament 1986-87. Part of Canada's ongoing effort to amend the 50-year old *Copyright Act*. This bill is notable for explicitly permitting backup copies for personal use, and for defining computer programs as copyrightable material. The bill has not been passed as at April 1988.

8.   Boebert, W. E., R. Y. Kain, and W. D. Young, "Secure Computing: the Secure ADA Target Approach," *Scientific Honeyweller*, July 1985.

9.   Bosworth, Bruce, *Codes, Ciphers and Computers*, Hayden Book Company, New York, 1982.

10.   Bosworth, Seymour, "Hardware Elements of Security," *Computer Security Handbook*, Macmillan Information, New York, 1973, p. 56.

11.   Brandon, Dick H., "Employees," in *Computer Security Handbook*, Douglas B. Hoyt (ed.), Macmillan Publishing Co., Inc., New York, 1973, p.102.

12.   Brandstad, Dennis K. (ed.), *Computer Security and the Data Encryption Standard*, National Bureau of Standards Special Publication 500-27, 1978.

13.   Carr, Peter F., "Most DP Centers Lax in Arranging Backup Facilities," *Computerworld*, July 15, 1970.

14.   *Computer Control Guidelines, Second Edition*, Canadian Institute of Chartered Accountants, February 1986.

15.   *Computer Security*, Time Life Books, Alexandria, Virginia, 1986.

16.   "Computer Systems Access Control Software," *Data Processing & Communications Security*, Madison, WI., September-October 1983, pp. 22-24.

17.   Cook, Rick, "Power Line Protection," *Popular Computing*, November 1984.

18.   Cromer, Robert, *Review Course Text for CDP Candidates*, Data Processing Management Association, Park Ridge, Illinois, 1987.

19.   "Data Encryption Standard," *Federal Information Processing Standards Publication 46*, National Bureau of Standards, Washington, D.C., January 1977, p. 4.

20.   "Datapac Improves Security, Message Delivery," *Canadian Datasystems*, August 1986, p. 69. Brief report on changes to Datapac network systems.

21.   Davies, D. W. and W. L. Price, *Security for Computer Networks*, John Wiley & Sons, New York, 1984.

22.   Deavours, Cipher A., and Louis Kruh, *Machine Cryptography and Modern Cryptanalysis*, Artech House, Dedham, Massachusets, 1985.

23.   "Department of Defense Trusted Computer System Evaluation Criteria," CSC-STD-001-83, Department of Defense Computer Security Center, Fort George G. Meade, Maryland, August 15, 1983.

24.   "Disaster Plan Saved Steinberg EDP," *Canadian Datasystems*, May 1987, p. 85. Brief description of recovery from fire at Steinberg's in Montreal. (See Also Garland, Jennifer, "Recovering from a Fiery Disaster," *Computing Canada*, June 11, 1987, p. 37ff.)

25.   "Dome's Bitter Lesson," *Canadian Business*, September 1985.

26.   "EDP Threat Assessments: Concepts and Planning Guide," *RCMP Security Information Publications #2*, RCMP "T" Directorate, Ottawa, January 1982.

27.   "Electronic Data Processing Security Standards and Practices for Departments and Agencies of the Government of Canada" (draft), GES/NGI-14/D03 - 1986-02-11, February 1986.

28.   Fisher, Royal, *Information Systems Security*, Prentice-Hall, Englewood Cliffs, New Jersey, 1984.

29.   Fites, Philip E., "Information Systems Security: Organizational Issues," in *Proceedings* of the Mid-Winter Meeting of the Alberta Branch, Canadian Bar Association, Edmonton, Alberta, January 1987. Paper contributed to supplement panel presentation. Reprinted in *Technology and the Law for General Practitioners*, Legal Education Society of Alberta, March 1987.

30.   Gallegos, Frederick, Dana R. (Rick) Richardson, and A. Faye Borthick, *Audit & Control of Information Systems*, South-Western Publishing Company, West Chicago, Illinois 1987.

31.   Gibb-Clark, Margot, "Line Blurs Between Fact and Fiction on Resumes," *Globe and Mail*, March 22, 1988, p. B1. Discussion of exaggeration and falsehood on resumes. Reports 10% - 30% estimated incidence. Most common are concealing gaps in history, degrees and certificates not actually held. Gray area in "puffery" vs "marketing."

32.   Glaser, Edward L. "A Brief Description of Privacy Measures in the Multics Operating System," *Proceedings*, Spring Joint Computer Conference, 1967.

33.   Glen, Ron, "Vendor Packs Now Hunt Pirates," *Canadian Datasystems* (*Software Canada* Section, p. 3), April 1987. Discusses cooperation of vendors in using active techniques to detect, catch, prosecute unauthorized copying.

34.   "Guidelines for Automatic Data Processing Physical Security and Risk Management," AFIPS Publication 31, U. S. Department of Commerce National Bureau of Standards, Washington D. C., June 1974.

35.   "Guidelines for Computer Security Certification and Accreditation," AFIPS Pub. 102, U.S. Department of Commerce National Bureau of Standards, Washington D. C., September 27, 1983, p. 12.

36.   "Guidelines for Implementing and Using the NBS Data Encryption Standard," AFIPS Publication 74, U. S. Department of Commerce National Bureau of Standards, Washington D. C., April 1981.

37. "Guidelines on User Authentication Techniques for Computer Network Access Control," AFIPS Publication 83, U. S. Department of Commerce National Bureau of Standards, Washington D. C., September 1980.

38. Hellman, Martin E., "The Mathematics of Public-Key Cryptography," *Scientific American,* August 1979.

39. Hogers, Hans, "Standby Power Takes on the Critical Jobs," *Canadian Datasystems*, May 1987, p. 34ff.

40. Hogers, Hans, "Staying On-line When the Power's Off," *Canadian Datasystems*, September, 1986, p. 61. Discussion of UPS systems.

41. Hooper, Paul, and John Page, "Internal Control Problems in Computer Systems," *Journal of Systems Management*, December 1982, p. 22.

42. Hoyt, Douglas B. et al. (eds.), *Computer Security Handbook*, Macmillan Publishing Co., Inc., New York, 1973.

43. IBM, "The Considerations of Physical Security in a Computer Environment," G520-2700-0, 1972.

44. IBM, "Data Security Controls and Procedures -- A Philosophy for DP Installations," G320-5049-1, 1977.

45. "Industrial Security Manual for Safeguarding Classified Information," Department of Defense 5220.22-M, Washington, D.C., January 1983.

46. "Report of Ad Hoc Meeting on Security," WOI Ad Hoc Group on Security (TC97/SC16/WG1), International Standards Organization, prepared for ISO after meeting in Washington, D.C., March 12-16, 1984.

47. Jeffrey, Liss, "The Real Odds on Computer Security," *Information Technology*, Canadian Business Publications, September 1985, p. 111.

48. Johnston, Peter, "Computer Hardware and Software Security Checklist," in *Proceedings* of the Mid-Winter Meeting of the Alberta Branch, Canadian Bar Association, Edmonton, Alberta, January 1987. Paper contributed to supplement panel presentation.

49. Kahn, David, *Kahn on Codes*, Macmillan Co., New York, 1983.

50. Karcher, P.A., and R.R.Shell, "MULTICS Security Evaluation: Vulnerability Analysis," ESD-TR-XXX, Electronics Systems Division (AFSC), L. G. Hanscombe Field, Bedford, Massachusets, July 11, 1983.

51. Kratz, Martin P. J., "Computer Abuse by Children," *Resource News*, Legal Resource Centre, Faculty of Extension, University of Alberta, April 1986, p. 18. Non-technical general public introduction.

52. Kratz, Martin P. J., "Computer Crime," *Resource News*, Legal Resource Centre, Faculty of Extension, University of Alberta, April 1986, p. 9. Nontechnical general public introduction.

53. Kratz, Martin P. J., "Evidentiary Problems of Computer-Generated Materials," in *Technology and the Law for General Practitioners*, Legal Education Society of Alberta, March, 1987. Somewhat technical, lawyer material.

54. Kratz, Martin P. J., "Introduction to Copyright Infringement," in *Technology and the Law for General Practitioners*, Legal Education Society of Alberta, March 1987. Intended for lawyers.

55. Kratz, Martin P. J., "ISS Information Systems Services Ltd. v. Hugh McColl's Southpark Motors Ltd," *Canadian Computer Law Reporter*, Volume 1, Issue 11, September 1984.

56. Krauss, Leonard L., *Safe: Security Audit and Field Evaluation for Computer Facilities and Information Systems*, American Management Association, New York, 1972.

57. Krauss, Leonard L. and Aileen MacGahan, *Computer Fraud and Countermeasures*, Prentice-Hall, Englewood Cliffs, New Jersey, 1979.

58. Landreth, Bill, with Howard Rheingold, *Out of the Inner Circle: A Hacker's Guide to Computer Security*, Microsoft Press, Bellevue, Washington, 1986 (Distributed by Simon & Schuster).

59. Legal Education Society of Alberta, *Technology and the Law for General Practitioners Featuring Computer Law*, collection of papers, Edmonton, Alberta, March 1987.

60. Lobel, J., "Risk Analysis Results," Computer Security and Privacy Symposium *Proceedings*, MEDW-359-801, Honeywell Information Systems, Phoenix, Arizona, April 2-3, 1979, pp. 79-84.

61. Lobel, J., *Foiling the System Breakers: Computer Security and Access Control*, McGraw-Hill, 1986.

62. Lord, Kenniston W., Jr., *The Data Center Disaster Consultant*, QED, Wellesley, Maryland, 1977.

63. Lord, Kenniston W., Jr., *CDP Review Manual: A Data Processing Handbook*, van Nostrand Reinhold, 1986.

64. Mair, William C., Donald R. Wood, and Keagle W. Davis, *Computer Control and Audit (2nd ed.)*, The Institute of Internal Auditors, Altamonte Springs, Fla., 1976.

65. Martin, James, *Principles of Data Base Management*, Prentice-Hall, Englewood Cliffs, New Jersey, 1976.

66. Martin, James, *Security, Accuracy, and Privacy in Computer Systems*, Prentice-Hall, Inc., Englewood Cliffs, New Jersey, 1973.

67. Meyer, Carl H., and Stephen M. Matyas, *Cryptography: A New Dimension in Computer Security*, John Wiley & Sons, New York, 1982.

68.   "Microcomputer Security -- Is There Anything Really New?," *Computer Security*, Number 56, January/February 1984.

69.   Miller, Howard W., CSP, "Disaster Recovery Planning," in *Journal of Systems Management*, March 1986, p. 25.

70.   Molho, Lee M. "Hardware Aspects of Secure Computing," *Proceedings* of the Spring Joint Computer Conference, 1970.

71.   "Multi-Use Micros Pose Greater Security Threat," *Data Management*, April 1987, p. 42ff. A brief discussion of increase in exposure with multi-user micros as opposed to single use.

72.   *MULTICS Data Security*, GA01-00, Honeywell Information Systems, Phoenix, Arizona, 1982.

73.   "New Code Is Broken," *Science*, May 1982.

74.   "OECD Guidelines Governing the Protection of Privacy and Transborder Flows of Personal Data," Recommendations of the Council of Europe, adopted at its 523d meeting on September 23, 1980.

75.   Ognibene, Peter J.,"Secret Ciphers Solved: Artificial Intelligence," *OMNI*, November 1984.

76.   Parker, Donn. B., *Computer Security Management*, Reston Publishing Company, Inc., Reston, Virginia, 1981.

77.   Parker, Donn. B., *Fighting Computer Crime*, Charles Scribner & Sons, New York, 1983.

78.   "Password Usage Standards," National Bureau of Standards Pub. (draft), National Bureau of Standards, Washington, D.C., 1984.

79.   Pettus, James, "64 Encryptor" in *Compute*, September 1986, p. 59.

80.   "Phone Fraud in U. S. is a Battle of Wits," *Globe and Mail, Report on Business*, April 23, 1987. Report of some sophisticated crimes/frauds involving US phone system.

81.   Pollock, Harvey, "How Encryption Secures Data," *Canadian Datasystems*, April 1987, pp. 72ff. A very brief nontechnical discussion of DES and other encryption methods.

82.   *The Privacy Act of 1974*, Public Law 93-579, 93d Cong., S.3418, December 31, 1974.

83.   "Response of the Government of Canada to the Report of the Parliamentary Sub-Committee on Computer Crime," Department of Justice Canada, October 1983.

84.   Ruthberg, Zella, and Robert G. McKenzie, *Audit and Evaluation of Computer Security*, National Bureau of Standards Special Publication 500-19, National Bureau of Standards, Washington, D.C., 1977.

85.　　　Schmucker, Kurt J., *Fuzzy Sets, Natural Language Computations, and Risk Analysis*, Computer Science Press, Rockville, Maryland, 1984.

86.　　　"Secure Storage," *Canadian Datasystems*, March 1987, p. 13. Product announcement for Modular Storage Subsystem.

87.　　　"Security Analysis and Enhancements of Computer Operating Systems," NBSIR 76-1041, National Bureau of Standards, Washington, D.C., April 1976, p. 3.

88.　　　"Security in the Computer Complex," *Computers and Automation*, November, 1970.

89.　　　"Security in the EDP Environment," *RCMP Security Information Publications #1*, 2nd ed., RCMP "T" Directorate, Ottawa, October 1981.

90.　　　"Security and VAX/VMS," *The DEC Professional*, December 1984.

91.　　　Smith, Jim, "Call-Back Security System Prevents Unauthorized Computer Access," *Mini-Micro Systems*, July 1984.

92.　　　"Staffing Dedication to Security Reduces Computer Abuse New Study Discovers," *Inside DPMA*, Summer 1987, p. 16. A report of a survey of DPMA members and analysis indicating that number of hours and staff dedicated to security are major factors; organizations using RACF or other products have significantly fewer problems than organizations without; 41% of organizations reported no security at all.

93.　　　Sullivan, Joseph, "Cryptography: Securing Computer Transmissions," *High Technology*, November 1983.

94.　　　Sykes, D.J., "Data Encryption Standards and Applications," Computer Security and Privacy Symposium *Proceedings*, DE89, Honeywell Information Systems, Phoenix, Arizona, 1981, pp. 91-93.

95.　　　Sykes, D.J., "Implementation of the NBS Encryption Standard," Computer Security and Privacy Symposium *Proceedings*, DF84, Honeywell Information Systems, Phoenix, Arizona, April 19-20, 1977, pp. 61-64.

96.　　　Sykes, D.J., "Generating Secure System Specification," Computer Security and Privacy Symposium *Proceedings*, DF 84, Honeywell Information Systems, Phoenix, Arizona, April 7-8, 1981, pp. 91-93.

97.　　　Sykes, David J., "Protecting Data by Encryption," *Datamation*, August 1976, p. 81.

98.　　　"Target Hardening," *RCMP Security Information Publications #3*, RCMP "T" Directorate, Ottawa, September 1983.

99.　　　Troy, Eugene F., Stuart W. Katzke, and Dennis D. Steinauer, *Technical Solutions to the Computer Security Intrusion Problem*, National Bureau of Standards, Washington, D. C., November 1984.

100.   Troy, Gene, "Thwarting the Hackers: New Security Protection Devices," *Datamation*, July 1, 1984.

101.   Turn, Rein, "Private Sector Needs for Trusted/Secure Computer Systems," *Report R-2811-DR&E Trusted Computer Systems: Needs and Incentives for Use in Government and the Private Sector*, The Rand Corporation, June 1981.

102.   van Tassel, Dennis, *Computer Security Management*, Prentice-Hall, Englewood Cliffs, New Jersey, 1972.

103.   van Tassel, Dennis, "Cryptographic Techniques for Computers: Substitution Methods," *Information Storage and Retrieval*, June, 1970.

104.   Wagner, Edward, "How to Make Networks Secure," *Canadian Datasystems*, September 1986, p. 66. Brief review of some products which can enhance network security.

INDEX